SLAVERY IN THE ROMAN EMPIRE

R.H. BARROW, M.A., B.LITT.

FORMERLY SENIOR SCHOLAR OF EXETER COLLEGE, OXFORD
CLASSICAL SIXTH MASTER AT SEDERGH SCHOOL

BARN
&No
BOO
NEW Y

*Orig

This edition published by Barnes & Noble, Inc.

1996 Barnes & Noble Books

ISBN 0-76070-081-8

Printed and bound in the United States of America

M 9 8 7 6 5 4 3 2 1

FG

PREFACE

THE following chapters attempt to review shortly the working of slavery in the first two centuries of the Roman Empire. Attention has been devoted to certain broad aspects, which, I hope, are the most interesting. At the same time a study of slavery leads to some obscure problems in Roman History; these have necessarily received brief treatment, but perhaps it has been worth while even to bring them together between two covers of a book.

For me it has been worth while, for a book may contain a preface, and a preface thanks. And so at last I may render thanks to Dr. B. W. Henderson, Fellow of Exeter College, Oxford, my former tutor in Ancient History; to his teaching and to his power of awaking curiosity I owe my interest in the Empire. But interest may be ill-equipped—how ill-equipped I have learnt from Mr. H. M. Last, Fellow of St. John's College, Oxford, who has saved me from errors and readily furnished me with information. Professor W. W. Buckland, of Cambridge University, was good enough to reply to a letter from an unknown inquirer; Dr. T. Ashby, late Director of the British School at Rome, helped me to obtain some photographs; three photographs I owe to the kindness of the Keeper of the Department of

Greek and Roman Antiquities, British Museum, others to the Direction des Antiquités de Tunisie, another to M. Emile Espérandieu. For all these services I am very grateful.

Finally, I thank Mr. E. W. S. Packard for his care in reading the proofs ; I wish that I could have made fuller use of his criticism.

R. H. B.

January 1928

CONTENTS

INTRODUCTION

F EW periods of two hundred years can offer so many and varied attractions as the first two centuries of the Roman Empire ; for few can present so many points of contact with our own age. And, as the attractions are varied, so are the men varied to whom they appeal. For the student of human character, great and puny figures pass across the stage—some with leisurely pace of philosopher or blasé noble, others hurrying rapidly to success or grief, to fame or obscurity, impelled by every motive and desire known to man. Monsters of inhuman passion, saintly examples of womanly devotion, stern and capable leaders of men and legions, the vulgar upstart gross in mind and body, the philosopher conscientiously supporting the burden of imperial rule, the loathsomeness and efficiency of a Nero—here is material for admiration or pity or ridicule. Or it may be the achievements of an imperial race that compels our interest—two centuries of experiment and experience in the ruling of subject peoples, of firmness not untempered by tact and sympathy, of hard work and abiding results with a minimum of talk. The civil servant may learn much of bureaucracy, the town-councillor of municipal finance ; here the novelist may go for material ; political theorists and writers of outlines with axes to grind may here make them a keen edge, if only for their own execution ; for it is easy but dangerous to draw the required lesson by forgetting the facts that are inconvenient. Moralists may find much to muse upon : Stoicism under other names is still fashionable to-day, and that was an age of spiritual unrest and vague, undirected impulse for good.

Municipalities and provinces, taxation and tariffs, conflict of creeds, frontier settlement, trade-guilds—it all sounds remarkably modern ; society was much the same then as now. But there was at least one great difference. ' Ancient society,' we are told, ' was founded on slavery.'

Or it may be attractive to point the differences between one age and another. The zealous optimist, inflamed with hopes of the future of man, is at pains to demonstrate advance in the past as an earnest for the future. And so he will fix his gaze on the evils inherent in that complex system of empire. He will turn page after page disfigured with vice and infamy, and the pages are there for all to read, and penned by a master. He will throw up his hands in horror at corruption in high places and the sham glitter of court and society ; nor can truth offer denial. The cruelty of the amphitheatre will repel him ; he will shudder at the outpouring of blood in wars of imperial expansion. And if modern parallels are quoted to him, perhaps disguised under fair-sounding names and therefore more insidious, then with confident smile he will play his trump card —slavery—and stretch out a hand to gather in the trick. ' Ancient society was founded on slavery.'

And it is an ill-sounding word. It brings with it the jangle of chains and the crack of the whip and the scream of victims not only from the ancient world of the Mediterranean. It calls forth impassioned declarations upon the tyranny of empire, and the exploitation of the native, eloquent perorations on liberty and equality and the rights of man. But it is also an ill-fated word. Slavery is viewed chiefly in its worst aspects : it is judged by its worst moments. Put on trial, it will no doubt be condemned at the last ; but if Roman law has taught us anything, a hearing must be given. It may be that all the charges cannot be proved, that the prisoner has been misunderstood ; he may turn out to be, if not a saint, at any rate in some ways a contributor, however humble, to civilization. We may indeed warn him not to appear in court again ; but we must not off-hand condemn his past as utterly and entirely bad.

Has slavery always been an evil? 'There are conditions,' says Lord Acton, 'in which it is scarcely an hyperbole to say that slavery itself is a stage on the road to freedom.' In the first two centuries of our era was done the spade-work in the task of civilizing the world, which is Rome's legacy to later generations. What part did slavery play in this work? Was it so immoral, so degrading (as some modern critics regard it) as to hamper the work of Romanization? Or was it even an instrument in that very process, which was being carried forward by many influences? Was slavery consciously used by far-sighted statesmen for this very purpose?

And was the lot of town or country slave as abject as has often been suggested? What chances were offered for release? Was slavery worse for the slave or master? 'It would be a mistake,' says a Church historian, 'to lay the chief stress on the sufferings of the slaves themselves.' And what of the records? Would a people be so ingenuous as to hand to posterity an indictment against themselves? Or was there no conscience to protest against the condition of slavery, and therefore no disposition to conceal its worst features?

The Romans wanted work done: they impressed non-Romans to do it. What was the nature of this work, and why the demand for labour? Was there a dearth of labour at home, and was slave labour cheap? Did slave labour throw out of work free men on farm and in factory? The foreign slave had something to give—labour, brains, skill often superior to those of the Roman: what did he receive in exchange? Again, having absorbed into the population vast numbers of foreigners, was imperial Rome alive to her responsibilities? Had she any motive at all besides that of exploitation, any conscious policy of training the best for positions of trust or responsibility? Did she wish to take them to herself as citizens? And lastly, what was the effect of this absorption of foreign blood upon the

Italian stock ? To what degree did the race degenerate as a result ?

When the conqueror's hand was stayed to spare the foe, the vast history of slavery began. To grant life instead of to destroy it was in itself a mark of progress,[1] even though the life spared was to be dragged out in the hewing of wood and the drawing of water. Enslavement was itself a concession ; and from that act of mercy or self-interest, a human institution began which is not yet ended. In early days the Latin, too, possessed his household slave whom he captured from rival neighbour. But such times are far from the Empire ; between the days of the Latin settlement and the fall of the Republic the Roman had learnt much from Carthage and had drawn from Greece her rich legacy of ideas and institutions. And a developed system of slavery is part of the legacy of Greece to Rome which Greece had in turn inherited from the East. Greece had adopted the system and rationalized it, offering after the event many sophistic justifications of it. In the study of Roman slavery defences will detain us little ; the Roman defence of slavery, as of most Roman institutions, will be found, if found at all, not in theoretic reasoning, but in a record of silent achievement.

---

[1] ' It is quite possible to hold that when, instead of devouring their captured enemies, men made slaves of them, the change was a step in advance ; and to hold that this slavery, though absolutely bad, was relatively good—was the best thing practicable for the time being.'— Herbert Spencer, *Study of Sociology*, p. 253 (London, 1878).

SLAVERY IN THE ROMAN
EMPIRE

CHAPTER I

THE MAKING OF SLAVES

Πόθεν δ' ἐστιν, ὦ ἄριστε, εἰδέναι ὅστις δοῦλος ἢ ὅστις ἐλεύθερος;
Dio Chr. xv. *ad init.*

ABOUT thirty years before our era, Octavian, then about thirty years old, took over that indescribable welter of corruption and misgovernment which was the Roman world. As the Emperor Augustus he left it an ordered Empire with all those opportunities for sound government of which advantage was taken later. To remote corners the Roman peace had penetrated; by the second century the world from Britain to Arabia and Armenia, from the Danube to the Sahara, was protected from foes without and to an amazing extent from misgovernment within: men had saluted Augustus by titles which to modern ears sound fulsome and extravagant, yet were the genuine expression of universal gratitude. And Gibbon is not alone in picking out the age from the death of Domitian to the accession of Commodus as 'the period in the history of the world during which the condition of the human race was most happy and prosperous.'[1]

Yet over the whole of this world, even to the farthest corners, were scattered those whom the Romans called *servi*, and we unfortunately call 'slaves.'

The sparing of the conquered enemy may have been the beginning of slavery;[2] but, as institutions became more elabo-

---

[1] *Decline and Fall*, ed. Bury, i. 78; Merivale and Dill would agree. For a different view, cf. J. A. Smith in *The Unity of Western Civilisation*, p. 88.

[2] For a short summary of the methods of enslavement, see Dio Chrys. xv. 453 and 454 R. War, he says, is the τρόπος . . . ὅσπερ οἶμαι πρεσβύτατος ἁπάντων ἐστί.

rate, so the reasons and methods of enslavement became more numerous : a device so obviously useful to the dominant race or family invited a wider application. To enslave an enemy rather than to slay him was a device to reap his labour, but it was also a way of enjoying a perpetual triumph over him ; it was at once a humiliation to him and a punishment for his presumption in taking up arms. Slavery as a punishment, therefore, becomes applicable not only to the foreigner but to the citizen also, who by crime, civil or religious, has shown himself unworthy of a citizen's privilege. Again, if the services of the slave are valuable, he himself is a valuable property ; it is but a small elaboration on primitive slavery by capture to enslave a free man who is unable to repay borrowed capital, especially if he has pledged his potential services as a slave against inability to repay. What a free man may suffer involuntarily, he may invite voluntarily, if he so will : a sheltered and tolerable slavery may be preferable to a precarious existence in freedom and poverty. A child exposed and left to die, but rescued by others, may be held to owe to his deliverers service and obedience in return for the supposedly invaluable gift of life. Accident of birth, lastly, condemns a child to a life similar to that of his parents : the children of slave-parents can scarcely be anything but slaves themselves. If none of these causes operate steadily and surely enough to keep the supply of slaves at the level needed—if wars have ceased, if exposure is condemned, or increase yields too few, then the conditions of warfare must be artificially restored, and brigandage and piracy and kidnapping become a profitable trade as the scarcity or the demand grows greater ; they become more dangerous and still more profitable as the Government takes stronger action to suppress them.

All these methods of enslavement had been known and used long before the history of Rome began : they had been practised in the Eastern and Hellenic and Carthaginian worlds.[1] Some of them Rome devised anew for herself ; but, as she extended her frontiers to include peoples and cultures in which slavery had been established for centuries, she acquired at once an apparent sanction and a greater desire for slave-labour.

[1] For the domestic slaves of the Etruscans, see Diod. v. 40 ; Fell, *Etruria and Rome*, p. 26.

The very elaboration of the system which she found there not only supplied justification and encouragement to enjoy its benefits, but offered the facilities of an organized traffic in slaves to absorb and distribute the tens of thousands of prisoners of war which fell to the victorious armies. But, though each method had operated at some time in Roman history, not all of them operated with steady or uniform effect ; by the time of the Empire some were almost or entirely obsolete, and compensation had to be found by stimulating others to keep the supply of slaves as constant as could be under altered conditions.

The temple of Janus was seldom closed in Roman history. During the last century and a half of the Republic the East had passed into Roman hands : Asiatic slaves perhaps first passed west as prisoners of war after the campaign against Antiochus in 189 B.C. ; and the victories of Pompey in Asia had benefited not only the merchant of goods, but the dealer in slaves. Hitherto slaves had come west chiefly by the channels of trade : now the vast reservoirs of slave-power themselves were thrown open. The campaigns in the West, culminating in Caesar's Gallic War, had worked the same effect : Gaul saw thousands of her sons sold beneath the yoke as the price of Roman rule. Under the Republic, war had seldom failed the demand for slave-labour. Mars was the enslaver, who enslaved as he conquered ; but his victims were foreigners from beyond the Roman frontier.

After victory, war should have given way to peace ; the conquered land had in theory become a province to be ruled by Roman law. If war had passed, then there was no longer enslavement by war. But under the Republic, peace and good government were too often ousted by greed : the province was to be the prey of its governor ; rebellion was provoked, wholesale kidnapping tolerated, publicans and slave-dealers were given a free hand, if only the governor shared in the profits. Enslavement by violence was common ; but it was sanctioned neither by war nor law.

With Augustus came a change. The 'boundaries' of Empire are observed, with now and then a forward move dictated by frontier needs. Absorption of territory on a vast scale is rare, and such territory is generally thinly populated ; consolidation is the watchword of imperial policy. The foreign enemy, therefore, can no longer furnish slaves as before. And with the Empire came a new life for the provinces ; the Emperors willed that peace and law should give to the lands now provinces such happiness as they had never known.[1] And their will became fact. Henceforth enslavement can take place on the frontiers only in defensive wars, or in such aggressive wars as defence demanded—and the enemy on the frontiers offered a less suitable type for slavery than the Asiatic, now a provincial ; or, enslavement must take place within the limits of Empire, and it must be sanctioned by law ; or it must be in violation of it, and therefore punishable, and under the Empire punished.

Yet enslavement by war within the Empire is not unknown in imperial times ; but now war and law go hand in hand. For the provincial turned rebel became a public enemy threatening the Roman peace, and as such he was liable to enslavement as a prisoner of war. It is on such grounds as this that Augustus had enslaved the cities of Cyzicus, Tyre, and Sidon ; party faction, the eternal trouble in these eastern cities, had broken out, and Roman citizens had been killed.[2] An example was made to teach the East, through the fate of three of her most famous cities, that peace and quietness shall reign. For long years Rome had shown more forbearance towards the troublesome Jews than to any other of her subject races. After a history of toleration on one side and broken promises and provocation on the other, the army of Titus took ninety-seven thousand prisoners and enslaved them all ;[3] most of them were sent to the mines of Egypt ; those under seventeen years old graced the victor's triumph before they were sold. A sterner, perhaps a kinder, fate was reserved for the Cantabri in the reign of Augustus. Some of them had been sold, but after killing their masters had returned to their homes, and stirred up rebellion. Even Agrippa failed at first to make headway against an enemy who had gained experience in slavery and fought with desperation, knowing that no quarter would be shown to slaves turned rebel ; they received none, nor their

---

[1] Abundantly illustrated in Rostovtzeff, *Social and Economic History of the Roman Empire*, chs. vi. and vii.

[2] Dio, liv. 7.

[3] Jos. *Bell.* vi. 9. 2 ; cf. also the enslavement of thousands in Hadrian's reign ; see B. W. Henderson, *Hadrian*, p. 218.

kinsmen, whom they had incited.[1] The Salassi, on the other
hand, a tribe in south-east Gaul, suffered only the enslavement
of those of military age on the understanding that they should
not be liberated for twenty years.[2] Such seems to have been
Augustus' usual treatment of rebellious tribes ; it earned the
approval of his biographer, Suetonius, who regards [3] it as
evidence of the general tendency to goodness and moderation
which caused peoples so remote as the Scythians and the Indians
to seek Augustus' friendship. ' He never visited with too severe
a punishment those who revolted too often or treacherously ;
he sold them as captives, with the proviso that they should
not be slaves in a district close to their own homes, and should
not be manumitted for thirty years.' If provincials refused to
take, when offered, the advantages of inclusion within the
Empire, they were to learn under compulsion to respect the
interests of those who wished to enjoy those advantages.

The other method of enslavement by violence within the
Empire is that of piracy and brigandage, both suppressed by
Government, but both existing precariously in the remoter
seas and distant mountains to a late date. Piracy had survived on a large scale into the Empire, encouraged by years
of civil war when thousands dispossessed of property and
fleeing for their lives had turned to piracy and robbery as the
only means of livelihood. Numbers of slaves, left uncared for
on their masters' death or flight, had no choice but to turn
brigands themselves, and join the pirate vessels which promised
an adventurous life and a rich reward. Indeed, in the latter
years of the Republic, piracy had fulfilled a useful function ; if
war failed to supply the increasing demand for slaves in Italy,
the pirate could be depended on to keep the markets full, while
the authorities looked on in well-paid complaisance.[4] Generals
engaged in civil war had found the pirate organization useful
too ; the pirates' numbers and daring, their specialized knowledge of tide and coast, had served more than one commander
in good stead. Sextus Pompeius enlisted pirates and slaves
and owed much of his success to their skill ; [5] from his fleet
Augustus handed back to their masters thirty thousand slaves.[6]

---

[1] Dio, liv. 5.   [2] liii. 25.   [3] Suet. *Aug.* 21.
[4] See H. A. Ormerod, *Piracy in the Ancient World*, p. 207.
[5] Dio, xlviii. 17.   [6] Mon. Anc. 25.

Even when defeated in the West, the pirate fleets maintained supremacy in the East as late as 25 B.C.,[1] until the organization of the Roman fleets won and maintained the command of the Mediterranean.   Epictetus [2] can say, ' You see that Caesar has given us a great peace ; no longer are there wars and battles or brigandage or piracy.   At all seasons we may travel by land or sea from the East to the West.'   Yet in the more remote seas it was still unsafe for trade vessels ; and the pirates often found the selling of their prisoners as slaves the most profitable part of a raid.   Even in Pliny's day the trade routes in the Bosporus and through the Red Sea to India were not free from danger, and armed guards escorted vessels.[3]   Yet it is clear that piracy on any scale was becoming a memory, suitable only for romance and the imaginary disputations of the rhetorical schools.[4]

That brigandage was common enough even in Italy for years after the battle of Actium is not surprising.   It would have been strange if life and property had suddenly become secure by the mere news of Augustus' victory : it was years before the first Emperor was sure even of his own safety.   But, his position established, peace and order in Italy were his first concern, and a firm hand was sadly needed.   Civil war had interfered with the supply of slaves by foreign conquest : confiscations and proscriptions, desolation and plunder, had made it easy for slaves to escape when their owners were with the armies, or in exile, or dead.   Augustus himself had enlisted thousands of them to man his fleets.   And so in the interval between the end of war and the return of peace lawlessness found its opportunity.   Citizens travelling by the main roads of Italy were carried off to fill the empty slave-prisons in the

---

[1] Cf., e.g., Strabo, 671.

[2] Diss. iii. 13, quoted Glover, *Virgil*, p. 144.

[3] On the route from Myos-hormos to India, see Ormerod, *op. cit.* p. 258 ; Charlesworth, *Trade Routes and Commerce of the Roman Empire*, p. 43. Plin. *N.H.* vi. 101 : ' quippe omnibus annis navigatur sagittariorum cohortibus impositis : etenim piratae maxime infestabant.'   For piracy off the Egyptian coast, see Philostr. *Vit. Ap.* iii. 24 (a carefully laid plan). Bosporus : Strabo, 495.

[4] Ormerod, *op. cit.* p. 264 : ' Capture by pirates formed a part of the stock-in-trade of the schools of rhetoric . . . in a period when piracy was practically non-existent.'   See reff. collected there.

south of Italy ; bands of unowned slaves lived as brigands in the highlands. It was unsafe to travel without escort ; for civil war had shown both landowners and slaves how to satisfy their wants. At last Tiberius was sent to the south of Italy with orders to restore law and order, and, though more is heard up to Claudius' reign of unruly gangs on estates, there is no explicit mention of kidnapping. But that mysterious disappearances ceased in Italy any more than a hundred years ago in England would be too much to expect. Pliny cites [1] examples of the disappearance of men while travelling ; one of them had only reached Ocriculum, forty miles from Rome, and Pliny suggests he was waylaid either by his servants or by brigands. Dio Chrysostom in a philosophical discussion can still quote kidnapping as a source of slavery.[2] Sometimes such captives were held to ransom, which would be safer than selling them, probably ; for by a *lex Cornelia* severe penalties were inflicted for selling a free man as a slave.[3]

Of the provinces it is less easy to say that liberty was certainly protected. As Roman influence penetrated into remote interiors and civilization secured a foothold, highway robbery and kidnapping decreased. In distant corners like the Bosporus slave-raids by local tribes were still carried on ; the Heniochoi, according to Strabo, raided by day or by night ;[4] neighbouring Governments sometimes combined to take reprisals, but Roman influence was not strong enough to suppress it, at any rate in his day. If the romance of Apuleius is to be taken as giving a fairly accurate account of prevailing conditions, Greece was the least orderly of the provinces. Especially in the north, robbery and violence were of daily occurrence.[5] At the same time, when peace was robbing the adventurous of much that enlivened life, the new art of the fairy story would make the most of its material. The brigand provided romantic material for the novelist, and safe and obsolete themes for the rhetorician, and Apuleius was both. Yet with all deduction made for invention it still remains true that Thessaly and Macedonia were among the most backward of all regions within the Empire,

[1] Plin. *Ep.* vi. 25.　　　　　[2] *Oratio* xv. 454 R.
[3] For ransom, *v.* Strabo, 496 ; for lex Cornelia, Apul. *Met.* viii. 24, e.g.
[4] ἀνδραποδισμοῦ χάριν. See passage of Strabo cited.
[5] See, e.g., *Met.* vii. 9.

and here, if anywhere, the seizure and sale of free men might take place.[1] At the same time it was strictly illegal, and a plea for the restoration of freedom—*causa liberalis*—might be brought by the slave before a magistrate in a province or before the praetor in Rome.[2] For the brigand the best chance of success lay in enslaving in a remote part and shipping the victim quickly and secretly to some other province to be put to work on an outlying estate.

So much for enslavement by violence. There were other methods, which were practised in the heart of the Empire. One at least was illegal, but was difficult to discover in practice ; others had the sanction and the active assistance of law.

At no time under the Republic or the early Empire was the practice of exposing new-born children forbidden by law.[3] Moralists might condemn it, statesmen who perceived the decrease of population might offer rewards for the upbringing of children, but the practice continued. Among the nobility there were more males than females, says Dio[4]—a strange proportion, especially after the civil wars, unless exposure reversed the natural tendency—and therefore Augustus allowed all who wished, except senators, to marry freedwomen, and gave to their offspring legitimacy of birth. Yet it was Augustus who wished to preserve the people free from all taint of servile blood. Children were more important than consistency.[5] At the other end of our period Christian apologists bear witness in no uncertain terms to the practice of exposure. They may exaggerate what they condemn ; but, since they quote exposure as a retort to the charges that at church meetings infants were slain and eaten, the countercharge depends for its point on the prevalence of the custom.[6] Minucius Felix asks in-

---

[1] Philostr. *Vit. Ap.* viii. 7 (xii) says kidnappers and slave-dealers never resort to Greece, least of all to Arcadia. But this occurs in Apollonius' speech in self-defence when accused of murdering an Arcadian boy.

[2] Buckland, *The Roman Law of Slavery*, pp. 652 sqq., deals with *causa liberalis*.

[3] *Id. Slavery*, p. 402. Other rights in the *patria potestas* had become obsolete ; but the right of exposure remained unforbidden till A.D. 374.

[4] liv. 16.   [5] See the chapter on Manumission.

[6] Tert. *Apol.* 9 : ' aut frigori et fami et canibus exponitis.' Cf. Justin Martyr, *Apol.* i. 27.

dignantly whether ' any one could have the heart to kill one just born, hardly entered upon life, and shed and drink its fresh young blood,' and turns the charge upon its inventors. ' No one can believe this unless he himself were capable of doing so. I see your newly born sons exposed by you to wild beasts and birds of prey and cruelly strangled to death.' [1]

That hundreds of exposed children died is certain ; perhaps fate was kind to them. Yet if they had survived, the law would not have been harsh ; in classical law exposed children never became slaves.[2] Actually, however, slavery claimed many ; those who found them brought them up as slaves or passed them on to dealers. The helpless babe could tell no tales. Sometimes they were reclaimed by parents, or evidence of free birth came to light. A slave who could produce evidence of free birth could set on foot a case at law provided he could find some one to support his case—an *assertor*—and the whole procedure gives the benefit of the doubt to the slave. It is difficult to say, however, to what extent the complicated rules applied to the provinces. Augustus, Vespasian, Titus, Domitian issued edicts and letters to regulate procedure in various provinces ; but Trajan, writing to Pliny, says that he can find no general rule ; he orders, however, that in Bithynia the claims of those who can prove a right to freedom are to be admitted, nor should it be required of them to buy their freedom by paying the cost of maintenance.[3] Such bias in favour of liberty—*favor libertatis*—is in agreement with the whole complex law of *causa liberalis*, which, of course, does not concern itself solely with the claims of the exposed.

At the same time the burden of proof lay with the slave ; and in the majority of cases such evidence would not be forthcoming. Often the slave would suppose he had been born such. It was not to the master's interest to reveal the truth, and he might justify his silence by reckoning up the cost of maintenance and tacitly promising manumission some day. Two cases, however, in which evidence was forthcoming, are mentioned by

[1] Minucius Felix, 30, transl. by J. H. Freese.
[2] Buckland, *Slavery*, p. 402. During the later Empire ' a harsher rule prevailed.'
[3] Plin. *Ep.* x. 65 sq. Mitteis, *Reichsrecht und Volksrecht*, p. 361, thinks that Trajan's decision can have had little effect.

Suetonius.[1] Gaius Melissus, a free-born native of Spoletium, was exposed owing to the disagreement of his parents. Brought up with care and patience, he was introduced by his protector to advanced studies, and was later given as *grammaticus* to Maecenas, with whom he lived on such terms of pleasant friendship that, in spite of the claim made by his mother, he remained in slavery, preferring his present status to that given him by birth.[2] Soon, however, he was freed, and passed into the service of Augustus, who put him in charge of the Octavian libraries. A few years before this a similar career had awaited M. Antonius Gnipho, who had been born a free native of Gaul, but had been exposed ; he had been educated and manumitted, and had acquired fame as a teacher of rhetoric, numbering Cicero among his pupils. But it would be unfair to argue from these two examples that the exposed child necessarily secured recognition of free birth ; all that can be said is that, if he could bring forward evidence, then the law asserted his freedom, and, if he had been manumitted, gave him back the status of ' free-born ' — *ingenuus* — instead of that of ' freedman.'

One of the rights given by the *patria potestas* from earliest times was the right to sell a child. It is true that certain conditions are made, but the right is not materially affected. Cicero [3] can speak of the sale of a child as possible in his time. If sold in a foreign country, the child became a slave ; if sold at home, he became a slave in private, but not in public law, ' and exchanges servitude to the father for that to the purchaser.' [4] But Paul the jurist lays down the rule of classical law that such a sale cannot prejudice the claim of the children to the right of free birth, since a free man ' is valued at no price.' [5] Still later, Constantine regards the sale of a new-born child as valid, and

---

[1] Suet. *de Gramm.* 21 and 7.

[2] ' Quamquam asserente matre, permansit tamen in statu servitutis praesentemque condicionem verae origini anteposuit.' For this attitude to slavery, cf. *C.I.L.* xiii. 7119 : 'servitus mihi nunquam invida fuisti.'

[3] *Pro Caec.* 34.

[4] Greenidge, *Roman Public Life*, p. 20, and cf. what is said there on ' the non-correspondence of fact and theory' in family life, and the law pertaining to it.

[5] P. v. 1. 1. Buckland, *Slavery*, p. 420. Confirmed by Caracalla.

says that this is a law established by earlier Emperors.[1] Here, then, is an exception to the classical law. But the information is very unsatisfactory; it is quite obscure whether Cicero is assuming the condition that the child must be new-born, or, if this condition is later than Cicero, who introduced it. It is equally obscure when or how it became admitted in classical law that sale was not prejudicial to free birth. All that can be said is that one of the Antonines seems to state in a rescript that the selling of children was illegal.[2] At the same time it is clear from legislation in the late Empire that the practice of selling children—not necessarily new-born—existed, especially in times of stress, and it would be hard to believe that in the first two centuries the temptation to relieve poverty in this way was always resisted. Such sale can safely be assumed for all periods in the history of slavery, yet little record would be left in the literature or inscriptions. The Phrygians, says Philostratus, see nothing shameful in selling their children into slavery. So, too, the Frisii sold herds, lands, wives, and children to pay the tribute, and, having exhausted these, revolted.[3]

Another source of slavery has been found in the selling of self; indeed, it has been claimed by a German scholar, Bang, that this was a method of enslavement extensively practised, and so prevalent as to warrant his statement that in the Empire Italy, next to the East, provided the greatest number of slaves. But Bang quite misunderstands the texts which he quotes to prove his point.[4] There was a rule, it is true, that a citizen of full age who sold himself to share in the price, could not claim his liberty. The point is exactly the opposite of what Bang needs. Such self-sale was a fraud, with the object of claiming liberty at once on the ground that a citizen could not be sold into valid slavery, and then pocketing the spoil in the form of the price paid. There is no sense in his sharing the price if he became a slave, for it would belong to his master. It is essentially a punishment that is inflicted, and it is essential

[1] *C. Th.* v. 10. 1. Buckland, *ibid.* Marquardt, *Vie privée*, p. 4, n. 1, does not help.

[2] *Cod. Iust.* vii. 16. 1. Hence Poste, Gaius, p. 40, 4th edition, says that *noxae deditio* was the only genuine sale of a child in Gaius' time.

[3] Philostr. *Vit. Ap.* viii. 7 (xii.); Tac. *Ann.* iv. 72. See Mitteis, *op. cit.* p. 359.

[4] *Röm. Mittheilungen*, vol. xxvii. p. 207.

that the buyer should be deceived.[1] At no historical date, so far as is known, did Roman law recognize self-sale into slavery.[2] It is possible that in times of difficulty men pretended to be slaves to make a living. But this did not make them slaves, and they could claim their liberty subject to payment of damages.[3] However, little is said of such voluntary slavery, if indeed it did exist to any degree. Ingenuus and Ingenua applied as names to slaves have been supposed to be evidence of free-birth ; Petronius mentions the case of a man who preferred to be a slave rather than a tax-burdened provincial.[4] Dio Chrysostom [5] says that thousands of men sold themselves into slavery ' under contract ' ; the contract, which would probably have a time-limit and might contain provisions about the man's family, somewhat takes the sting out of slavery ; but Dio is writing for Greeks at a time when they still lived for many purposes under Greek law, which did allow temporary slavery. How far Roman law in such matters was supposed to supersede local law is obscure ; but as it is probable that in the provinces, particularly in the East, self-sale, whether forbidden or not, did exist, so it is certain that Roman law regarded temporary slavery as a contradiction in terms, and never recognized self-sale as a valid method of enslavement.[6]

Enslavement might follow as a result of condemnation in the law-courts. Enslavement for theft, for evading the census

[1] See Buckland, *Slavery*, p. 427.

[2] With the possible exception of self-sale by *nexum*, abolished by the ex Poetelia, perhaps 326 B.C. But it is uncertain whether *nexum* implied self-sale. See de Zulueta, *The Recent Controversy about Nexum* (Oxford, 1912), esp. p. 9, and p. 26, where he sums up ' the theory of self-mancipation is juristically objectionable.'

[3] *Dig.* xl. 12. 7. pr. and h.t. 14 sq. ; for lapse of time barring this claim, see Buckland, *Slavery*, p. 648.

[4] 57.   [5] 453 R.

[6] The confident tone of this paragraph is due to a letter kindly written to me by Professor Buckland, who supports me in challenging Bang's evidence and conclusions. To him I owe one or two of the points made. See further, Mitteis, *op. cit.* pp. 359–361. Mommsen treated it as an open question whether ' es dem freien Peregrinen des römischen Reichs gestattet war, sich in die Gewalt eines Dritten zu begeben.' Mitteis, relying on Callistratus in *Dig.* xl. 12. 37, ' Conventio privata neque servum quemquam neque libertum alicuius facere potest,' and considering the circumstances under which he wrote, regards self-sale as forbidden to provincials ; the *Reichsrecht* has superseded the *Landsrecht*.

or military service, had by the Empire become obsolete ; but there still remained enslavement for serious crime, when the sentence involved loss of civil rights. Such criminals were generally sent to work in mines or marble or sulphur quarries. In the legal phrase they were condemned *in metallum* and became *servi poenae*; on the other hand, a temporary term of labour was distinguished by the phrase *ad ministerium metallicorum*, and sentence to this did not involve enslavement. Sometimes criminals were condemned to *ludus venatorius* or the gladiatorial arena, and were so employed till their death-sentence was carried out ; sometimes they won pardon and freedom by successful efforts to satisfy the blood-lust of the populace. But sentence to penal slavery (*servitus poenae*) applied only to the lower order of free men ; decurions were for practical purposes exempt, so too soldiers and veterans. Sometimes an Emperor exerted his will to override the established usage of the law.[1] Augustus sold into slavery a Roman knight who had mutilated his sons so that they should not be able to serve in the army.[2] Titus ordered that professional informers (*delatores*) should be scourged and sold into slavery.[3] Meantime the principle that a free man 'is valued at no price' is preserved. Technically, the convict is not enslaved ; no price has been paid for him ; he abdicates his rights, and in theory at least belongs as a slave to no one.[4]

As akin to penal slavery may be mentioned enslavement under the SC. Claudianum of A.D. 53. The provisions of this rule, and their significance, will be considered later, but for the moment they may be summed up by saying that a free woman who persisted, after warning, in living with a slave, might be claimed as a slave by the slave's master, if he so wished. Whatever the difficulties attached[5] to the interpretation of this decree, it is clear that for at least three centuries this danger overhung any free woman who so demeaned herself, and it is clearly a punishment and a deterrent, which aimed at protecting the

---

[1] For *servi poenae*, see Buckland, *Slavery*, 403 ; Mommsen, *Droit pénal romain*, iii. 292.

[2] Suet. *Aug.* 24.   [3] Suet. *Tit.* 8.

[4] Hence there can be no manumission, only restoration to freedom. See Buckland, *loc. cit.*

[5] Buckland, *Slavery*, p. 412.

interest of the master, and preserving society from a multitude of anomalies which would otherwise have arisen.

There remains finally the commonest method of enslavement under the Empire—namely, birth. Here the rule may be quite simply put : if the mother of the child is a slave, the child is a slave whatever the status of the father. The most important exception is a provision of the SC. Claudianum. By it the children of the free woman were slaves whether the master of the slave exercised his right to enslave her or not. It was left for the humane Hadrian to abolish this provision as harsh and inelegant.[1]   Henceforth the child takes the status of the mother, in this case as in the rest. On the other hand, there are cases in which the child of the slave mother is regarded as freeborn. But all such cases presuppose the eventual manumission of the mother, which, for various legal reasons, may have been delayed ; again the law is wholly on the side of liberty.[2]

This short summary of enslavement started with war and ended with birth ; and this is the true order in the history of slavery. It ceases to be profitable to buy slaves, work them to death, and replace them by the purchase of more. As wars ceased and slaves became more scarce, the source of supply became in the main the birth of children of slave-parents.

The change from enslavement without the Empire to enslavement within the Empire, and from enslavement by capture to enslavement by birth, is of the utmost importance, and has far-reaching effects both upon the history of slavery and the history of the Empire. The making of slaves is taking place in the heart of the city and in the home ; it ceases to be the triumphal retribution upon foes, and so loses much of its prima facie justification ; it becomes commonest not where are strife and bloodshed, but where peace and kindliness flourish most. The nearer the life of the slave approximates to the free family life of the free man, the more will the increase of slaves be encouraged. And so the change, helped by other influences, altered the type of slave and modified very profoundly the attitude of master to slave ; it had a very real

---

[1] Tac. *Ann.* xii. 53. (Suet. *Vesp.* 11, is erroneous.)   Modified by Hadrian. See Gaius, i. 84–92.

[2] Buckland, *Slavery*, p. 399.

bearing on manumission, and the assumption of freed slaves into the citizen roll is of great concern to the State. To trace this process from enslavement to citizenship, and to indicate the issues involved for individual and Empire, is the main interest in a study of Roman slavery.

Meantime, whatever the method of enslavement, whence came the majority of slaves ?

To answer this question use may be made of an elaborate collection of references to slave nationality compiled by Bang.[1] Divided into two sections, Republican and Imperial, the collection gives an opportunity of reviewing quickly the nationalities which provided slaves, though the conclusions drawn by the compiler seem of unequal value. Under the Republic slaves are, on the whole, drawn from outside the limits of Roman rule ; under the Empire the vast majority are necessarily drawn from within. But in the imperial section appears a large sub-section devoted to slaves drawn from Italy. A slave who is described in the inscriptions as ' natione Florentinus ' is, according to the author of the article, a real Italian, who has been enslaved by one of the peaceful processes mentioned above ; on the other hand, the son of an Egyptian slave, a son born in Italy and speaking no language but Latin, still remains ' natione Aegyptius.' [2] The list of Italian slaves is, it is true, fairly long,[3] and includes slaves and freedmen who are natives of all parts of Italy—natione Florentinus, Puteolanus, Ferrariensis, domo Veronae, domo Aquileiae. That Italy played some part in the making of slaves would seem to follow from these cases ; but it would be unjustifiable to conclude, as Bang does,[4] from the frequency of such references, that Italy, next to the East, provided the greatest number of slaves, and provided them by direct enslavement and not by birth. The mere counting of instances will give uncertain results. It is true that the East provided the greatest number of slaves at all times, and this is revealed not by any counting of references to Oriental

---

[1] *Die Herkunft der röm. Sklaven*, in *Röm. Mittheilungen*, vols. xxv. and xxvii. The collection is fairly exhaustive, though one or two additions can be made. See also an article, *J.R.S.* vol. xiv., by M. L. Gordon, which uses Bang and Tenney Frank, *American Historical Review*, xxi. p. 689.

[2] Bang. *op. cit.* p. 220.   [3] It covers two and a half pages.

[4] P. 219.

slaves—though the numerous examples, especially in the inscriptions, must be given their due weight—but from express statements in the literature. On this point the statistics of Bang give corroboration. But thousands of Syrians may be enslaved in a single sentence of the literature : the references to Italian slaves mention only one individual, for most of them are sepulchral inscriptions. When all are cited individually, the list may seem imposing. But it thus gains a false value. There are only two known cases of Pannonian slaves ; yet it would be rash to argue that more Italians than Pannonians were enslaved.[1] The problem turns upon the relative likelihood of the survival of records. The Italian enslaved for whatever reason was still proud of his free birth : [2] his Italian blood marked him off from the Oriental, his birth distinguished him from the *verna* ; the title ' natione Florentinus ' records both. On the other hand, the slave from the western frontiers, though he may have treasured the memory of freedom, had less opportunity to record it. Wilder in nature and illiterate, he worked in farm or mine, and when he died no monument bore witness to his race. Thousands from the western frontiers served in the auxiliary troops, it is true ; but none the less thousands were enslaved : yet the individual references to Dacians or Pannonians or Noricans are so few as to be negligible.

Nor need it be assumed that, because under the Empire there are more references to the enslavement of individual Italians than there are under the Republic, the enslavement of Italians therefore increased. The overwhelming majority of inscriptions of most kinds date from imperial times : this consideration alone vitiates any comparison of republican and imperial inscriptions on a merely numerical basis.

The stream of slavery set from the East along well-established channels worn deep by the traffic of slaves for hundreds of years ; a channel of movement in the opposite direction was provided by the army ; the West produced the soldiers, who

---

[1] For enslavement of Pannonians by Tiberius, see Dio, liv. 31.

[2] Cf. Ingenuus and Ingenua as slave-names. And not only Italian pride. Cf. *C.I.L.* x. 388=Dess. 7791. L. Manneius Q. libertus medicus, φύσει δὲ Μενεκράτης Δημητρίου Τραλλιανός. For a different explanation of Ingenuus, see M. L. Gordon, *J.R.S.* xiv. p. 109.

were often quartered in the East.[1]   The stream started as far east as Parthia and Persia, gathered much of its strength from Asia Minor and Syria, with contributions from Egypt, Thrace, and Greece ; as it made for Rome it gathered a little from the north shores of the Adriatic and was joined at Rome by a tributary from Africa and smaller rivulets from the northern and western provinces.   To realize the origin of the slaves scattered over the Empire is of importance for the two last chapters of this essay ; but all that need be done here is to mention the chief nationalities and add notes on the type of work in which they were employed and some of their characteristics.[2]

From Asia Minor come Phrygians, Lydians, Cappadocians, Bithynians, Carians ; from beyond, Persians, Arabians, Parthians ; from the south of the Aegean, Alexandrians, Egyptians, Ethiopians.   These ' Asiatics ' were used chiefly for domestic service of any kind ; they were civilized, more so than their masters often, for much of Syria and Asia Minor was overlaid with Greek manners.   But that was not necessarily an advantage.   What Greek manners taught in versatility was undone often by laxity of morals.   Syrians are venal and the more worthless as they know Greek, says Cicero ;[3] their morals are gross, their music unendurable.[4]   I know your Cappadocian, says a character in Petronius ; he does not rob himself of much. And so, having some pretence to manners, these races serve in every capacity within the house—in the kitchen, in the dining-room, in office, in library, everywhere.   A Syrian porter is mentioned by Lucian,[5] and a Libyan nomenclator. Cappadocians are familiar as litter-bearers, but Bithynians, Moesians, Liburnians are also found in this employment.[6] Syrians steal plate from a dining-room ;[7] while Carians are

---

[1] Syrians served in the army, even in the first century, but they would be stationed in the west, e.g. the Leg. iii. Augusta at Lambaesis contained Syrians.   The effect of Syria on the legions from the west was bad ; cf. the indiscipline which Corbulo found and remedied.   See Henderson, *The Life and Principate of the Emperor Nero*, p. 166 sq.

[2] Bang gives the nationalities.   Employments and characteristics can be found incompletely in Marquardt, *Vie privée*, i., and Mayor's Juvenal. The list in the text is compiled more or less at random from the literature.

[3] *De Or.* ii. 66.   [4] Juv. iii. 62.   [5] *De mercede conductis*, 10.

[6] Mart. vi. 77 ; Marquardt, i. 175, n. 4 ; and Mayor on Juvenal, i. 65.

[7] Petr. 22.

offered for sale with the recommendation that they are not thieves—which condemns the whole race.[1] Sardians were proverbially dishonest. Whole droves from Pontus, Lydia, Phrygia, may be seen at Rome, writes Philostratus of Domitian's time ; [2] hither, too, Egyptians, Ethiopians, Asiatics were brought by Caligula for plays and spectacles.[3] An inscription found at Rome commemorates Trophimus, an imperial freedman : he was once a Phrygian shepherd.[4] From Pontus, too, came L. Lutatius Paccius, a *turarius*, from the staff of Mithradates ; if captured by Pompey and sold as a boy, he could easily have lived till the time of Augustus.[5] Another freedman came from Nisibis, in Syria, another from Palmyra.[6] Jews are common enough, and not popular.[7] Persians are rare, and few Parthians care to reveal themselves as such.[8] A traffic in Indian slaves is attested in the *Periplus of the Red Sea*.[9] Petronius mentions Arabians with bored ears,[10] and Nubians were somewhat of a curiosity. Numidians and Africans were employed as litter-bearers and outriders. ' I should like Cato to see one of our dandies with his outriders and Numidians,' writes Seneca.[11] So also Gaetulians were employed.

Slaves from the western frontiers are less frequent in the literature and inscriptions. Julius Caesar is said to have surrounded himself with a Spanish bodyguard.[12] Augustus similarly used Germans and Batavians, whom he dismissed after the defeat of Varus.[13] Germans were carried off in numbers by Germanicus and attached to his household to form a guard ; among them were Batavians, Frisians, Suevi, Ubians, and Bataesians.[14] And Germans are again to be found as an imperial guard under Gaius and Nero, till they were dismissed, probably finally, by Galba.[15]

---

[1] Philostr. *Vit. Ap.* iii. 25.

[2] viii. 7. (xii.).   [3] Suet. *Calig.* 57 and 58.   [4] Dess. 8070.

[5] See Dess. on 7612.   [6] 3944, 7063.

[7] Juv. iii. 296 ; Petr. 68 ; Dess. 8193. See Friedländer (9th ed.), iii. pp. 206–208.

[8] Cf., however, *C.I.L.* vi. 23959, if Mithres and Persis are any indication.

[9] 36.   [10] 102.   [11] *Ep.* lxxxvii. 9.   [12] Suet. *Div. Iul.* 86.

[13] Tac. *Ann.* i. 24 ; Dio, lv. 24 ; Suet. *Aug.* 49.

[14] Dess. 1724 sqq.

[15] Suet. *Calig.* 43 ; Tac. *Ann.* xiii. 18, xv. 58 ; Suet. *Galba*, 12.

The northern frontiers provided other slaves : ' send me a slave bought from a Mytilenian dealer,' writes Martial,[1] ' and I will send you a Danubian only fit to tend sheep.' Sarmatians, too, are known, and Siracians,[2] a Sarmatian tribe ; Iazyges [3] and Dacians. From Thrace came a number employed in domestic duties or as gladiators. The monument of the Statilian family records some twelve Thracians serving as litter-bearers, valets, cooks, and so forth. Augustus had freed a slave of the name of Bithus,[4] and Horace mentions a famous gladiator of that name ; [5] a Bessian, a Thracian tribe enslaved in 11 B.C., is to be found as an oil-dealer.[6] But the Thracians are less important as recruits to slavery than as recruits to the army. In the first century many Thracian slaves but no soldiers are to be found among the inscriptions of Rome ; in the second century Thracians flock into the army, whereas no datable inscription occurs which mentions a Thracian slave or freedman.[7]

Such accumulation of foreign elements was no sudden phenomenon of the Empire ; it was a process which had started long ago when foreign slaves first began to be imported, but under the last years of the Republic it had undoubtedly been speeded up.[8] During the years of the Augustan peace the vast number of foreigners began to attract serious attention, and became during the progress of the first century a commonplace of conversation and literature, forcing its way into the deliberations of senate and the decisions of Emperors.

The literature makes clear enough the enormous number of

---

[1] vii. 80.

[2] Tac. *Ann.* xii. 17. In A.D. 49, Zorsines, king of the Siracians, offered the Romans 10,000 ' slaves ' in return for the lives of free men.

[3] Dio, lxix. 22.   [4] *C.I.L.* vi. 20666.   [5] *Sat.* i. 7. 20.

[6] Dio, liv. 34 ; Dess. 7492.

[7] With the possible exception of *C.I.L.* vi. 1052. A most exhaustive treatment of the subject is to be found in an article of 233 pages, *I traci nelle epigrafi di Roma*, by G. G. Mateescu, in *Ephemeris Dacoromana I*, to which Mr. H. M. Last has referred me. The author produces by various tests, chiefly of nomenclature, an amazing mass of evidence to show the large number of Thracians in the army in the second and third centuries, and the same tests determine the nationality of many slaves and freedmen, providing at the same time fresh proof of the cosmopolitan character of the population of Rome.

[8] See a dissertation by M. E. Park on *The Plebs Urbana in Cicero's Day*, 1918.

slaves in Rome, where barbarian servants jostled staid senators
from the path, and made a city, once the home of the purest
Latin, horrid with the outlandish accents of foreign tongues.
Few of the Satires of Juvenal fail to contain some caustic
reference to the ubiquitous Oriental.[1]   In Rome on carnival
nights, says Statius, Lydian beauties clap their hands ; the
clashing of cymbals, the jingling music of Spain, the noise of
Syrian troupes make the night barbaric.[2]   Musical slaves were
common throughout the Empire, and when L. Verus returned
from the East to Italy with scores of musicians he is said to
have altered the musical taste of the times.[3]   Rome might be
described, says Athenaeus,[4] as the world in miniature ; here
all nations may be seen firmly established, whole nations are
settled—Cappadocians and Scythians, dwellers in Pontus, and
many others.   Similar is the description of Alexandria by Dio
Chrysostom,[5] ' here I see not only Greeks and Italians, Syrians,
Libyans, Cilicians, Ethiopians, Arabians, but Bactrians and
Scythians and Persians and Indians,' and both passages recall
a more famous.   Rome had become as cosmopolitan as the
most famous cities of the East.   A proposal to differentiate by
dress between slave and free man had been rejected in the
Senate through sheer fright ; slaves would thus discover their
tremendous majority in the city, and the lives of the few free
men still remaining would at once be endangered.[6]   Rome was
trembling, says Tacitus, at the vast size of slave establishments,
while the free people daily decreased.   To overawe these
multitudes Augustus selected one of the ex-consuls as city-
prefect, and in time of famine hoped to relieve it by the expulsion from the city of the thousands of unnecessary slaves
consuming the remaining stores.[7]

Attempts have been made to estimate the population of
Rome.   Different methods of reckoning and checking have
given some fairly definite results for the free population ; but
unfortunately it is precisely in the number of slaves that the

---

[1] Cf. iii. 60, the Orontes passage.   [2] Statius, *Silv.* i. 6. 65.
[3] Script. hist. aug. *Verus*, 8.   Alexandrian musicians have been found
at Cologne ; *C.I.L.* xiii. 8343.
[4] i. 36, p. 20 b.c. ; cf. Mart. vii. 30.   [5] xxxii. 672 R.
[6] Sen. *de clem.* i. 24. 1.
[7] Tac. *Ann.* iv. 27, vi. 11 ; Suet. *Aug.* 42.

investigations show the greatest divergence of opinion. For there is little evidence on which to work ; and every worker in this field must hazard his own guess as to the relation between slave and free, relying to a great extent upon the vague impressions conveyed by the literature. One reckoning assumes a free population in Rome of 520,000, a slave population of 280,000 ;[1] another, a free population of 710,000, while the number of slaves is placed as high as 900,000.[2] A more recent estimate suggests the figures 781,000 for the free population, 200,000 for the slaves.[3] Thus on the lowest computation of slaves there would be about four free men in Rome for every slave, a proportion which would justify Tacitus' statement.

[1] Beloch.

[2] Marquardt, *L'Organisation financière*, p. 151. Friedländer suggests that 900,000 is too large, *Roman Life and Manners*, vol. iv. p. 19 (Eng. trans.).

[3] Kahrstedt, in 9th ed. of Friedländer, *Sittengeschichte*, vol. iv., where reff. may be found.

CHAPTER II

IN THE HOUSEHOLD

Οἰκία δὲ τέλειος ἐκ δούλων καὶ ἐλευθέρων.
Aristotle, *Pol.* 1253b.

τῶν μὲν γὰρ λεγομένων δούλων πολλοὺς ὁμολογήσομεν δήπου εἶναι ἐλευθερίους,
τῶν δέ γε ἐλευθέρων πολλοὺς πάνυ δουλοπρεπεῖς.
Dio Chrysostom, xv. 456 R.

διχῶς γὰρ λέγεται τὸ δουλεύειν καὶ ὁ δοῦλος.
Aristotle, *Pol.* 1255a.

THE title of this chapter is somewhat misleading. The present survey limits itself to an attempt to show the influence of the system upon the moral and spiritual conditions of the day, and its implications of this nature for both master and slave. Fact must support and illustrate the more general statements, while law is relevant as reflecting and guiding public opinion. But exhaustiveness of detail must be sought elsewhere ; [1] on the other hand, the proportion here observed is somewhat novel ; slaves in education receive fuller treatment than slaves in the dining-room.

The effects of household slavery upon the mind and body of the slave-owning classes are subtle and far-reaching ; correct description of an insidious disease, whose destructiveness is little apparent to the sufferer himself, is not easy. Mistakes may be made in the sequence of symptoms ; what is diagnosed as a cause may be merely a result. Atrophy can only be understood in the light of a lesion elsewhere ; debility of one kind predisposes to disease of a more deadly nature. Here we must be content with artificial analysis, and consider the effects of the abuse of household slavery upon body and health and upon mind. Absolute control leads to the satisfaction of every bodily whim, and creates a despotic and irresponsible temper insensible to the happiness of others and blind to moral values. To depend

[1] e.g. Marquardt, *Vie privée*, i ; Becker's *Gallus*.

22

upon slaves is to give them power, which in turn is to be feared ; irresponsible power joined with fear causes the bluntness of feeling which increases into hideous cruelty ; the circle turns, and cruelty inflicted brings haunting terror of revenge to come ; insensibility swings back to debauchery and vice. If such were the effects upon men and women, what of the children reared in such an atmosphere, and deliberately thrust into the arms of slave nurses and tutors ?

I

Roman luxury is a theme which has held many by the double fascination of the attractive and the repellent. But luckily it need not detain us. Our concern is rather with the foundation upon which Roman luxury was built ; except for slavery, it would never have reared so vast a superstructure.

Let us review, then, the household of Trimalchio. At the moment he is away at the public baths, amusing himself with a game of ball. A slave hands him a new ball as he drops the other ; a slave boy stands by to offer his mop of hair for the great man to wipe his hands upon. After strenuous exercise there follows massage by skilled masseurs ; then home in a litter, four bemedalled runners going before him, a musician playing to him, and his favourite riding in a rickshaw by his side. At the door is a porter in green livery ; at the entrance to the dining-room sits a steward receiving payments ; here, too, a slave is stationed to remind guests to enter the room right foot foremost. Alexandrian boys pour water over the guests' hands ; others manicure them. The banquet begins ; waiters pass fussily everywhere. Ethiopians, Syrians, Jews, Egyptians perform their tasks ; cooks or butlers are commended or reproached. Lest the banquet should pall, entertainers of all kinds make their appearance, acrobats and comedians, mimics of the cries of mule-driver or hawker or of the nightingale's song. There follow musicians, reciters of Homer, dancers, actors, even huntsmen to enact the slaying of the wild boar, fowlers to snare the game. It is a wild scene—a masterpiece of conception and description. We may leave Trimalchio to his banquet and take a glance at the rest of his staff, so large that it was organized in *decuriae,* so large that not one in ten knew his master by sight, while even the domestic staff were compelled to take their meals in relays. Valets and bath attendants are present in abundance ; bailiffs and agents administer the numerous properties; foresters dwell in their cottages on the outlying lands; tavern-keepers carry on their business for their master ; couriers keep communication between the estates and carry the enormous correspondence involved by such manifold activities ; and when at night those activities cease, nightwatchmen come on duty to guard the whole.

The story is mere caricature. True, but as far as regards the domestic staff of a rich household rather its restraint is to be remarked. It is the inscriptions that read as romance ; in them most of Trimalchio's slaves can be found, and there are scores besides. The tomb erected by the Statilian family for their slaves and freedmen, and found in 1875 on the Esquiline, contains over five hundred epitaphs. It is true that the tomb may represent the staff of more than one generation, and certainly a good number refer to slaves engaged in business rather than in domestic duties, e.g. 'porter and rent-collector,' 'warehouseman '—*insularius, horrearius*; but, even so, there remain masseurs, bath attendants, litter-bearers — *unctores, balneatores, lecticarii*—and the rest. The imperial houses contain the greatest variety, duties being subdivided with an amazing minuteness.[1] Thus a slave solemnly records his duty as 'in charge of silver drinking vessels,' or 'brooches,' or 'perfumes,' or 'pearls '—*ab argento potorio, a fibulis, ad ungenta, ad margarita* ; it seems impossible not to believe that he must have combined these duties with others of which he was less able to make a suitable title, especially as we hear of no specialists whose duty it was to sweep or dust or wash dishes. Just as Trimalchio asks a slave to what division of the staff he belongs and how he came into his possession, so Seneca's imaginary critic retorts that the Stoic philosopher in his Epicureanism has more slaves than he can remember.[2] Not that this in itself is a matter of disgrace ; even in the present age the owner of a large house may never have seen or spoken to his scullery maid ; but there is evidence that the enormous staff of Trimalchio was not unparalleled in fact. Pedanius Secundus, a consular, is

---

[1] Cf., e.g., Dessau's Indices, or Marquardt, *op. cit.*
[2] Petr. 47, cf. 53. Sen. *de vit. beat.* xvii. 2.

said to have employed four hundred slaves in domestic duties alone.[1] Seneca speaks of the mob of well-groomed slaves to be found in every rich house,[2] and draws a revolting picture of their duties in the dining-room, where silent ranks of slaves stand round watching the gluttony of their master, and leaping forward only to perform some disgusting office. Should they but cough or sneeze, punishment follows. And what a life! For one of them the whole of life is summed up in his skill to carve a fowl—if, indeed, the tutor of the art is not more debased than his pupil. Others in degrading costumes pour out wine, and divide the night between the drunkenness and debauchery of their masters. Here are chefs skilled in sauces and piquant dishes who must note what taste their lord approves, who must study his palate and devise new flavours to whip into life his jaded senses. 'Di melius! Quot ex istis dominos habet!'[3] Regardless of numbers, slaves were everywhere to minister to their owners' pleasures and gratify every sense. The pleasures of eating and drinking, of dress and display, of self-indulgence and lust are everywhere apparent; the desire to rival a neighbour or friend led to the enlargement of slave-staffs and the introduction of fresh extravagances and luxuries. Handsome slaves of the same age, gathered from the markets of the world, were matched with fastidious taste,[4] much as chestnuts or bays were matched some years ago. The mere multiplication of slaves becomes an ambition in itself;[5] they must attend on walk or journey for mere appearance's sake.[6] No matter what they cost, no matter what economies must be effected elsewhere, slaves cannot be sacrificed.[7] The man of dignity must have his crowd of servants, whom merely to feed is so costly that Seneca sighs for the proverbial fertility of foreign climes.[8]

'The Roman of the Empire becomes tired, effeminate, sleepy. Of all the furniture in his house his bed is that which he uses most willingly; he lies down to sleep, he lies down to eat, he

---

[1] Tac. *Ann.* xiv. 43.　　[2] Sen. *Ep.* cx. 17, 'cohors culta servorum.'
[3] *Ep.* xlvii.　　[4] Tac. *Ann.* xv. 69.　　[5] Tac. *Hist.* ii. 78.
[6] Mart. ii. 57; Hor. *Sat.* i. 6. 101; Juv. vii. 141, vi. 352; and Sen. *Ep.* cx. 17; those handsome litter-bearers! Why marvel at them! 'Pompa est, ostenduntur istae res, non possidentur.' Cf. Hor. *Sat.* i. 1. 47, vi. 108; Apul. *Met.* ii. 2.
[7] Lucian, πρὸς τὸν ἀπαίδευτον, 25.　　[8] *Ep.* xvii. 3.

lies down to read and to think.'[1] And it is true that some circles at Rome seemed to be penetrated by that paralysis of body and mind which demands that others shall wait upon it. ' Alienis pedibus ambulamus : alienis oculis agnoscimus : aliena memoria salutamus : aliena vivimus opera. Perieruntque rerum naturae pretia et vitae argumenta. Nihil aliud pro nostro habemus quam delicias.'[2] That was the trouble ; all natural values had gone, all reasons for living. Occasionally a new sensation might be sought even in a return to the simple life. For two days Seneca and Maximus rough it. They take with them no luggage ; their fare is of the plainest ; they sleep upon the ground, wrapped in greatcoats. Thus they learn how much is superfluous in life, how mighty is the mind which has laid aside the need for the ministrations of others, which by desiring nothing creates its own riches. For two days these philosopher-gipsies live in camp. But how did they fare forth ? —with stick and stout boots to cover long miles ? They rode in a cart. True, it was a farm-cart. Unattended ? Behind followed another, filled with slaves. But only a few—' a few slaves, only as many as one wagon would hold.'[3] ' Perieruntque rerum naturae pretia ! '

Some elements of Roman luxury were definitely Roman ; gluttonous feasting was no part of the Oriental or Greek legacy, even though Greek cooks or Eastern delicacies were necessary to it. But many methods of extravagant spending were learnt in the East, and tutors of the new pleasures were ready to hand in those free, freed, or slave dependents of the great houses, who were only too anxious to start some novelty or set on foot a new fashion which presently was to become a necessity. Many masters learnt as much evil of one kind from their slaves as they taught of another ; the Syrian profligate stood by as a tempter to whisper the promise of new vice in the ear of the descendant of a Roman family once famous for hardness and simplicity, but now too enervated to resist. Given the depravity of master or slave or both, given the relation between them as supreme control on one side and fear or sycophancy on the other, the result can scarcely be anything but the bestiality which disfigures so much of the literature of the early Empire.

[1] Boissier, *Religion Romaine*, ii. 314.   [2] Plin. *N.H.* xxix. 19.
[3] *Ep.* lxxxvii. 2 ; for a similar picnic, cf. Statius, *Silv.* iii. 1. 77.

If all that may be summed up under the phrase ' flos Asiae '
is thus briefly dismissed, it is not because we minimize either
the extent or the effects of this prostitution of household slavery.
Not that slavery alone was responsible for the corruption. Rome
may have been no worse than London of to-day ; she talked
more freely and not without exaggeration of her vice, which
slavery made more easy but also more open. Unfortunately
it cannot be said that the presence of a slave class protected
the free classes from corruption within themselves. Lust is a
disease which does not confine itself to any one class ; and if it
looked downwards into slavery, it soon was encouraged to raise
its eyes higher till it scored its greatest triumphs in the *magna
adulteria* of the early Empire.

The dependence of society upon slaves produced natural
results of another kind. Both in big things and in small, society
put itself into the hands of its servants and laid itself open to
attack. ' Il est de règle que dans la vie privée, comme ailleurs,
le pouvoir finit toujours par appartenir à l'intelligence ' ;[1] but
the observation is true also of the unintelligent household slave.
' Quot servi tot hostes.' There is no secret of the house that
will not be divulged : ' you shall now know the whole state of
affairs in our house,' says Fotis in Apuleius :[2] life is not worth
living, whines a rich owner ; blackmail by friends is always
threatening.[3] The goodwill of an influential slave must be
secured by ' The Dependent Scholar ' of Lucian,[4] who must
slip some shillings into his hand as he brings an invitation to
dinner ; a slave secretary was bribed to cut out passages of
his master's private diaries.[5] Often, however, more serious
results depended on the word of a slave, which, purposely or
accidentally dropped, might lead to momentous results. The
most worthless slaves came forward with information as to
their masters' wealth on the accession of Vespasian ;[6] a chance
remark led to the burning of Cremona in the civil wars, and a

[1] Boissier, *Rel. Rom.* ii. 335.

[2] iii. 15. Cf. Prop. ii. 22*a.* 49; ii. 23. 2 ; iv. 8. 37. Slaves were the
agents used in Propertius' love affairs, and reported on his mistress'
attitude to him, etc.

[3] Philostr. *Vit. Ap.* vii. 23.   [4] *De mercede conductis,* 14. Cf. 28.

[5] Plin. *Ep.* vi. 22. Cf. Petr. 43, ' oricularios servos ' ; Plut. *de cap. ex.
in. util.* 87C, 91D.

[6] Tac. *Hist.* iv. 1.

slave of Verginius Capito deserted to L. Vitellius with promises
to hand over Tarracina to him by treachery.[1] Covert information gave place to open threats. The slave was often a real
menace to his master, whom he would openly threaten ; others
assailed their masters with false accusations.[2] So audacious
became the enterprise of clever slaves that impostors and
pretenders threatened the security of individuals and the safety
of the State. By clever impersonations they attempted to
make history and very nearly succeeded. Clemens, says
Tacitus, was the author of ' a scheme beyond a slave's conception.' Impersonating Postumus Agrippa, he landed in
Etruria and secured a considerable following in the towns.
Crowds of adherents followed his lead in Ostia and even in
Rome itself. So menacing was his approach that Tiberius
seriously considered the use of military force, but in the end,
by accomplishing the murder of the leader, dispersed his
followers.[3] A counterfeit Drusus appeared in the East and
was joined by many of the Emperor's freedmen ; so, too, a
certain Geta impersonated Scribonianus Camerinus murdered
by Nero.[4] Slaves had even laid claim to the Empire ; Telephus
had believed himself to be marked out by destiny for the rule
of the world and laid plans for an attack on Augustus.[5] In
the short reign of Otho a slave from Pontus had gathered
together deserters, and trading upon the popular belief that
Nero was not dead, rallied even soldiers and sailors to his cause
by the magic of that name. This rising became threatening
till by luck its leader was entrapped and murdered. In the
reign of Pertinax a similar slave pretender was lucky to escape
with a flogging.[6]

From these two roots, luxury and fear, sprang the callous-
ness to the happiness of the slave which developed into foul
cruelty. Indifference to the feelings of the slave was nothing

[1] iii. 32, ' vernile dictum ' ; iii. 77. He was given equestrian rank, and
later crucified.
[2] Nero refused the trial of Celer on the prosecution of a slave. Tac.
Ann. xiii. 10. For Pertinax' attitude, cf. Script. hist. aug. *Pert.* ix. 10 ;
cf. x. 10.
[3] Tac. *Ann.* ii. 39 and 40 ; Dio, lvii. 16 ; Suet. *Tib.* 25.
[4] Tac. *Hist.* ii. 72 ; *Ann.* v. 10.
[5] ' Quasi debita sibi fato dominatione.' Suet. *Aug.* 19.
[6] Tac. *Hist.* ii. 9 ; Script. hist. aug. *Pert.* x. 2.

new, and in the Roman was due to many causes. It was part of the legacy from the past history of slavery ; the victorious wars of Rome had enslaved many more thousands than the East had ever seen ; at the beginning of the Empire slaves were still cheap, and their lives were of little value compared with the pleasures of the conqueror, whose heart had been hardened by success. To this rather than to the brutalizing influence of warfare, which may be greatly exaggerated, may be attributed the insensibility of the Roman to suffering in slave or animal. The stern struggle may have produced a stock that was hard and unyielding, but stubbornness is not cruelty. It was the very success of Empire, the enjoyment of absolute power, that changed ruthless steadfastness to the blindness of heart which rejoices in gratuitous cruelty. Add to these craven fear, and the bully stands complete. But it was not only slave-blood that was freely poured.

The lives of slaves were freely expended in the mad freaks of masters who aimed at eclipsing their predecessors or contemporaries by some gorgeous show or atrocious novelty, or attempt to perform the impossible. To give point to a jest, life or limb was accounted cheap ; to demonstrate the owner's generosity, slaves were given away as presents, torn from their kindred or uprooted from surroundings where they were at last making for themselves some comfort and success.[1] The Roman matron, who might otherwise be a paragon of motherly care and kindliness, could keep by her side miserable slave-children deformed by nature or art, dwarfs and freaks, whom she fondled and displayed to her friends, asking them to admire their quaintness.[2] The shedding of the blood of slave gladiators or wild beasts in the arena could be tolerated, let alone enjoyed, only by those who were indifferent to the welfare of either in life, and such spectacles reacted to kill completely a moral sense by this time almost dead. To deadening influence of this kind no limit can be set ; it is its very curse that it spreads unsuspected to every phase of life, and it must be held as contributory cause of the cold-blooded carnage of the civil wars and the merciless exploitation of the provincials under

---

[1] Cf., e.g., Suet. *Nero*, 11 ; Script. hist. aug. *Ver.* v. 2, etc. etc.

[2] See Marquardt, *Vie privée*, i. 178 and 179, notes. Seneca (*Ep.* 1. 2) says he hates them ; cf. **xv.** 10.

the Republic. It is significant that a change in the treatment of provincials coincides fairly accurately with a change in the treatment of slaves, and both are symptoms of the healthier influences which produce the glory of the Antonine age. Unfortunately the arena still claims its victims in unabated numbers.[1]

Seneca complains that masters have greater power of punishment than the Emperor himself. ' We punish for absurd reasons—an obscure answer, an impertinent look, a whisper so subdued that we cannot even hear it. And, after all, who are we that our ears should not be offended ? Enemies of State have received their pardon, and shall not the idle, the careless, the talkative slave ? ' ' Some excuse can be found for all: if it is his first offence, let us remember rather how long he has given satisfaction ; if he has often offended, let us endure further what we have hitherto endured. And if we must punish, then let us be careful not to act in the heat of the moment ; realize the gravity of sending an unfortunate slave-boy to work in a slave-prison. Why should we be in a hurry to flog or maim ? Wait a little ; the power of punishment is not destroyed, if punishment itself is delayed.' ' And think less of your rights. Your slave answers you pertly, and you cry that liberty is vanished. If he were silent, you would complain of his insolence. Let him laugh and talk. Before his master ? Certainly ! Uproar and silence would vex you equally. Are your ears so delicate that they can listen only to certain sounds ? You had better train them ; for sensitive as you are, you will have to listen to thunder.' [2]

Individual cases of cruelty must be left to the curious, and surely he will be satisfied. Agrippina, suspecting poison hidden in fruit, hands it first to her slaves.[3] The children of the Pisonian conspirators, together with their tutors and attendants, all drink the fatal cup prepared for them.[4] Sick slaves exposed to die in the island of Aesculapius,[5] the mistress flogging her slave in a fit of temper,[6] felling Plecusa to the ground with a

---

[1] For Pliny's protest, see *Ep*. iv. 22, ad fin.

[2] Paraphrased from Sen. *de ira*, iii. 24. 2 and 3, iii. 32. 1, 35. 1 to 3 ; Marcus Aur. xi. 30.

[3] Tac. *Ann*. iv. 54.   [4] Suet. *Nero*, 36.

[5] *Id. Claud*. 25.   [6] Apul. *Met*. iii. 16.

mirror when a wayward ringlet was out of place,[1] or hanging
Lalage by her twisted hair [2]—floggings [3] and brandings [4] by
masters, who, as Martial said, but leave an indelible record of
their own infamy [5]—burning and maiming and fighting with
wild beasts [6]—Vedius Pollio flinging his living victims to the
lampreys [7]—crucifixion [8]—these will serve to whet his appetite.
But he must steel his heart ; for even the ' impassivity ' of the
Stoic admitted that the terrors of the prison and the cross, the
rack, the hook, the shirt of fire, were real.[9]

Such cases may be given their full value. But for assessing
the general Roman attitude in this matter of cruelty, and dis-
covering what progress was made in the direction of humanity,
we may with greater confidence turn to another source of evidence, which cannot indeed be accused of representing the
abnormal ; for law is seldom in advance of opinion.

Slaves gave evidence under torture. It is a favourite indictment to bring against ancient slavery. It cannot be denied,
indeed, for it is substantiated both in the manuals and practice
of law. Nor apparently can the slave give evidence except
under torture.[10] The charge grows blacker still ; and, when it
is added that the reason is to be found in the belief that the
slave is unable to tell the truth except upon the rack, then the
Roman seems to stand self-convicted not only of cruelty, or of a
gratuitously harsh verdict upon a large proportion of his fellow-
men, but of an entirely mistaken calculation as to the efficacy
of torture to obtain the truth ; and many would regard the last
as the most serious offence.

Actually the charge is as true as most unqualified assertions ;
very serious modifications qualified not, indeed, the principle
involved, but the practice of it.

---

[1] Mart. ii. 66. [2] Prop. iv. 7. 45.
[3] Mart. iii. 94, viii. 23 ; Petr. 28, 30, 54.
[4] Petr. 107 ; Mart. x. 56. [5] iii. 21.
[6] Petr. 115 ; Suet. *Calig.* 32 ; Mart. ii. 82 ; Petr. 45.
[7] Plin. *N.H.* ix. 77 ; Sen. *de ira.* iii. 40 ; Dio, liv. 23, evidently a
famous story.
[8] Tac. *Hist.* ii. 72 ; Petr. 53 ; Dio, liv. 3, etc. Cf. Hor. *Sat.* i. 3. 80.
[9] Sen. *Ep.* xiv. 5 and 6. For other methods of torture, see Marquardt,
Vie privée, i. 215.
[10] Tac. *Ann.* ii. 30 illustrates the rule ' negante reo adgnoscentes servos
per tormenta interrogari placuit.'

Normally the evidence of slaves was not allowed in civil cases. This, however, was bound to lead to miscarriages of justice ; and certain exceptions make their appearance, of which the general nature may be shown by saying that when the case concerned actions of the slave himself and there were no other witnesses, then such evidence was allowed. At the same time, it is probable that such cases would not arise very often. In business the slave was generally acting under the express or general orders of his master ; and many occasions of dispute or wrong-doing never proceeded to the courts owing to the power of punishment which the master had over his slave, and the possibility of making good from his private property—*peculium*—any damages which might be incurred.

In criminal cases, however, evidence under torture was permissible, again subject to great restrictions. It is fairly clear that not only the degree of torture to be employed,[1] but the decision whether evidence should be taken by this means or not, rested with the court ; slaves were not to be at the mercy of whatever passions swayed the parties concerned. Further, it is clear that, for the guidance of the court, general regulations were from time to time laid down, and commented upon by the lawyers. Some of these cannot certainly be assigned to the first two centuries ; but those which bear a date may be briefly mentioned.

Augustus' declaration is definite ; torture is to be resorted to when capital crimes ' cannot be investigated except by the torture of slaves ' ; in such cases torture is most efficacious in disclosing the truth.[2] But elsewhere his opinion as to this latter point is less positive ; he rules that evidence under torture should not open a case, nor should too much credence be placed in it.[3] Trajan insists that in investigating a case by torture the question should not be put in the form, ' Did So-and-so do this ? ' but rather ' Who did this ? '[4] Hadrian reaffirms the Augustan principle. Torture can only be used if the case hangs upon slave-evidence ; and in a joint theft by master and slave the slave cannot be interrogated about his master. To Marcus Aurelius is attributed the rule that slaves from the house

---

[1] *Dig.* xlviii. 18. 10. 3.   [2] xlviii. 18. 8.   [3] xlviii. 18. 1. pr.
[4] ' Alterum enim magis suggerentis quam requirentis videtur,' xlviii. 18. 1. 21.

of the prosecutor must not be taken too readily. Antoninus, in allowing slave-evidence on a money matter, insists that it shall be regarded as a last resort. Such being the spirit of the imperial rescripts, it is permissible to quote passages from the lawyers, which, though bearing no exact date, are comments on the rescripts. Slave-evidence under torture is 'a fragile and dangerous thing, likely to cheat the truth.' Many can resist torture, and their statements are not true; others tell falsehood to escape. Personal animosity may show itself even under torture; at the same time, such evidence is not necessarily false because such feelings are known to exist. Much more of similar wisdom may be found in the *Digest*, lib. xlviii.[1]

There are further limitations; but unfortunately the details are not very clear. There seems to have been an ancient rule of the Republic that slaves could not give evidence against their masters when defendants.[2] Julius Caesar is said to have confirmed it.[3] But there were times when it was convenient that the rule should be circumvented. By a *lex Julia* such evidence was allowed in cases of adultery. In a case of *maiestas* in 8 B.C., Augustus ordered the accused man's slaves to be sold to the State agent, and then examined. A section of public opinion protested against this nullification of the law; others, however, regarded it as justifiable under the circumstances, since many took advantage of the old regulation and conspired against Emperor and magistrates.[4] Tiberius resorted to the same device. Treason may be held to justify the evasion of law. The cases are Libo Drusus, C. Silanus, Vibius Serenus.[5] So, too, Piso, when on trial for the murder of Germanicus, offered his slaves for torture, and invited the prosecution to submit those of Germanicus.[6] His guilt was established otherwise, but it seems that a similar fiction would have been necessary if such evidence had been wanted. In the case of Lepida there were other charges besides that of treason, but though Lepida's own slaves and those of P. Quirinius, whose death Lepida was charged with attempting, were examined under torture, there

---

[1] Including the remark that slaves are not to be killed under torture 'ut salvi sint innocentiae aut supplicio.'
[2] Tac. *Ann.* ii. 30. [3] Dio, xli. 38. [4] Dio, lv. 5.
[5] Tac. *Ann.* ii. 30, iii. 67, iv. 29. [6] iii. 14.

is no mention of the device of selling them to the State agent.[1] Either Tacitus omits it, or, amid the terror, the ancient rule was omitted. But that it was not forgotten by the majority is shown by the implied censure in Dio's brief reference: ' He welcomed informers, not letting it make any difference if a slave gave evidence against his master or a son against his father.' [2] Caligula seems to have admitted such evidence, and even gave a reward to a freedwoman who, though tortured, had concealed her patron's crime. And in the days of Nero's great fear, when Petronius was charged with treason, Tigellinus is said to have bribed a slave and to have robbed the defence of witnesses by imprisoning the greater part of Petronius' domestic slaves.[3] From these exceptional cases it is difficult to argue that the ancient rule was cancelled, or that in civil or criminal cases generally, in which the Emperor was not concerned, the rule excluding such evidence was deliberately set aside. Imperial needs or imperial terrors must be held to account for it, especially since little is heard of the question later. Since the whole tendency of the law is towards the exclusion of slave-evidence, it may be assumed that evidence against the master is all the more excluded, except in cases of treason and the like, when Emperors' interests are affected.

There seems to be one kindred reference in later literature. A mother lost her son, and accused his freedmen, who were co-heirs of the estate, of having forged the will and poisoned their patron. Pliny the Younger defended the freedmen, who were acquitted on the evidence of slaves. Whose slaves they were is not stated, and Pliny offers no comment.[4] It is possible, however, that the evidence of slaves against their masters was more freely admitted when those masters were freedmen ; for the exclusion of evidence against a master was due not to any desire to spare the slaves, but to spare the master from the ignominy of being so condemned ; and the feelings of freedmen might naturally be less consulted.

The only conclusion from the contradictory evidence is that on the whole slaves did not give evidence against their

[1] iii. 22, 23: ' actor publicus.'

[2] lvii. 19. 1b ; cf. lx. 15, Messalina and Narcissus employed slaves as informers against their masters.

[3] Tac. *Ann.* xvi. 18.   [4] *Ep.* vii. 6.

masters unless there was some overriding consideration—generally that of treason.[1]

The admissibility of evidence for the master may be more shortly dismissed. The case of Piso mentioned above seems to support it ; he asked the prosecution to examine their slaves thus. There is, however, nothing to show that the demand was legal, and further the case was exceptional, being nothing less than the murder of the Emperor's probable successor. Hadrian seems to have allowed it in the case of joint ownership of a slave.[2] But the general view of the Corpus is overwhelmingly against the admissibility of such evidence.[3]

Torture, then, from the earliest days of the Empire, is the subject of regulation, which did much to narrow down its scope, and to ensure its use only in the interests of justice. At the same time, its value as an instrument for the discovery of the truth is more and more called into question, especially in the comments of jurists later than the limit of our period. This indictment of ancient slavery must stand, but only on the understanding that those who bring it realize its limits, even if they refuse to derive any comfort from the heroism of slaves under torture. When the gentle Octavia was accused by Poppaea, most of her slave-girls showed their love of their mistress by the most constant assertion of her innocence, and endured torture which they might have been spared had they uttered a word against her.[4] But all must yield to Epicharis, an ex-slave and the heroine of the Pisonian conspiracy, who endured unspeakable torments rather than betray her fellow-conspirators, thereby putting to shame the senators and knights and soldiers who played a sorry part in an ill-starred enterprise.[5]

Hitherto it is the unconscious or half-conscious influence of slavery upon the whole of the slave-owning classes that has been pressed. Such influence was penetrating enough, but not every one had the wit or the insight to see the devastating effect of the slaves whom they despised upon the moral health

[1] Prop. iii. 6. 19 seems to suggest torture against master on a charge of perjury. Apul. *Met.* vii. 2, against master on a charge of theft. In x. 7–12, there seems to be evidence taken from a witness not under torture. Later, when his statements are denied, he is tortured ; it is a case of poisoning. Little, however, can be built on such references.

[2] *Dig.* xlviii. 18. 17. 2.   [3] Buckland, *Slavery*, p. 88.
[4] Tac. *Ann.* xiv. 60.   [5] xv. 57.

of society, still less had they the conscience to care. In one sphere, however, the influence of slavery was more conscious and more direct ; it is to be found in a region where one unfamiliar with the ancient life of the Mediterranean would least seek it. The Romans have often been charged with an indifference to education ; Polybius early expressed his dissatisfaction, and Cicero's defence [1] that the lack of system was intentional has found no favour with modern historians, though it may find a warmer welcome among schoolmasters. Early Roman education needed no surer foundation than the *patria potestas* ; round the central hearth were gathered all those religious and moral influences which were potent enough to shape character in the time-honoured moulds of conservatism. ' What, then, Laelius, do you think we ought to learn ? ' and the answer comes quick enough, ' Such arts as make us useful to the State.' It contains nothing new ; Plato had devoted a considerable portion of the *Republic* to the same theme, even though his successors had lost sight of it. But it is a useful key to the whole development of Roman education ; everything depends upon the conception of the ' State ' ; if the nature of this changes, so will the ideal of the citizen change, and with it the method of education. To cling to the mother's skirts and thus learn the elements of a simple faith and the rudiments of a primitive literature, to follow the father round the land picking up now a hint on the management of the estate, now a reminiscence of the good days when true Romans lived, to accompany him to market and council and hear him debate great things and small with Roman ' gravity ' and no less characteristic shrewdness—this was, no doubt, an excellent training for the citizen of the infant Republic ; in this stern nursery character was surely formed by the training of a high moral sense still oblivious of the glittering toy of Hellenic culture.

But as the State grew and absorbed within it men of different race and morals and heritage, as the city-state ceased to be an adequate political ideal, many grew tired of the perpetual refrain of *mos maiorum* ; they realized as they came in contact with Greeks, whose wits had been sharpened by a vast literature, that the narrow field of ancestral ideals, productive as it may

[1] *De Rep.* iv. 3. 3.

be to a point, becomes a barren soil when perpetually ploughed to receive the same seed generation after generation. The old training had nursed a conquering race, but it had failed to produce a breadth of outlook, an adaptability, an individual culture which would enable that race to meet on equal terms of intellect those peoples whom it had subdued by superior arms. And so the broader minds braved the Catos of their age, and, without necessarily wishing to overthrow the moral basis of the old ideal, welcomed teachers of Greek, being influenced first by practical motives, later by an appreciation of its literature. Even Cato himself had yielded in his old age so far as to study Demosthenes and Thucydides before venturing upon the writing of a handbook of rhetoric for his son; still he resolutely 'refused to have his son reprimanded by a slave, or pulled, it may be, by the ears when found tardy in his lesson; nor would he have him owe to a servant the obligation of so great a thing as his learning.' [1]

The growing needs of the imperial Republic summoned overseas the heads of families whose task it had once been to educate the coming generation; the increase of wealth had opened up a fuller social life for women, who found their time filled with other occupations than the education of their children. Simultaneous with these two movements there was another, the steady flow of Greek slaves and teachers into Italy, making easier both tendencies and filling the gap in the educational system of which their presence in Italy was partly the cause, partly the effect. By the time of the Empire, teachers of writing, literature, science, rhetoric, are to be found in many well-to-do families either as slaves, or as freedmen, or as free men nominally independent but often living in degrading dependence on their patron. From the cradle to old age a scion of an old Roman family might be dependent for his teaching upon the degenerate descendant of a Periclean Athenian, and in some cases it would be difficult to pronounce which was the more debased, pupil or tutor; in other cases it is certain that both owed much to the differing gifts of the other.

Of nurses under the Empire more is heard for evil than for good, as is perhaps true of modern times also. But on the positive side it is possible to say that the nurse, generally a

[1] Clough's translation of Plut. *Cato*, 20.

'Graecula ancilla' chosen for her quickness, often earned and received grateful recognition from her charges ; though perhaps she more often earned it than received it. The inscriptions preserve the pride of the slaves or freedwomen who had nursed Nero's unhappy wife, Octavia, and the children of Germanicus and the grandchildren of Vespasian ; [1] no less is the pride of another whose charges grew to be senators ; another—' nutrix mellitissima '—laments the death of an eight months' old baby.[2] Round these at least the nursery had woven its spell. Nor were the children themselves unconscious of their debt ; Pliny made over land worth 100,000 sesterces to produce an income for his nurse, and, in writing to Verus, who managed the land for him, emphasized that he was handing over to his care not so much the trees and the soil as the gift itself ; for he himself was as anxious as his nurse that it should bring in a good return.[3] When the fourteen-year-old daughter of Fundanus died, Pliny writes of her: 'How she loved her nurses and teachers and tutors, each according to their station ! ' The calculated measure in which she distributes her affection rather depreciates from its value ; but Pliny expressly includes in a long list of her other virtues ' the common sense of a grown woman.'[4] An ex-consul remembers to dedicate a monument to his slave nurse—' nutrici et mammulariae '—whom he had freed ; and Q. Pescennius Chrestio, using the language of his nursery, writes an inscription ' nonnae suae.' [5]

From the hands of the nurse the boy, perhaps, too, the girl, was received by the *paedagogus* ; his title is difficult to render, his work not easy to define or his reputation to defend. He is spared neither by the comic playwright copying from Greek originals, nor by the satirist's caricature, nor the moralist's gloomy broodings. All present one side of the case, no doubt. For the other side evidence is not so plentiful ; nor could it be expected. In all ages the humble work well done finds little record, and not least is this true of education.

Usually a Greek, by descent at any rate, the paedagogus was expected to familiarize his pupil with the Greek language, though the Emperor Claudius was placed in his unhappy youth under the care of a barbarian who had lately been head

[1] Dess. 1837 sqq.   [2] Dess. 8531, 8537.   [3] Plin. *Ep.* vi. 3.
[4] *Ep.* v. 16 : ' anilis prudentia.'   [5] Dess. 8532 (cf. 8536), 8542.

driver of the beasts of burden.[1] Accompanying his pupil to school and to the theatre, where special seats were reserved for paedagogi, and being present at games and pastimes, the paedagogus, half tutor, half attendant, was expected to exert an influence by example and contact rather than by systematic instruction. It was an anomalous position ; conscious often of ability superior to that of his owner, with whose parental authority he was invested, he was at the same time the tutor of that pupil from whose goodwill he might one day hope to receive his freedom. To him was committed the child for good or evil.

And a mixture of good and evil is generally the fruit of compromise ; for Roman education was compromising. The old system demanded too much from parents now called elsewhere ; it failed to satisfy the increasing craving for individual culture, of which it had not known the need or the value. The new plan, loth to surrender entirely that close personal contact, in which it had seen the best method of training character, and clinging to the formation of character as the end of education, half-heartedly hoped to find in the paedagogus the means of combining the merits of the old training with the attractive advantages of the new knowledge. To this end the enslavement of Greeks was the obvious, if not the only, solution.

The compromise might have been as successful as most, if Greeks had not been Greeks, if paedagogi had not been slaves, if parents had not been lax. For such, in short, is the criticism made by the reaction, which swung back to emphasis on morals rather than on culture.

The criticism comes from Tacitus, anxious to trace back evils to their cause ; from Juvenal, who regarded all things as within his mission ; from Quintilian, the first State-paid Professor of Rhetoric, who fulfilled many of the duties which we should require from a Professor of Education ; from Plutarch, the kindly moralist, whose philosophy, if neither very original nor very profound, had the supreme advantage in educational theorizing of two feet firmly planted on the ground. Their criticism is levelled neither against the Government, which hardly interfered with education, nor against the schools, for Quintilian at least recognizes [2] that they only supply what is

---

[1] Suet. *Claud.* 2.   [2] Cf. x. 5. 21.

demanded, nor against Hellenic culture, for the city of Rome, says Plutarch,[1] has risen to its greatest heights while entertaining Greek learning ; it is levelled against the parents.

> Velocius et citius nos
> Corrumpunt vitiorum exempla domestica, magnis
> Cum subeunt animos auctoribus.[2]

The young master rattles the dice-box specially made for him, for his small fingers cannot grasp the larger size ; the little mistress knows by heart the long list of her mother's lovers, and learns at her dictation how to pen her earliest billets. The children are spoilt from their earliest years ; in mind and body they are ruined by that soft upbringing which is called gentle nurture. They crawl on purple and cry if they are set down on a cheaper brand of scarlet ; their palates are taught to discriminate before their lips are taught to speak. Laughter and a kiss reward the pert answer. But it is the parents who are to blame ; the children see their elders' vice ; they see mistresses and favourites ; every dinner-party rings with foul songs. The children learn all this before they know it is wrong ; so far from being corrupted at school, they actually introduce vice among their fellow-pupils.[3] Against so powerful a home influence education is useless.

But many parents, perhaps even the majority, could claim exemption from Juvenal's tirades, and plead not guilty to Quintilian's accusations ; yet, even so, they would encounter Plutarch's rebuke. Even though they may set a tolerable example themselves, they are careless in choosing the influences to which they expose their children. The present practice is ' excessively ridiculous.'[4] Children are handed over to the care of slaves of barbarian race and unsteady character.[5] And other critics agree. The infant is entrusted to a Greek slave-girl, who takes the place of some elderly and trusted member of the family under the old system ; she fills its mind with silly stories and mistaken notions, and teaches incorrect modes of speech which later must be unlearnt.[6] She ought to be a philosopher

---

[1] Plut. *Cato*, 23.　　　[2] Juv. xiv. 31.　　　[3] Quint. i. 2. 6–8.

[4] ὑπερκαταγελαστόν, Plut. *de educ. lib.* 4a. It is not certain that Plutarch wrote this treatise ; for convenience I regard it as his.

[5] ἀνδραπόδοις ἢ βαρβάροις ἢ παλιμβόλοις.　　　[6] Tac. *Dial.* 29.

(pity the child !), but, failing that, she should be of good character, for the worst impressions are the most lasting.[1]

But it is in choosing the paedagogus, Plutarch continues, that the greatest folly is shown. The best slaves are turned into farmers, captains of vessels, merchants, stewards, and bankers' agents ; whenever a slave turns out to be a drunkard, a glutton, worthless for every good purpose, he is converted into a paedagogus. At the moment it may be more economical ; yet it would pay to regard Phoenix as the ideal tutor, and search for a tutor of ' irreproachable character.' [2] Other parents descend to such miserliness, utterly regardless of their children's interest, that they deliberately buy the cheapest slaves they can, ' in their hunt for ignorance at a bargain price,' [3] and show surprise when the morals of their children leave much to be desired.[4] And, even apart from morals, says Quintilian, the teaching which the paedagogus gives is often bad ; he should have had a thorough education or he should know that he knows nothing. There is none worse than the tutor who believes that he possesses real knowledge when he has hardly left the alphabet behind. He refuses to condescend to the humdrum work of teaching ; he thinks he has a title to power, and becomes imperious or brutal in teaching his own unsound knowledge.[5]

Little is known about individual paedagogi ; it is possible that Suetonius' list of famous *grammatici* contains men who formerly served in a humbler capacity. One at least certainly did so, though the record of his career does not suggest that he fulfilled the high requirements of his pupil, Quintilian. Q. Remmius Palaemon, a *verna* born at Vicentia, learnt letters while accompanying his young master to school. Afterwards manumitted, he set up a school at Rome and held the first place among the *grammatici*. By his fluency and retentive memory he attracted large audiences, and gave displays of extempore versification. But his moral character was such that Tiberius and Claudius could declare that there was no one to whose care boys could less fittingly be entrusted. His arrogance was insufferable, and his luxurious tastes were scarcely satisfied by the revenues from his lecture-room, his factories, and vineyards.[6]

[1] Quint. i. 1. 5.　　[2] τοῖς τρόποις ἀνεπίληπτος, Plut. *op. cit.* 4b.
[3] εὔωνον ἀμαθίαν διώκοντες, Plut. *op. cit.* 4f.　　[4] 5b; cf. Quint. i. 2. 7.
[5] i. 1. 8–9.　　[6] Suet. *de gramm.* 23.

To this the epitaph of a freedman, once a paedagogus, affords a grateful contrast. 'I have lived as long as I could ; I have lived without lawsuit, without quarrel or dispute, without debt ; to my friends I have always been loyal ; my savings are small, my mind well stored.' [1]   And self-praise is sometimes less extravagant than praise by another, though to Aristophanes 'without lawsuit' would have sounded odd in the mouth of one who was perhaps a descendant of the fifth-century Athenian.

If it is possible to draw a deduction from the nationalities of freedmen rhetoricians given in Suetonius' list, the nationality of paedagogi would not be entirely Greek.   Claudius' barbarian ex-groom was probably an exception, but Spain and N. Italy and Syria provided rhetoricians and possibly tutors.   And in the inscriptions, attendants—*custodes*—and footmen—*pedisequi*—who occasionally fulfilled the duties of paedagogi, are derived from a variety of nations neither Greek nor Graecized.

Cato's hatred of things Greek was in part a pose maintained by pride, as Plutarch saw ; but most Romans were conscious of a contempt and suspicion of a race which, lacking all patriotism, was as ready to adapt its conduct to meet circumstances as it was to justify whatever suited the moment.   Versatile still, the Greek had lost in the judgment of the Roman whatever stability had once made his versatility a safe possession ; and had developed at the same time a power to maintain the unjust argument among a people more easily captivated than Strepsiades, and less ready to burn down the whole paraphernalia about the heads of its ingenious devisers.   A semi-Graecized Oriental, professing a smattering of letters and relying on the sanction of a debased cult to be indifferent to morality, was capable of inflicting lasting harm on the child committed to him. 'How much will you charge to teach my son ? ' Aristippus was asked. 'A thousand drachmae.' 'But I can buy a slave for that.' 'Then you'll have two slaves—your son and the one you buy.' [2]   There was truth in this, as the critics saw.

Yet Aristippus' answer contains only half the truth.   For busy parents there might be no better solution than to hand over a child to a trusted slave, who, born of parents devoted to the family and himself brought up in the household, had come into such close contact with his master as to be a suitable

[1] Dess. 8436.   [2] Plut. *op. cit.* 4 F.

tutor. 'It was you, Charidemus, who rocked my cradle,' says Martial, 'and now you rule me with "your father never did such things." You are a Cato, but I'm a man now.'[1] In other cases it was certainly more desirable that a child should be exposed to the influence of many a typical paedagogus than to the undesirable example of its own parents. There seems to be no reason why, in a slave-owning society, a child should not receive from a slave that education which to Plutarch is the 'fount and root of good breeding'; the danger lies in the temptation to the parent to shirk his own share, and in the temptation to the child to doubt the value of what he receives as coming from a slave; if, however, he valued it, he must often have been led to doubt the justice of the system which could make him indebted to slaves for his most precious possession—or, at least, to use, under the influence of humane letters, every opportunity of lessening the gulf between slave and master, and humanizing a system which to him may have seemed indispensable.

II

Luxury in slaves and cruelty in the treatment of them reached their climax some time between Augustus and Nero. The attitude of Augustus towards slavery must be reserved for treatment in a later chapter on Manumission, in which it is suggested that he first formulated clearly a new view as to the function of slavery in society. In comparison with his legislation on manumission, brief notices in the literature about his treatment of slaves or his severity towards cruel masters are insignificant. Twice in Tiberius' reign an attempt was made to introduce legislation which should check luxury, and twice Tiberius refused to take any steps, on the ground that sumptuary laws create greater evils than they set out to cure. 'And where was he to begin, with the vast numbers of slaves of every nationality?'[2] Private example would do more than penal codes. He himself kept slaves on a very moderate scale,[3] and encouraged public thrift by his own modest table.[4] From his reign, Tacitus dates a movement towards economy which was maintained even to his own day. Noble families had been ruined through their own extravagance; or their pre-

[1] xi. 39.   [2] Tac. *Ann.* ii. 33, iii. 53.   [3] iv. 7.   [4] Suet. *Tib.* 34.

eminence had made them a mark for the informer. Voluntary economy was often a means of survival. On the other hand, new men of simpler habits were emerging from the townships ; the thrifty example of Vespasian, the Sabine farmer, was a powerful motive ; and possibly there are cycles in these things.[1] Further causes Tacitus omits, which will be noticed in their place.

If Claudius was under the control of his freedmen, he was willing to hold the balance between slave and master. When a tribune beat an imperial slave in public, Claudius made no protest ; on the contrary, when one of his own slaves insulted a prominent man he sent him off to the forum to meet with due punishment.[2] Yet he could be sympathetic ; the cruel exposure of sick slaves on the island of Aesculapius he heartily condemned, ordering the slaves to be free if they recovered.[3]

Nero handed back to their masters slaves who had been guilty of intrigue against their masters, many of whom refused to take back such scoundrels.[4] He freely gave away slaves as presents at the musical festivals to those who applauded his efforts.[5]

Galba kept up the old custom of having his household slaves and freedmen appear before him night and morning to salute him,[6] and it was to a freedman, Argius, that he owed his burial.[7] Vitellius was more interested in the recipes of his cooks than in the men themselves, and was deserted by his household when his end was obviously approaching.[8]

The civil wars resulted in financial exhaustion and the ruin of many noble families, though the damage done by them can be exaggerated. From the strife emerged Vespasian, the man of sound sense rather than genius, and under the Flavians autocracy flung aside the mask of the Augustan diarchy. This was inevitable, and its effects were far-reaching, being relevant even to slavery. For it was by virtue of censorial office that the Flavians asserted their control of the senate, acquiring thus the right of revising the senatorial roll, and admitting new members. The senate was ripe for it, and an aristocracy arose new in personnel and, when Vespasian was the arbiter, new in ideals. Coming frequently from the provinces and

[1] Tac. *Ann.* iii. 55.   [2] Dio, lx. 12.   [3] Suet. *Claud.* 25.
[4] Dio, lxiii. 3. 4a, 4b.   [5] Dio, lxi. 18.   [6] Suet. *Galba,* 4.
[7] Tac. *Hist.* i. 49.   [8] Tac. *Hist.* iii. 84.

representing broad and imperial rather than narrow and
senatorial interests, their habits were simpler, their manners
less fettered by convention, their sympathies larger, and, since
they owed their places to the Emperor's choice, they were
subservient to him, and, while destroying thus the last traces
of political liberty, inaugurated a new epoch in which the
Emperor's example became of paramount authority. Further,
this period saw a great forward movement in the granting of
Roman citizenship to townships. Everywhere new blood was
obtaining power and recognition.[1] Society followed the imperial lead, and when thrift or philosophy sat upon the throne
habits became simpler and wealth less ostentatious, in spite of
the survival of extremes of poverty and riches. With fresh
blood invigorating society a reaction set in against the excesses
of luxury and extravagance prevalent under the Julio-Claudians ;
even pleasure palls, and even the blasé, because of their very
weariness, were caught in the fashionable stoicism or embraced
it with genuine enthusiasm. Comfort and plenty remained,
conventionality hardened, ostentation became bad form ; if
there was progress in ideals, it was in the sphere of humanity
and kindliness.

Domitian endeavoured by vengeance upon Nero's freedman, Epaphroditus, to terrorize his own freedmen ;[2] his body
was rescued and buried by Phyllis, his nurse.[3] The tendency
to economy was further encouraged by Nerva, who is also said
to have put to death slaves and freedmen who brought charges
against their masters.[4] Hadrian refused to allow his freedmen
to have any control over himself or over public affairs, con-
demning all his predecessors for their indulgence to their dependants.[5] Yet when his freedmen were ill he visited them
two or three times a day and cheered them ;[6] he treated
Heliodorus and Epictetus with the greatest friendliness. His
treatment of slaves may be inferred from three episodes. Seeing
one of his slaves walking away between two senators, he sent
some one to box his ear, and to tell him not to walk between
those whose slave he might one day be.[7] On another occasion
he was attacked while walking in his host's garden by a slave ;

---

[1] Rostovtzeff, p. 106. [2] Dio, lxvii. 14. [3] Dio, lxvii. 18.
[4] Dio, lxviii. 2. [5] Script. hist. aug. *Hadr.* xxi. 2.
[6] ix. 7. [7] xxi. 3.

he handed over his assailant to physicians for treatment, who pronounced him insane.[1]   That he disliked cruelty is shown by his banishment of Umbricia, a Roman lady who had ill-treated her slave-girls for trifling reasons.[2]   He refused to free a charioteer who had pleased the populace.[3]

Antoninus Pius cut down imperial expenses with the greatest economy, in spite of the opposition of the imperial servants.[4]   His own slaves, fowlers and fishermen and hunts-men, furnished his modest table.[5]   So, too, Pertinax, who was hated by his freedmen for compelling them to surrender their gains,[6] set such an example of economy as to cause a drop in the cost of living.[7]

Under the Republic the power of the master over his slave was unlimited by law.   Actually it was limited by self-interest and a vague power of the censor to supervise morals which cannot have resulted in any effective repression of cruelty. Under the Empire regulations begin to appear ; growing luxury and cruelty may have made them necessary.   On the other hand, increasing humanity and the influence of Stoicism on law may undoubtedly be detected.   By the *lex Petronia* of uncertain date [8] masters were forbidden to hand over at their own dis-cretion their slaves to fight with wild beasts ; their charges against the slave had first to be examined before a *iudex*.[9] A decree of the senate of A.D. 20 lays down the same procedure in the trial of criminal slaves as obtained in the case of free men.[10]   The punishment of crime in slaves is thus taken from their masters.   Hadrian forbade the selling of a slave to a gladiatorial trainer without good reason.[11]   Yet the master can still put his slave to death.[12]   Not until the time of Antoninus was any order passed making an owner liable for the death of his slave ; and, as will be seen later, a slave complaining of in-tolerable cruelty was ordered by the same Emperor to be sold

[1] xii. 5.   [2] *Dig.* i. 6. 2.   [3] Dio, lxix. 16.
[4] Script. hist. aug. *Pius*, vi. 4.   [5] vii. 5.
[6] *Pert.* viii. 1, xi. 5, xiii. 9, xiv. 6.   [7] viii. 8 and 10.
      [8] There was a Petronius consul in A.D. 6, and the law is as old as A.D. 79, since a mention of it occurs at Pompeii.
      [9] *Dig.* xlviii. 8. 11. 12.   [10] *Dig.* xlviii. 2. 12. 3.
      [11] Script. hist. aug. *Hadr.* xviii. 8.
      [12] *Ibid.* 7, 'servos a dominis occidi vetuit,' said of Hadrian, conflicts with Gaius, i. 53.   See Mommsen, *Droit pénal*, ii. p. 330, n. 4.

to another master. There seems even a note of pride in the lawyer's brief paragraph ; by *ius gentium*, he says, slaves are in the power of their owners, for in all nations we can see that masters have power of life and death ; but in our day neither Roman citizens nor any other member of the Roman Empire may use excessive or groundless cruelty against their slaves.[1]

Mutilation of free men or of slaves was forbidden by Domitian,[2] prostitution of slaves not till the time of Severus. At the same time *infamis iniuria* came under the heading of cruelty, and was a valid ground of complaint before the prefect at least as early as Gaius.[3] And much earlier it had been possible for an owner when selling a slave to enforce a restrictive covenant ' ne prostituatur ' in the interest of morality and the slave ; for Vespasian it is ' clearly an existing institution '[4] that even a verbal proviso that a slave-woman should be freed on prostitution should be upheld.[5] In other cases a proviso was made ' ne prostituatur ' giving the vendor power of recovering the slave on breach of the condition.[6] Hadrian forbade the selling of a slave-woman for immoral purposes unless for good reason,[7] and probably increased the penalty for mutilation.[8] It was left for Marcus Aurelius to add that on the breach of the proviso the slave should be free even if the owner's goods were under pledge, so that in the ordinary course of events he could not have been manumitted.[9]

III

Even in the most extravagant periods of these two centuries there was often need neither of preventive law nor imperial example. Hitherto it is the repulsive side of household slavery that has been sketched. There is also another aspect. The literature reveals the vast household as normal. It is, of course,

---

[1] Gaius, *loc. cit.*, ' supra modum et sine causa ' ; *Dig.* i. 6. 1. 2, quoting this paragraph, adds ' legibus cognita.'

[2] Stat. *Silv.* iv. 3. 13 ; cf. Mart. ix. 7 ; Philostr. *Vit. Ap.* vi. 42 ; Justin Martyr, *Apol.* i. 29 ; and see Mayor on Juvenal, x. 307.

[3] i. 53.   [4] Buckland, *Slavery*, p. 603.

[5] *Dig.* xxxvii. 14. 7 pr.

[6] If the vendor refused to exert his right of *manus iniectio*, freedom followed ; *Dig.* xl. 8. 7.

[7] Script. hist. aug. *Hadr.* xviii. 7.   [8] Buckland, *Slavery*, p. 37.

[9] *Dig.* xviii. 7. 6. 1, xl. 8. 6.

the exception. Large slave staffs undoubtedly existed, and they are generally to be found in Rome. But even in Rome it was not necessary to feed regiments of slaves to be respectable. Horace, in his early days, had only three slaves to attend to his wants.[1] Umbricius could put his whole household on a single wagon ;[2] and, even if Naevolus were to have 20,000 sesterces per annum, he would need only four slaves, two being skilled craftsmen to support the others.[3] Augustus ordered that men in exile should not possess more than 500,000 sesterces or more than twenty slaves, and it has been suggested that these two figures were meant to bear some relation to one another.[4] It should be remembered that the knight's property qualification was 400,000 sesterces, a senator's one million.

In Italy and the provinces there was less need of display ; many of the staff of the villa were engaged in productive work connected with the land and its produce. The old-fashioned relationship between farmer and slave remained there ; the slave was often a fellow-worker. The kindliness of Pliny towards his staff is well known. It is in no spirit of self-righteousness, and in no wish to appear in a favourable light in the eyes of the future generations which he hoped would read his letters, that he tells of his distress at the illness and death of his slaves. And, even if such were his motive, it is not entirely without credit to him that he chose the rôle of philanthropist in which to appear before posterity. His distress is genuine enough. He derives some comfort, however, from the reflection that he has manumitted readily. The death of a slave while still a slave seemed to him to cut off something before it had reached maturity ; even before the complete status of freedom was won, he allowed him some of its privileges and rights ; the household is the slaves' republic. And so his staff made valid wills, which Pliny observed with exactness. ' Pareo ut iussus.'[5] A portion of one wing of his elaborate villa was reserved for their use, and such pleasant rooms provided for them that occasionally they were used to accommodate guests. Thence

---

[1] *Sat.* i. 6. 116.   [2] Juv. iii. 10.   [3] *Id.* ix. 64–66, 142–146.

[4] Friedländer, iv. 20 (Eng. trans.), and see Kahrstedt in 9th ed. **Val. Max.** iv. 4. 11 speaks of an heir who was left 37,000 HS. and ten slaves.

[5] *Ep.* viii. 16.

the noise of their laughter resounded far, and particularly at
the time of the Saturnalia this indulgent master retired to a
small study to secure, not always successfully, quiet and soli-
tude.[1] His freedmen frequently dined with him ; in every
respect they were treated as equals ; for, as he said, it was to
dine that he invited them, not to grade them in varying degrees
of rank or to decide accordingly the vintage to be set before
them. ' It must cost you much.' ' No ! my freedmen do not
drink the same wine as I do ; but I drink the same as they.' [2]
Pliny's kindliness is large-hearted and observant ; there is no
difference, he complains, between slaves and free men when in
ill-health, yet free men receive gentler treatment from their
doctors.[3] But in such matters his own sympathy was beyond
reproach. The care which he took of his consumptive freedman
might have provoked the envy of many an ailing free man.
But such indulgence seems sometimes to have awakened no
answering dutifulness ; Pliny hopes that Pompeia Celerina, if
ever she stays at a villa belonging to him, will be attentively
received by his servants ; to him they are lax ; their fear of
a good master grows less as they come to know him ; but a
visitor to the house recalls them to a sense of their duties, for
they try to win their master's praise by their care for his
guest.[4]

Pliny's account of his treatment of his slaves is sometimes
regarded as so much in advance of general or even occasional
practice as to be valueless as evidence. There is no reason for
this attitude. Pliny was a liberal benefactor to his native
town : he endowed charities for children ; he built schools and
libraries ; he paid teachers ; he granted a dowry to a friend's
daughter. In all this there is nothing exceptional ; very many
inscriptions dug up by accident show carefully framed schemes
initiated by private bequest to relieve distress among poor
children, and philanthropy is the motive.[5] Private munificence,
often at personal sacrifice, is a commonplace of the inscriptions,
and a due proportion of it was inspired by genuine humanity.
If, then, other phases of Pliny's character are admittedly re-

---

[1] ii. 17.   [2] ii. 6.   [3] viii. 24.   [4] i. 4.
[5] There is no direct evidence that the *alimenta* of individuals or of the
State were started with the idea either of assisting agriculture or increasing the population.

presentative of a common tendency, there is no reason why his treatment of slaves should be singled out as exceptional. The very improvement in the position of slaves so marked during these centuries compels the existence of many a Pliny, who, to our loss, have not left a candid record of themselves in their letters. Pliny seldom touches upon slavery, and only once does he refer to his friends' treatment of their slaves. He sends Zosimus to be cared for at a friend's country house, which had the reputation of having a healthy climate. ' I see,' he says to Paulinus, ' how leniently you treat your slaves.' Here, at least, is another Pliny, hailing from Forum Julii and the friend of Vespasian. He may be taken as typical of that new aristocracy recruited under the Flavians, which did so much to alter standards of life and morality. The Lucilius of Seneca's correspondence wins the sage's approval for his friendly relations with his slaves, and calls forth the famous forty-seventh letter, which, if he is not the most unabashed hypocrite who ever posed as philosopher, must reflect some fragment, at any rate, of Seneca's own practice.[1]

It may be a further indication of the improved lot of slaves under the Empire that ' verna ' seems to have changed its implications. The word always meant a slave born in the household, but under the Republic the fact of such origin seemed to be viewed from the standpoint of the master; it was a method of acquiring slaves. Such seems to be Cato's attitude at any rate. But, as slave families were encouraged, partly owing to a diminished supply from war, but partly also owing to more humane treatment, ' verna ' later seems to suggest rather the slave's side of the relationship; it served to differentiate him from the imported slave in origin, but also in status, responsibility, and accomplishments, until it became a title which many were glad to record on their tombs; and, indeed, freedmen also retained this title as a mark almost of rank. In the literature the licence allowed to insolent *vernae* is frequently mentioned and sometimes deplored;[2] those of more sober manners do not attract so much attention. But this is in a

---

[1] In *de vit. beat:* 17, Seneca replies to the imaginary charge, ' quare ergo tu fortius loqueris quam vivis ? ' The answer is ' non sum sapiens . . . hoc mihi satis est, cotidie aliquid ex vitiis demere.'

[2] See Marquardt, *Vie privée,* i. 195, n. 4 ; Mayor on Juvenal, v. 74.

sense an accident. The references to 'pertness' are made in half-deprecating amusement at the toleration which masters extended to intelligent slave-boys ; and in such a mood both toleration and licence would easily be exaggerated. In many of the inscriptions *verna* seems to denote just the reverse— responsibility and tried service ; [1] but the ideas are not inconsistent, for pertness in youth might naturally develop into steady and intelligent service later. At any rate the *verna* occupied a privileged position, and this position accorded to an increasing number might have a beneficial effect on slavery in general. A slave of A. Furius Festus ' is regarded as a son ' ; [2] a boy of sixteen described himself as ' slave and yet son, a slave born in the household ' ; [3] and the *Silvae* of Statius contain poems about two slaves who had been adopted by their masters.[4] Statius' own adopted son had died, and his grief was genuine enough. It was no pert, chattering boy whom he had bought, trained in the impudence of his native Nile. ' Meus ille, meus.' He saw him as a new-born babe ; he had rocked him to sleep. A second birth he had given him ; he had freed him while yet a babe ; haste, however, was needful lest such brief freedom should lose a single day. ' Shall I not mourn for thee, dear boy ? While thou wert alive, I yearned not for sons ; from thine earliest birth my heart wrapped thee round and would not let thee go. I taught thee words and sounds ; as thou didst creep on the ground, I bent down and lifted thee up with mine own hands to be kissed ; when thy cheeks were wet with tears I made thee hide them in my welcoming arms and court sweet sleep.' [5] In view of this charming piece, the ' consolation' addressed to Melior gains in sincerity, despite its length and mythological extravagances. Glaucias had been to Melior a haven of rest, a welcome solace in old age, a delight, a precious anxiety. He had never known the whirling throng of the slave-cage.[6] 'Hic domus, hinc ortus'; his father and mother had long been dear to their master, and had been

---

[1] Cf. also the distinction between *novicius* and *veteranus*. Dess. 7424a, 7432d ; *Dig.* xxxix. 4. 16. 3.

[2] Dess. 8554.   [3] Dess. 7479.

[4] On the adoption of sons from the legal point of view, see Aul. Gell. v. 19.

[5] *Silvae*, v. 5.   [6] Cf. Mart. vi. 28, 29.

freed to please their son, whom their master accounted as his own, for

> ' 'Tis often seen
> Adoption strives with nature, and choice breeds
> A native slip to us from foreign seeds.' [1]

IV

Turn now to slavery and its implications for the slave. Some details of the conditions of labour must be left to be dealt with as they become relevant in later chapters ; here one or two general considerations may be offered.

For the slave almost everything depended on the character of the master ; for the protection of the law did not and could not extend to every relationship between slave and free. Within slavery were possible virtue, happiness, culture, wealth ; but whether the slave enjoyed any of these depended on his master. This is the condemnation of slavery, that under it the character of one man or one class should have the power to insist upon a relationship which could give or withhold happiness, could stifle or encourage the goodness of another. Without slavery there can be cruel oppression, tyranny, and persecution, with its train of misery, corruption, and vice ; but there is generally some measure of opportunity for severing the relationship either in whole or in part. It is idle to condemn slavery lightly or hurriedly ; many a slave would readily have admitted that he owed everything to slavery, and many did so whether they would have admitted it or not. Neither the crushing of individuality nor the refusal of personal growth was necessarily inherent in Roman slavery. It can be condemned only on the ground that it was a gamble in human lives which might attach them, by mere chance often, to a destiny which, owing to the limitations of slavery, it might not be in their power to shape. Man's power of guiding his destiny is limited ; he is perpetually striving to direct it according to his choice. It is the sin of

---

[1] Thus *All's Well that Ends Well*, i. 3. 150–152, may translate (as a note in D. A. Slater's translation suggests), *Silvae*, ii. 1. 84–87 :

> ' non omnia sanguis
> proximus aut serie generis demissa propago
> alligat : interius nova saepe adscitaque serpunt
> pignora conexis.'

slavery that it *may* so limit the power of choice as to destroy it. But to banish an institution to prevent its misuse may be to banish much good with the bad.

Reasonably hard work can hardly be made a ground of complaint against any system of employing labour, whether slavery or other; if in agriculture or industry there was merciless driving of slaves, in the households of the rich criticism must be directed against the nature of the work performed and its insufficiency rather than excess. It has already been suggested that the employer learnt much evil from his own slaves, and to tutor in vice is naturally to grow in its proficiency. To set a premium on the services of those who will pander to excess of every kind is to corrupt still further both teacher and taught, and the cramping limits of slavery, with its veiled threats of punishment, must have left many slaves no alternative but to provide for themselves temporary security at the cost of their own honour and self-respect; ' nec turpe est quod dominus iubet.' [1] And still more true is this of the Western slave. Tacitus draws a picture of the primitive simplicity of the German tribes, and possibly he exaggerates to point a contrast with Rome. But it is obvious that to take a native from the Western frontiers and to plant him in a Roman household is to expose him to influences which may be utterly harmful. If not the example of society, at any rate many of the Eastern slaves with whom he would be thrown into contact would spoil his more artless nature. Either from his fellow-slaves or from the very conditions of slavery, he would learn to ease its burdens. Obsequiousness and hypocrisy were so often the best policy as to become recognized characteristics of the slave; the 'servilis animus' became a type apart. Ill-treatment must be avoided no matter by what methods. A timely suggestion to a dishonest master, whose good graces must be cultivated at all costs, may earn promotion and an easier lot. Theft or sharp practice by a slave trading for his master may increase his own *peculium*, with which he may eventually bargain for his freedom; information may be sold or fees levied by the slaves of influential masters from those who would seek audience of him. At any moment it might be profitable to betray an old master to gain the favour

[1] Petr. 75.

of a new. Set amid conditions of material prosperity, amid a society bent upon the pursuit of pleasure, yet debarred from the real enjoyment of either by the restraints of his status, the slave might well set before himself no other ambition than his own comfort to be enjoyed as far as possible now, but certainly in the far-off days when manumission would give him the opportunity ; and if he could bring that day nearer, what matter by what means ? Not to labour the obvious, it may be said that slavery might be a persistent and compelling education in false ideals set before the slave either by the fear of punishment and cruelty or the hope of material gain.

V

To the slave meeting with cruelty there remained several courses—to endure, to run away, to put himself to death, to retaliate, to obtain justice.

Those were wise, perhaps, who endured, though it might lead to further degradation of themselves and their masters.

' Reflecting upon my mistress's character, . . . at last I decided to run away.' [1] But flight was not easy, except in time of civil war, and recapture meant stern punishment ; [2] for there were few masters who would echo Diogenes' dictum on the flight of his slave, ' turpe est Manen sine Diogene posse vivere, Diogenen sine Mane non posse,' [3] and the law, though giving the benefit of the doubt to the slave in ambiguous cases, recognized that *fugitivi* were a public danger. And therefore failure to report them was penal for those who sheltered them.[4] But the right to search other people's property was not given till the time of Antoninus Pius, when slaves were increasingly valuable, and Marcus Aurelius extended this right to the lands of Caesar and the fisc—as in fairness he had to do—and insisted that local authorities should lend their help in search,

---

[1] Apul. *Met.* iii. 16.

[2] Petr. 107 suggests that the penitence of a *fugitivus* sometimes had a humanizing effect on a cruel master. *Fugitivi* were called *cervi*, Mart. iii. 91.

[3] Sen. *de tranq.* viii. 7.

[4] Apul. *Met.* vi. 4 ; cf. *Dig.* xi. 3, ' de servo corrupto.' For the lex Fabia, a SC. ad legem Fabiam and several rescripts, see *Dig.* xlviii. 15 ; *Cod. Iust.* ix. 20.

and their power in punishment.[1] For no doubt there was a temptation to harbour runaways, when the market was empty and prices dear ; but Roman law always upheld the rights of property.

Suicide might be a happy release. ' Death is coming to you—don't you see for what trifling reasons it is despised ? ' asks Seneca. A slave hurls himself from the roof to avoid a stormy outburst of his master's wrath; a runaway stabs himself rather than be recaptured; a German gladiator rams a sponge down his throat till he is suffocated; another thrusts his head between the spokes of a wheel, just as a Spartan boy dashes his head against the wall rather than perform a menial service. ' Is Freedom so close at hand, yet is there any one a slave ? ' is Seneca's helpful question. Happy the sage ![2]

But the worm turns. Lucilius, complaining that his slaves have taken advantage of his recent preoccupation to run away, is told he is lucky. ' Left you ? Others they have stripped and robbed, attacked with malicious charges, betrayed, trodden under foot, poisoned, slain.'[3] ' Every slave has the power of life and death over you. Thus I assert : whoever despises his own life is lord of yours. Call to mind the cases where masters have fallen victims within their own houses to plots of open violence or of craft ; you will realize that as many have fallen through the rage of slaves as of sovereigns.'[4] ' Quisquis vitam suam contempsit ' ; many thought revenge not dearly bought with their lives. For they could scarcely expect it at a cheaper price.[5]

There was an ancient tradition that, if any slave had murdered his master, then all his slaves should be put to death.[6] So

---

[1] *Dig.* xi. 4.

[2] Sen. *Ep.* iv. 4, lxx. 20, lxxvii. 14 ; cf. *de ira*, iii. 5. 4. The case of the slave flinging himself into the river Moenus is mentioned *infra*, p. 87. Dess. 8476, ' d.m. Philumeni et Eutychiae Menander et Vestina domini iuvenum benemerentium qui cum simul quietem sani petissent in complexu pari exanimes inventi sunt ' might be an agreed suicide.

[3] Sen. *Ep.* cvii. 5.

[4] Sen. *Ep.* iv. 8 ; cf. Hor. *Sat.* i. 1. 99. ' At hunc liberta securi Divisit medium fortissima Tyndaridarum.'

[5] Sen. *de clem.* i. 26. 1. ' Crudelitatem privatorum serviles quoque manus sub certo crucis periculo ultae sunt.'

[6] Mentioned by Tac. *Ann.* xiv. 42 ; implied by Cicero, *ad fam.* iv. 12. 3,

harsh a rule seems almost unintelligible ; it assumes the complicity of the rest of the slaves, and if no other objection can be found, it seems unnecessarily hard upon the heir. With one solitary exception the rule does not hold good during the Empire, though the murder of masters by slaves was by no means unknown, and even indulgent masters express their consciousness of the dangers to be apprehended ; no one can feel safe, however easy and good tempered he is, ' for villainy, not deliberation, murders masters.' [1]   ' Unrestrained anger begets madness,' says Seneca,[2] and slave-owners should realize this. ' Quot servi tot hostes.' [3]   That the fault often lay with masters is equally admitted, and on the murder of a notoriously obscene master Augustus practically agreed that the slaves had done right to murder him, and refused to punish.[4]   It was a dangerous precedent, no doubt, if unaccompanied by rule ; and this rule was expressed in the SC. Silanianum of A.D. 10, which provided for the torture, not necessarily the death, of ' all the slaves within the house, or those outside the house who were present at the murder ' ; only the guilty were to be put to death.[5] By the SC. Claudianum of A.D. 57, slaves manumitted by the will of the murdered man—that is, freedmen at the time of the investigation, but slaves at the time of the murder—were to be punished as though still slaves ; [6] there was to be no inducement for a slave to murder his master, relying upon the manumission so secured to excuse him from torture.

So far there is a movement towards justice and clemency. But four years later—in A.D. 61—occurred the famous case of the murder of Pedanius Secundus, the city prefect, by one of his slaves. There were four hundred slaves in the household, and the *vetus mos*, still not without fascination to some zealous republicans, condemned them all to death. The mob angrily demanded mercy, and besieged the senate-house, wherein an old jurist, C. Cassius, pressed for the drastic penalty, on the ground that, unless an example were made, there would be no security for Roman masters henceforth. The Senate divided ;

---

[1] Pliny, *Ep.* iii. 14.   [2] *Ep.* xviii. 15.   [3] Cf. Sen. *Ep.* xlvii. 5.
[4] ' Et tantum non pronuntiavit iure caesum videri.' Sen. *N.Q.* i. 16. 1.
[5] *Dig.* xxix. 5. Cf. Buckland, *Slavery*, p. 95.
[6] Tac. *Ann.* xiii. 32 ; *Dig.* xxix. 5. 3. 17, ' nam aequissimum ultioni dominorum non obstare indulgentiam ipsorum.'

the ancient rule was triumphant, and Nero refused to interfere
with the considered judgment of the Senate whom he was
striving to conciliate. The four hundred died.

Such is the outline of the story as given by Tacitus ; but it
is by no means free from difficulties.[1] The existence of the
SC. Silanianum is ignored ; yet it was not a dead letter, for it
was confirmed and extended by the SC. Claudianum. The
protest of the mob, which was so violent that soldiers were
ordered out to line the streets, seems unusual in such a case ;
the cognizance by the Senate of a case which was undoubtedly
within the province of a minor court seems uncalled for. The
great number of the victims is often advanced in explanation ; but, at the most, this can meet only the second of these
difficulties.

It is tempting to believe that Tacitus has not accurately
reported the point at issue. The question was not whether
the *vetus mos* was to be upheld, nor is Cassius pleading for its
observance as current law ; the point is rather whether the
existing law, i.e. the SC. Silanianum and the SC. Claudianum,
shall be suspended and replaced by the very *vetus mos* which
had become obsolete. The senate is desperate ; what had
happened to the city prefect might well happen to themselves.
C. Cassius, no doubt an admirer of republican institutions—his
phrase ' contrary to the ordinances and laws of our forefathers '
seems to stamp him as a reactionary—and certainly a jurist,
remembered the old rule, and in a panic these noble senators
cancelled the earlier decision of their own body. Rules made
in the imperial age were thus set aside, and no doubt Cassius

---

[1] Nor is the interpretation of the text. In Tac. *Ann.* xiv. 43, the
statement of Cassius, ' quamvis nondum concusso senatus consulto,'
must be a mistake or confusion, as Furneaux suggests ; ' the reference
does not seem to be strictly to the recent decree xiii. 32, but to the *vetus
mos* . . .' The *vetus mos* had been already shaken by the SC. Silanianum,
which the republican bias of Cassius ignores (it has been suspected that
the text is unsound). Furneaux's sentence continues, ' but to the *vetus
mos* presupposed and extended by it ' (' it '=the SC. Claudianum).
But the SC. Claudianum extended only the SC. Silanianum, which modified
very much the *vetus mos* (*quaestio* plus death of guilty *vice* death of all).
Nor does the note on xiv. 42 seem accurate ; there is no ' increased
stringency of subsequent laws ' in relation to the *vetus mos* ; the increased
stringency is only in relation to the SC. Silanianum, which, however, is
itself modified by Hadrian, *v. infra*, p. 59.

regarded it as a worthy offering to the name he bore. For Nero did not interfere with this cruel piece of antiquarianism,[1] which must be regarded as a solitary reactionary step in the history of the question, which otherwise shows progress in the direction of mercy from Augustus to Marcus Aurelius.

Cassius' object was not realized ; even after A.D. 61 masters perished at their slaves' hands. Largius Macedo, of praetorian rank, was a notoriously overbearing and cruel master ; he forgot, says Pliny [2]—or rather he remembered too keenly—that his father had been a slave. While he was bathing at his Formian villa he was attacked by some of his slaves and left for dead. But the murderers had not completed their task ; tended by the more faithful of his staff, he lived for a few days and enjoyed the satisfaction of seeing the guilty suffer the full punishment usually exacted when the victim died. But only the guilty were put to death, as the SC. Silanianum demanded. Afranius Dexter, a consul, had met with a violent end, but the circumstances were not clear ; he may have been killed by his freedmen, and even so he may have commanded them to kill him. Again the question was raised in the senate, and three different courses were suggested. Pliny himself advised torture, and freedom if the accused were guiltless, which would be the normal procedure ; others urged either banishment or death. By a long speech on the procedure of debate, Pliny [3] eventually persuaded the proposer of death to withdraw his suggestion ; but he neglects to tell us which of the remaining courses was adopted, or why the question reached the senate. Possibly it was because the dead man was consul, possibly because there was a suspicion of virtual suicide. Indeed, the habit of suicide, so frequent under the early Empire, bore hardly upon slaves ; to order slaves to deal the fatal blow, if courage was lacking, was an easy but selfish way out of life, for it left him who was the instrument of death to prove that he was not the agent. For this reason the Emperor Otho, whose death was as noble as any Roman's, if less theatrical than many,

---

[1] For the reasons, see B. W. Henderson, *Nero*, p. 92, though there a different view of the whole incident is taken.

[2] Plin. *Ep*. iii. 14. Two friends of Pliny disappeared while travelling, possibly murdered by their own slaves, *Ep*. vi. 25.

[3] *Ep*. viii. 14.

commanded his freedman to show himself to the legions, lest he should afterwards be charged with the murder of his Emperor.[1] Such virtual suicide was fair neither to the master nor to the slave, and therefore Domitian warned slaves that to help their master to die was criminal, and promptly put to death Epaphroditus for so assisting Nero.[2]

About later legislation little need be said. The savage practice does not appear again ; only the guilty are to be punished, and Hadrian makes it clear that only slaves near enough the scene of murder to know anything about it are to be examined by torture, which is thus further restricted.[3] At the same time, he expects a slave ' to prefer his master's safety to his own.'[4] And with this reconciliation between the interests of the master and the slave the Roman law remained satisfied.[5]

For the ill-treated slave there also remained the Emperor's statue. He might appeal to law. When this practice was established is uncertain. The biographer of Nero claims this act of justice for his Emperor, suggesting that it was perhaps even the affair of Pedanius Secundus that prompted it.[6] ' Some one was appointed to hear cases of wrong done to slaves by their masters,' says Seneca, and the official concerned was the city prefect.[7] ' Slaves have the right to take refuge at the Emperor's statue,' he says elsewhere.[8] If to fly to the Emperor's statue is equivalent to lodging a complaint before the city prefect, then either the credit is not Nero's or Tacitus is in error ; for in the reign of Tiberius there were bitter complaints that slaves took advantage of such asylum and were becoming a real terror to society.[9] Is Augustus the real author of this concession to

---

[1] So Vocula's slaves and freedmen prevented his suicide, Tac. *Hist.* iv. 59 ; possibly for this reason. Cf. Sen. *Ep.* lxxvii. 6–8.

[2] Suet. *Dom.* 14.

[3] Script. hist. aug. *Hadr.* xviii. 11 ; *Dig.* xxix. 5. 1. 28.

[4] *Dig., loc. cit.* ; Script. hist. aug. *Hadr.* xviii. 7 says he deprived a master of the power to put a slave to death, but Gaius, *Inst.* i. 53, contradicts this.

[5] Other legislation deals with smaller points, too technical or trivial to be dealt with here. See *Dig.* xxix. and xlviii. in particular.

[6] B. W. Henderson, *Nero*, p. 94.

[7] *de ben.* iii. 22 ; cf. *Dig.* i. 12. 1. 1 and 8. Mommsen, *D.P.R.* v. 367 ; *Droit pénal*, ii. 144 ; cf., perhaps, Stat. *Silv.* i. 4. 43.

[8] *de clem.* i. 18. 1–3 ; cf. *Dig.* xxi. 1. 17. 12.

[9] Tac. *Ann.* iii. 36.

slaves ?   And do the complaints about their growing insolence, which are loudest between Tiberius and Nero, really reflect the indignation of the owning classes at having their rights curtailed ?   Every case of insubordination would be made the most of as evidence of the harmful result of the law's interference between master and slave.   On the other hand, it is just this same period between Tiberius and Nero which contains some of the most glaring cases of cruelty.   But, whatever the date, the right seems to be established under Nero, and by the time of Pliny seems to be upheld throughout the Empire, the place of the prefect at Rome being taken by other magistrates. In Bithynia a slave who thus took refuge at Trajan's statue was brought to Pliny's notice.[1]   Plutarch, too, moralizing upon the fate of the superstitious man who can never escape from the tyranny of the god which he has imagined, considers that he is in worse plight than the slave, who by law is entitled to throw himself before the altar and demand that he should be sold to a kinder master.[2]   Here is a further step, a right to sale, which is generally attributed to Antoninus on the authority of Gaius.[3] However the contradiction is solved, it is clear that, some time about the middle of the second century, law will protect the slaves who appeal to it, even to the extent of insisting upon sale.

VI

Turn to the other side of the picture and ask whether the slave could put down anything of value as owed to slavery.

Society may often have turned the slave's activities into foolish and unproductive channels.   But it is certainly true that often slavery was a compulsory apprenticeship in a business

---

[1] And eventually sent to Trajan, *Ep.* x. 74, for he was an important slave. He was a slave of Laberius Maximus before capture, and had been sent to the King of Parthia by Decebalus, and was therefore evidence, and is our sole evidence, of communication between these foes of Rome at the time of the Dacian wars.

[2] ἐστὶ καὶ δούλοις νόμος ἐλευθερίαν ἀπογνοῦσι πρᾶσιν αἰτεῖσθαι καὶ δεσπότην μεταβάλλειν ἐπιεικέστερον, *de superst.* 166D. ἐστὶ δούλῳ φεύξιμος βωμός 166 E. Perhaps—1. Plut. is not referring to Roman law ; 2. there is a distinction between altar and statue ; 3. Gaius is wrong ; 4. the treatise is not by Plutarch, who cannot have lived much beyond A.D. 120:

[3] i. 53.

or craft or art. The enslavement of highly skilled Greeks or Orientals had been a feature under the Republic; during the course of the Empire there can have been little supply of slaves educated or trained before enslavement. The alternative was to train them when young slaves [1] in domestic work or in skilled craft, as was indeed done to some extent before the Empire, by Cato the Elder, for example.[2] The training was done by the owner and his existing staff, with a view to employment or sale; indeed, the households of the rich contained special paedagogi for this purpose.[3] Such training took many forms; industry and trade provide the most conspicuous examples, and must be reserved for later treatment, but a word may be said here of arts and letters.

From reasons both of display and genuine literary interest, the rich families attached to their households slaves trained in literature and art. Calvisius Sabinus is said by Seneca to have had eleven slaves taught to recite Homer, Hesiod, and the nine lyric poets by heart. Bookcases would be cheaper, said a rude friend. 'No; what the household knows the master knows,' was the answer.[4] But, apart from such abuses, educated slaves must have been a necessity in the absence of printing; not even the public recitations, which were such a trial to Juvenal, could make up for this deficiency. The busy lawyer, the dilettante poet, the philosopher and educated gentleman of literary tastes had need of copyists and readers and secretaries. Such men were naturally linguists also; a *librarius* who dies at the age of twenty boasts that he was 'litteratus Graecis et Latinis.'[5] *Amanuenses* were common enough; librarians are to be found in public and private libraries.[6]

Shorthand writing was in common use under the Empire, and slave *notarii* were regularly so employed.[7] Pliny the Elder,

---

[1] Cf., e.g., 'd.m. Hilarioni pammuso,' aged fifteen years; Dess. 8482a.
[2] Plut. *Cato*, 21.
[3] *v.* Marquardt, *Vie privée*, i. 186. See Dess. 7446 for a paedagogus in the house of L. Volusius Saturninus; 1825 sqq. for imperial paedagogi.
[4] Sen. *Ep.* xxvii. 6; cf. Petr. 46.   [5] Dess. 7753.
[6] *v.* Marquardt, *op. cit.* p. 177. Dess. 7398 sqq.; 1970 sq.
[7] Maecenas is said by Dio, lv. 7, to have invented it. But Suet. *de gramm.* 1, together with Isidore, *Etymologiae*, i. 22, suggests that Ennius may claim the credit. Tiro, Cicero's secretary, also elaborated a system, Isidore, *loc. cit.*, cf. 'notae Tironianae.' For *notarii*, see Dess. 7402, 7756 sqq.

when travelling, always took with him a shorthand writer ;
whom, even in winter, the polymath's observations kept busy,
his hands covered in woollen mittens.[1] And some of these
men must have reached a high pitch of skill, if the epitaph of
one of them may be believed :

> ' iam doctus in compendia
> tot literarum et nominum
> notare currenti stilo
> quod (sic) lingua currens diceret.' [2]

Many freedmen rhetoricians and grammarians are collected
by Suetonius in a special treatise. Verrius Flaccus was tutor
to Augustus' grandsons, and at death was publicly honoured
by a statue. Scribonius Aphrodisius was the slave and disciple
of Orbilius, and was afterwards freed by Scribonia. Hyginus
was librarian of the Palatine library, in which office he was
followed by Julius Modestus, his own freedman.

We hear of freedmen historians,[3] of a slave philosopher who
was encouraged to argue with his master's friends,[4] of slave
and freed architects.[5] Freedmen as doctors occur frequently
in the inscriptions, some of them specialists ; they had been
trained in big households as slaves, as is shown by one or two
examples ;[6] after manumission they rose to eminence and
became notorious for their high fees. The record of P. Decimus
Eros Merula is instructive ; he was ' medicus, clinicus, chirurgus,
ocularius ' ; for liberty he had paid fifty thousand sesterces, for
the sevirate two thousand. In dedicating statues in the temple
of Hercules he expended thirty thousand, in paving roads for

---

[1] Plin. *Ep.* iii. 5.

[2] Dess. 7756. Dessau compares Ausonius, *epigr.* 114.

[3] ' Legisse me apud Aelium Maurum Phlegontis Hadriani libertum
memini. . . .' Script. hist. aug. *Hadr.* xvi. 1. Part of Phlegon's work is
extant (the *de mirabilibus*). See Westermann, *Scriptores rerum mirabilium
Graeci*, pp. xxxvii, 117 foll.

[4] ' Nequam homini et contumaci sed libris disputationibusque philo-
sophiae aures imbutas habenti. . . .' Gellius, i. 26.

[5] Dess. 7733a, belonging to Domitian ; cf. M. Artorius M. l(ibertus)
Primus, who built the large amphitheatre at Pompeii ; Mau-Kelsey,
Pompeii, p. 144.

[6] e.g. Secunda Livillaes (Caligula's youngest sister), medica ; Dess.
7803. Celadus . . . medicus chirurg., 7811. The latter died at the age
of seventeen. For Antonius Musa, who cured Augustus' fever by cold
baths (but killed Marcellus), and the honours granted to the profession,
see Dio, liii. 30 ; Hermogenes (Hadrian's doctor), Dio, lxix. 22.

his township thirty-seven thousand. At his death he left four hundred and twenty thousand. Slavery had not been unprofitable to him.[1]

The tastes of some sections of society demanded that dancers, singers, musicians,[2] mountebanks, variety artistes, athletic trainers, and masseurs should be forthcoming. All these are to be found in slavery, often trained by teachers who had acquired some reputation. Ummidia Quadratilla, even at the age of eighty, kept a troupe of pantomimic performers to whom she showed extravagant favour.[3] Seneca had his *progymnastes*, and declaims against the tyranny which slave trainers exercised over their pupils.[4]

But whatever the skill required, it is clear that the slave received some training which would enable him to support himself when freed, and often gave opportunities for a fuller life than he could otherwise have enjoyed. And even though the apprenticeship was neither very advanced in subject nor thorough in tuition, even though it went no further than elementary accounts, it was often invaluable and paved the way to later success. Trimalchio came while still young to Rome, learnt to figure, became a *dispensator*, and reached affluence with a smattering of letters.[5] The son of one of his guests, a freedman also, can do his four times table and never has his eyes off his book.[6] Education, boasts another, made me what I am ; and his education did not extend further than reading, writing, and arithmetic.[7] ' I became master in the house, and had my master's brains in my own keeping,' says another ; [8] and such was often true of many a quick-witted slave who benefited by his master's elementary teaching. In short, slavery must often have meant the exchange of semi-barbarism for Roman civilization, a vague enough gift but none the less real. The full opportunities for civilized life could only be fully used in freedom, no doubt, but slavery was an apprenticeship.

[1] Dess. 7812.
[2] Cf. Dess. 9345, Ode, the slave of C. Cassius Symphoniacus ; Marquardt, *Vie privée*, i. 178.
[3] Plin. *Ep.* vii. 24.
[4] Sen. *Ep.* xv. 3. ' Accedunt pessimae notae mancipia in magisterium recepta.'
[5] Petr. 29, etc.   [6] 46 ; cf. 75.
[7] 58 ; cf. Dess. 7753, ' partes dixit CCC.'   [8] Petr. 76.

Further consideration of this, however, must be deferred to the chapter on Manumission.

The consciousness of kindly treatment and the recognition of a debt to the master brought in return a disinterested devotion of slaves to their master. The domestic slave living in close association with his owner's family found his life bound up with theirs, and often became attached by ties of affection and common interest. Inscriptions testify to the devotion of slaves not only to an Octavia but to humble masters not long promoted from slavery. Many of these records, as will be seen later, refer to the gratitude of freedmen, but it was not only manumission that secured such gratitude.

Treat your slaves kindly, says Seneca, and they will repay you ; forbid them to speak in your presence, and they will speak to good purpose about you abroad ; allow them freedom of speech, and they will divert danger to themselves, and lay down their lives for you. 'They may have chattered as they waited on you, but on the rack they held their tongues.'[1] When assassins were hot upon the track of L. Piso, a single slave stood on their path. 'Art thou Piso ? ' they cried through the darkness. 'I am he,' and he fell without a moan. 'A noble lie ! '—even Tacitus[2] condescends. Can a slave confer a benefit ? asks Seneca, and devotes eight pages to the discussion of the problem, bringing forward case after case of devotion. A beleaguered city can hold out no longer ; a mistress's slaves desert to the enemy. On the fall of the city the victors rush wildly in, bent upon bloodshed, among them the slaves, who save their mistress by pretending to hale her off to cruel punishment. Their previous desertion was necessary to convince the enemy of the reality of their hatred for their mistress : ' So vital they deemed it to seem to have slain their mistress, if they were to save her.' Other cases of bravery are quoted, others of cleverness and forethought in the interests of masters ; but this list of Seneca, together with another compiled by Valerius Maximus, leaves no doubt that slaves could confer a benefit, and that Romans could be grateful.[3]

---

[1] *Ep.* xlvii. 4.   [2] Tac. *Hist.* iv. 50.

[3] Seneca, *de ben.* iii. 18–28. Some of his instances are from the Republic, some from the Empire. Valerius Maximus' instances are from the Republic (vi. 8).

ON THE LAND

Quonam igitur modo utilissime colentur agri ?
Pliny, *N.H.* xviii. 39.

I

THE Romans shared with the rest of mankind an irresistible tendency to throw back into the past the golden age of agriculture; seasons were faultless, land fertile; labour was cheap, if indeed men did not gather of the bounties of the soil without the labour of plough and sickle. Crops were heavy, flocks and herds multiplied manifold. Even the dreamer of a golden age to come must cast his vision back to that glorious day—*redeunt Saturnia regna*—and prophesy that earth will see again its wonders.

Such visions add the poet's sanction to the farmer's established privilege of grumbling: the soil is not what it was, nor the seasons; the labourer knows no longer that in the sweat of his brow he must eat his bread; the very beasts have degenerated in stock; everything conspires against the success of the farm; the land, the weather, the government are all in league against the farmer—except in the fat years, when he confesses his gains and grumbles still because he cannot deny. Meantime the general public eat their bread, and, believing that the proof of the pudding is in the eating, discount the laments of agriculture—and turn from meals to more exciting things.

And history is often equally indifferent. The crops grow

---

[1] This chapter was written before the appearance of Rostovtzeff's *Social and Economic History* and the 2nd ed. of Tenney Frank's *Economic History*, containing additional chapters. But reff. to both have been added, and certain conclusions of Rostovtzeff have been quoted in the last paragraph.

silently, the deeds and misdeeds of men clamour for attention. And in the study of the Roman Empire attention is rightly turned to the great problems of imperial consolidation. When agriculture thrusts itself to the fore, it is because famine or social disorder or poverty or failure of recruits compel the historian to inquire into the condition of the land. And, if things go ill there, the scanty contemporary evidence must be searched and a reason found.

But in searching for that reason it may be well to remember that the farmer's complaint need not necessarily be believed entirely in the face of a moderate prosperity, nor need the complaint of conditions here be taken to prove equally bad conditions there. Nor, if conditions are admittedly bad, need they be accounted for by one single cause. The lament may often be heard during the Empire that agriculture is decaying ; and a variety of reasons is offered to account for the decay— the attraction of Rome for an idle peasantry,[1] the demoraliza- tion of the civil wars,[2] the slave gangs of the *latifundia*,[3] the exhaustion of the soil, the importation of foreign corn, and the absence of a protective tariff. But history would become intolerably easy and dull if one cause alone always sufficed to explain each event, or if it were possible to label each pheno- menon as productive entirely of good or entirely of bad. One formula will not explain agricultural conditions throughout the whole of Italy during even the first two centuries of the Empire, and mere condemnation of this or that does not lead to the understanding of them. If slave-labour in agriculture is to be blamed for the decay of Italian farming—if that decay is true—then it must be proved that slave-labour preponderated on the land, and that it was inferior to free labour. If it is inferior, then it must be explained why it preponderated ; either the inferiority is thought to be counterbalanced by cheap- ness, and free labour is therefore driven out, or slave-labour is a second best, made necessary by the dearth of free labour ; in this case slave-labour is hardly to be blamed for the decay of agriculture, unless it is also proved that it prevented free labour when available from returning to the land.

From a very early date in Roman History the problems of land, franchise, and military service had been inextricably

[1] Varro, *R.R.* ii. 1. 3.   [2] Lucan, vii. 399.   [3] Pliny, *N.H.* xviii. 35.

interwoven. The Punic Wars and the struggles of the revolutionary period had taught the Government that a power embarking on a career of imperial expansion, whether voluntary or not, must sooner or later draw a dividing line between the farmer and the soldier in the interests of both army and agriculture. The soil may, indeed, provide the sturdiest of recruits, but there is a point beyond which it is not wise to exhaust this source by ceaseless war or intolerable conditions ; [1] the land may be the natural place in which to resettle ex-service men, but the land is often unwilling to absorb back in changed form what it has sent out, and the very men may cease to be satisfied with a bucolic life.

If the social unrest and economic confusion which followed immediately after the Punic Wars suggest the need for the division of labour between the soldier and the farmer, the support given to the Gracchi and to Livius Drusus was a very plain expression of that need ; to some the demand for land may not have been the most urgent demand of those troubled days.[2] The demand for the franchise is the claim of the Italian to serve as soldier on the same terms as the Roman ; [3] it is the refusal of the farmer and the unprivileged to fight the battles of the town and the privileged. The army reforms of Marius, whatever their cause, conceded much to the Italian, and insomuch as a distinction was now made between farmer and soldier, a prosperous future may have awaited agriculture. If the Social War followed, it was due not to grievances with regard to military service, but to the Italian demand for full and equal citizenship, and the protection and privileges which it gave. If the new professional army[4] destroyed vast tracts of rich farming land in the struggle to solve the problem of the central Government—which was the cause of the fall of the Republic—and the equally pressing problem of the future of

---

[1] For Ti. Gracchus' time, cf. Plut. *Ti. Gr.* 8, ἠμέλουν τε παίδων ἀνατροφῆς ὡς τάχυ τὴν Ἰταλίαν ἅπασαν ὀλιγανδρίας ἐλευθέρων αἰσθέσθαι.

[2] Cf. App. i. 21. προτιθέντες τῶν χωρίων τὴν πολιτείαν. In 125 B.C., when some at Rome preferred to give the franchise rather than divide their lands, ἐδέχοντο ἅσμενοι . . . οἱ Ἰταλιῶται.

[3] Cf. Plut. *Ti. Gr.* 8, οὔτε ταῖς στρατείαις ἔτι προθύμους παρεῖχον ἑαυτούς. Vell. ii. 15.

[4] Heitland, *Agricola*, p. 176, suggests that Marius drew on the free *mercennarii*.

the provinces—which was the justification for the fall—it does not disprove the thesis that in the establishment of a professional army lay the main hope of farming in Italy. Nor could the victory of the Italians remedy at once evils inherited from the Punic Wars. And not the least of those evils was the encouragement given to the large estate worked by slave-labour.

It is, however, quite possible to overestimate the evil effects of the large estates, to distribute them over the map of Italy too freely, and to lay too much stress on the greed of the wicked capitalist. The picture is often drawn in dismal colours. The primitive simplicity of the Cincinnati and the Fabricii [1] is a thing of the past. Then the yeoman farmer lived with his family on the land ; he and his son, his wife and his sons' wives did the work—he ploughed, she spun and made clothes. From the land the household was fed, clothed, and furnished with utensils ; the larger the household, the greater the economy. The estate produced little more than it consumed ; there was no incentive to produce more, for there was little demand either for food or for goods in the small country towns. Into this idyll broke the Punic Wars, in which the Senate at first engaged with reluctance, seeing no gain to be reaped from such a conflict, as indeed little at first was reaped. The country population was drained to the utmost to fill the legions ; the casualties were enormous.[2] The enemy lived upon the country, and destroyed what he could not consume ; cornlands reverted to fallow. Small farms, even outside the devastated area, were left idle for lack of labourers ; the larger farms were turned over to grazing, which needed less labour and less skill ; small holdings were mortgaged and lost. Returning from the wars,[3] the small farmer had not the courage to start anew, coming back perhaps broken in health or spirit, perhaps rich in purse,

---

[1] Colum. *prooem.* 13.

[2] The census lists for 234 B.C. give a roll of 270,713 citizens ; for 209 B.C., 137,108, though Beloch would write 237,108, on the ground that manumission made up the losses ; *v.* M. E. Park, *The Plebs Urbana in Cicero's Day*, where, on p. 16, a list of casualties is given ; but the evidence is very scanty.

[3] M. E. Park, *op. cit.*, estimates that, between 200 and 190 B.C., 15 per cent. of the citizens were absent on military service ; the percentage of allies would be very much greater.

and changed in ideals. He had seen something of life; he had
yielded to the allurement of the town; he saw unlimited
opportunities in the provinces, whither he went in the employ
of the tax-farmers, or as independent merchant or trader.
Wealth poured into Italy, and with wealth came slaves, and
slaves took the place of son and daughter, who found pleasanter
places than the dairy or the stable in which to spend their time.
And, to pass into the later Republic and early Empire, foreign
imports took the heart out of the farmer, who found it impossible to plant and sow to his profit ; the smallholder was squeezed
out, for the large estate, by the natural attraction of the larger
unit for the smaller, absorbed the small farm which could not
face the competition of cheap slave-labour, and had not any
capital behind it for development or improvement. Pasturing
would pay only on a large scale ; the capitalist would sink his
money in flocks of sheep and herds of slaves, both of which
he treated as beasts of the field. While Rome fed on the
luxuries of the East, Italy wasted away, bled by capitalists who
put their gains to usury or squandered them in the pleasure
resorts of Campania.

II

But the picture may be overdrawn. The growth of the
latifundia is due to many causes.

It has been estimated that two million acres were left
devastated after the Punic Wars, or were forfeited to the
conqueror ; and, if some of them passed back into the occupation of their original owners, many were undoubtedly left idle,
passing easily into the hands of those who had the capital to
work them, without those hands necessarily being guilty of
rapacity or oppression. If private lands lay idle, the same is
more true of vast tracts of *ager publicus*, and the State acquiesced
only too gladly in the grazing of more acres of public land by
the herds of those who were lucky enough to possess them than
the law allowed. If the Government and capital were in league,
or if those who governed were also capitalists, then both might
plead that the wealth of the State was increased and no harm
done. But when land is concerned, the distinction between
occupation and possession is easily obscured. In the revolutionary period, by which time the people had recovered and

the Italian land-hunger was being felt at its keenest, the State
had need to repent bitterly of its former generosity.   Then
the occupiers of much land were cursed for their greed.   Earlier,
no doubt, many had been praised for their enterprise ; but,
whether they were cursed or praised, it is clear that the public
land was not merely in the hands of a few Roman capitalists, for the Italians opposed the Gracchan and Livian land
reforms.   In another way, too, the State sometimes encouraged
unintentionally the large farm, while attempting to encourage
the small holding.   In the founding of new colonies the land
was not always distributed in equal lots ; men of distinction
or influence sometimes secured large plots without being compelled to live on them.   Nor was the success of military colonies
assured.[1]   The State advanced neither capital nor tools, and
the failure of one veteran must often have meant the moderate
accumulation of land by his more fortunate neighbour.   But
such causes as these latter could hardly lead to the making of
vast estates ; the Sullan proscription and later confiscations
undoubtedly led to greater accumulation of land, much of
which was left idle and unoccupied.

The appropriation of ' public land ' took place under the
Republic ; yet it is none the less relevant to the time of the
Empire, for in the causes of the growth of the *latifundia* is to
be found a clue to their distribution.   The devastated regions
and the ' public land ' lay chiefly in the south of Italy, in Apulia
and Lucania ; here high grasslands were suitable for nothing
but grazing by hardy mountain sheep or cattle which could
live on poor grass during the summer, if they had large enough
areas over which to range, while in winter they were driven
down to lowland pastures.   Elsewhere, too, grazing farms
existed in the mountainous districts, where long stretches of
rugged country could no more be divided into productive allotments than thousands of acres of Scotch or Yorkshire moorland.
The lands confiscated by Sulla lay throughout Italy ; many
acres were given to faithful supporters of the Sullan cause,
and, often allowed to go to ruin, were bought up cheaply ;
much of the confiscated property, however, was set apart for
colonies and military holdings, whence the occupiers often
drifted back to Rome.   On the whole, the Sullan distributions

[1] Cf. Tac. *Ann.* xiv. 27.

tended to break up large estates ; so, too, the expenditure by Augustus of six million sesterces in Italy, and 160 millions in the provinces, in buying land for his veterans.

There is another alleged cause for the growth of the large estate—a cause which is said to have ruined Italian farming ; this is the importation of foreign corn. Whether it is assumed that Italy had originally fed Rome, and was ruined by the lack of demand when Rome was flooded with imported corn, or whether it is assumed that the imported corn found its way into the remote townships of Italy, the theory seems to raise more problems than it solves.

The first foreign corn was imported into Italy during the first Punic War. Rome adopted the Carthaginian theory of sovereignty, and diverted to herself the tribute in kind which had formerly made up much of the wealth of Carthage. The war had obviously drained agriculture of much labour ; but no Government was likely to commit the folly of bringing to Italy the corn which would ruin her own agriculture. And the senators themselves were in those days landlords. Some other reason must be suggested, and it has been found by some in the exhaustion of the Latin soil. Nor was Gaius Gracchus likely to excite opposition in landed quarters by proposing a *lex frumentaria,* if there was to be competition between home-grown and foreign corn in the city markets. Before the days of imported corn, oxen no more dragged to Rome corn-laden wagons at slow and laborious pace over hill and down dale than in later days they carried African or Sicilian corn to starving Italian farmhouses. The cost of transport made both economically impossible ;[1] the rich might pay for peaches brought from Verona, asparagus from Ravenna, roses from Paestum,[2] but these are the luxuries of a few. Rome never had drawn on Italy for her bread ; she had drawn on Latium ; as her population had increased she had exhausted too rapidly

[1] ' The highways of the Empire were constructed with a view to military or administrative ends, and not for purposes of trade,' Stuart Jones, *Companion to Roman History,* p. 45. Columella, i. 5. 6, advises a farm well away from main roads, which suggests that the supply of the urban market was not his aim. Yet he thinks a river is useful, a wish not often fulfilled in Italy ; but cf. Pliny, *Ep.* v. 6, who sent grain by the Tiber.

[2] Stuart Jones, *Companion to Roman History,* p. 312.

the resources of a restricted area.[1]   Round Rome large estates had been in evidence a hundred and fifty years before the fall of the Republic.   Originally, economic competition for the growing Roman markets had favoured the farmer who could produce grain in quantities; later, an exhausted soil possibly, certainly the growing population, and the constant encroachment of the parks and pleasure-grounds of rich city officials, had made imperative the importation of corn, since the area on which Rome had formerly drawn had become too small to supply her needs.   Transport by sea was cheap, in spite of the danger of storms; economically Rome was nearer Egypt and Africa than the Po Valley; the sea was less of a barrier than the Apennines.   Once this practice of importation was established, the zone round Rome was released from the duty it could no longer fulfil.   If corn was grown in this zone, it was grown to gratify the vanity of the rich, who prided themselves sometimes on a table supplied by home production, more often on the procuring of every rarity from the East; but parks, vineyards, and market-gardens occupied many acres, and grazing was common in the neglected countryside of Etruria; close to Rome vegetables were grown and hawked in the streets of the city.   The city and the area round it barren of corn together make up one unit; foreign corn is distributed in the city and sold in the area; if the cornships are delayed, the country round about suffers as the city suffers.   When in time of famine Augustus banished slaves and other unnecessary mouths a hundred miles from the city, he did not send them to starve in the country, which would be equally hungry if it depended on foreign imports; he sent them outside the cornless area, that the State reserves of grain might suffice for citizens within it.[2]

Even apart from considerations of transport, the influence of imported corn could not make itself felt very far.   In the time of Augustus, the yearly imports into Rome amounted to

[1] Tenney Frank, *Economic History*, 2nd ed. pp. 56–57, suggests that a thin soil laid upon an underlying deposit of volcanic tufa had been exploited too cruelly. Rostovtzeff, p. 329, says the exhaustion of the soil was not general in Italy or the provinces. Columella denies this exhaustion to Italy as a whole, *v. infra*, p. 75.

[2] Dio, lv. 25; Suet. *Aug.* 42.

sixty million *modii*. The yearly consumption of the city was twenty-eight millions in Cicero's time ; about half the supply was taken by Rome ; the rest was sold in the districts round Rome,[1] where it would feed a population about as large as that of Rome. If Rome contained under a million souls and Italy four and three-quarter millions (Beloch's figures), 76 per cent. of Italians would be fed by home-grown corn ; if Rome contained one and a quarter millions and Italy fourteen and three-quarter millions (Nissen's figures), only 9 per cent. of Italians would be dependent on foreign corn.

It has been contended that the cause of the growth of *latifundia* gives a clue to their distribution. There still remains another aspect, which will make clear the reason for their growth and for their failure to extend over the whole of Italy. As has been suggested already, the perpetual problem of agriculture is the problem of labour. The summons of war, the devastation of land, the gayer life of the town, the possibilities of the provinces had made the question of labour acute. It was solved, so it was thought, by slave-labour. Slaves had worked on the land before the Punic Wars ; Carthaginian practice had shown how to apply their labour on a large scale ;[2] the supply of this labour was well-nigh inexhaustible. The wars and the capture of the East, with its slave trade established and organized for centuries, made certain a steady flow of slaves at low prices. Here was the solution of the problem, and the

---

[1] See Salvioli, *Le capitalisme dans le monde antique*, p. 171, and Tenney Frank, *Economic History*, p. 430, for reff. Salvioli deduces from the yearly consumption of corn the probable population of Rome, which he puts at under a million. This would agree fairly closely with Beloch, who puts the number at 800,000. Nissen estimates the yearly consumption at $27,375,000 \times 2 = 54,750,000$ (= double the figure quoted for the time of Septimius Severus) ; ' this, however, allows a consumption of 60 modii per head per annum, and Beloch believes 36 to be the correct figure,' Stuart Jones, *Companion to Roman History*, p. 40. But Nissen gives the population at from 1,200,000 to 1,300,000, which gives 45 modii per head, and this is nearer Beloch's figure. Either the whole supply was taken by Rome, or if 36 represents the maximum consumption per head, only one-quarter was available for the country districts, and would feed 300,000. As Nissen puts the population of Italy at $14\frac{3}{4}$ millions, excluding Rome, only about 9 per cent. of [them would taste foreign corn.

[2] But see Rostovtzeff, p. 277.

enterprising capitalist sunk vast sums in slaves, whom he hoped
to work at the highest pitch to redeem their cost ; he need
pay no wages, and he need no longer fear that this labour would
be called up for service, or drift away to the towns. Slave-
labour came in to take the place of the decreasing country
population, and was recommended to the landlord by its
exemption from military service,[1] and by the necessity imposed
on it of remaining on the land. The dealer and the landowner
combined to remedy by one method the very evil which the
Government was later compelled to deal with on other lines by
the pressure of the Italians and their supporters at Rome. And
so for the time the dealer reaped his profits ; for long years
the uplands of Italy claimed the whip-driven labour of thousands
of barbarian herdsmen, and soon gave a resting-place to their
worn-out bodies.

The evils of the *latifundia* reached their climax sometime
during the later years of the Republic. In Augustus' day
vast gangs still overran the south of Italy, and he was compelled to send Tiberius to deal with the organized kidnapping
of travellers and children, who were carried off to work in the
ergastula ; even deserters from the army had betaken themselves there to hide.[2] Perhaps already the *pax Romana* was
beginning to diminish the supply of slaves, and open kidnapping was necessary. In A.D. 24 there was the germ of a
slave revolt at Brundisium, luckily prevented from developing
into serious trouble by the presence of a force of marines ; [3]
in A.D. 29 Tiberius dispatched a force to Apulia *ad servos
torquendos* ; [4] in Claudius' reign Lepida was said to be disturb-
ing the peace by her imperfect control of her numerous slaves
in Calabria.[5]

But during the first two centuries of the Empire the tendency was for the large estates with their slave-labour to grow
less numerous. The supply of slaves diminished as wars
became less frequent ; the free labourer and small farmer,

[1] Cf. τοῦ μὴ τοὺς ἐλευθέρους ἐς τὰς στρατείας ἀπὸ τῆς γεωργίας περισπᾶν,
App. i. 7.

[2] Suet. *Aug.* 32 ; *Tib.* 8.   [3] Tac. *Ann.* iv. 27.

[4] Dess. 961 ; the date depends upon Hirschfeld's restoration. For a
rising in the East, serious enough to make Vespasian dispatch a force to
deal with it, see Tac. *Hist.* iii. 47.

[5] Tac. *Ann.* xii. 65.

either as owner or tenant, was by no means extinguished, and appeared in greater numbers ; but, above all, the flaw in the brilliant solution made itself manifest — slave-labour was expensive and inefficient.

On this point Columella, writing about the time of Nero, is emphatic. Observing that countries each have their own peculiar gifts, he reviews the districts of Italy, and praises the produce of each, second to none in the world—Campanian and Apulian grain, Ligurian cattle, the vineyards of the *agri Massici*, and so on. His panegyric closes with a moral : Italy has been the most responsive of lands ; it has learnt to bear the fruits and crops of the whole world—but on one condition, *adhibito studio colonorum*—'given the devotion of its cultivators.'[1] The depression of Italian agriculture is due, he urges in his preface, not to the exhaustion of the soil,[2] but to the abandonment of that land which the noblest of ancestors nobly worked, to the lowest of the slave class. The art of agriculture, though of blood relationship with wisdom, is alone in lacking alike pupils and professors, else more care would be taken in choosing a slave farm-bailiff (*vilicus*) who had some knowledge of the work, or was quick to learn it. The rich man sends to his land worn-out lackeys and litter-bearers, feeble and aged ; sometimes a free man, refusing any longer the daily task of fawning to a patron, is appointed, but he does not always know the work which he is to supervise.[3] But, even supposing the bailiff is of average ability, he needs to be constantly kept up to the mark ; and a bailiff is necessary, unless the ideal is followed that a landlord should farm his own land. But ambition calls most men elsewhither. Yet the absentee landlord is at the mercy of his agents, who take advantage of the rareness of his visits, and, going from misdeed to misdeed, eventually devote their attention to their own enrichment rather than to the tilling of their masters' estates ;[4] even the announcement of more visits to be paid in the future than in the past would be a device which would soon lose its effect.[5] In crop-producing farms, therefore, a tenant—*colonus*—is pre-

---

[1] iii. 8. 5.
[2] Cf. Tac. *Ann*. xii. 43, ' nec nunc infecunditate laboratur.'
[3] i. *prooem*. 11–12.
[4] i. 1. 18–20, ' sub expectatione successorum.'   [5] i. 2. 1.

ferable to a slave-bailiff, who will find too many opportunities
to steal, to let out for hire the animals of his farm, to be careless
in work, and negligent in book-keeping.[1] Yet, even supposing
that he adds honesty to ability, even so the labour of those
under him is inefficient and careless. And for a good reason, as
Columella recognizes : [2] the interest of slave and master have
nothing in common. The slave was careless of beast and
tool ; he had no interest in the success of the farm or the
efficient performance of his own work ; the bankruptcy of the
estate and a change of master might be a good thing for him.
At all times he can rely on food and clothing, for without his
health the master would gain no profit on his original outlay.
In agriculture, as in industry, the problem is how to reconcile
the interests of slave and master. 'My practice,' says
Columella, ' and I do not regret it, is to be on easier terms
with my country slaves than with my town slaves. I realize
that their labours can be made more tolerable by the kindliness of their master towards them. I even joke with them.
I consult the most skilled about new work ; they always
do better a job which they think is due to their own
suggestion.' [3]

But the problem was incapable of solution even by Columella's condescension, and opposition of the interest of slave
and owner in agriculture and industry led neither to efficiency
nor economy.[4] A reading of the agricultural writers makes
clear how much time and money was wasted on the unproductive task of mere supervision. In the vineyard the slaves
should work in groups of ten : thus they will be most readily
supervised ; they should not be allowed to disperse in twos
and threes ; over four or five an older or more competent slave
may be placed, himself supervised by a foreman, who in turn
is subject to the bailiff, who may be responsible to a *procurator*,
who is the agent of the landlord—an elaborate system of checks
devised to produce work from an unwilling worker. Not that

---

[1] i. 7. 6; for corn-producing districts free men were preferred.

[2] i. 8. 15 sqq.

[3] So, too, Varro, *R.R.* i. 17. 6, ' minus se putant despici atque aliquo
numero haberi a domino.'

[4] Cf. Philostr. *Ep. Ap.* xli. οὐδὲ τοὺς οἰκέτας ὑμῖν εὐνοεῖν εἰκός, πρῶτον μὲν
ὅτι οἰκέται, εἶτα ὅτι . . .

cruelty need be employed, for the bailiff must be—' as far as slave nature allows '—' possessed of such qualities of mind that his rule is neither lax nor harsh.'[1]

For work on the land the hardier type of slave was necessary, but it was also a less intelligent type. It was certain loss of capital to place a delicate Greek or Syrian on a farm, even if his brains did not make him too expensive for such a purpose. But a Dacian or Thracian needed a longer period of training, and probably never reached a very high pitch of skill. Rascally slaves are often possessed of quicker wits, says Columella, and should be used in the vineyards— not that he prefers to work ' per noxios quam per innocentes ' ; an honest man of the same mental alertness will do, if he can be found.[2]

But, whichever type is bought, slaves cost money, and they all need to be maintained. The capital spent in buying them is money taken out of productive enterprise and locked up in human labour—money which might be used in development of the farm, if free labour were employed. Loss of a slave is loss of capital. Even if he works for many years, his labour cannot be regarded as good interest on the price paid. To determine the ratio of efficiency of free labour to slave-labour no figures exist for ancient times ; in 1789 in the West Indies the relative value of work done was variously estimated at 8 to 2, 9 to 5, 3 to 1.[3] If these figures are of any use for ancient times, about three times as many slaves as free men would be needed, and each slave represents capital which is extinguished by his death. Against the profits of his labour must be set the cost of maintenance.[4] The difference between the cost of living of the poor free man (for his wages would not be much more than the cost of living) and the cost of mainten-

---

[1] Colum. i. 8. 10.   [2] i. 8.

[3] Summary of evidence ' taken before a Committee of the whole House, to whom it was referred to consider the slave trade,' in 1789 ; ii. 52, 74, iv. 32.

[4] About one-twentieth of the purchase price ? average price for good slave is 8000 sest. ? Hor. *Ep.* ii. 2. 5 ; Colum. iii. 3. 8 (for other prices see app.). Bare subsistence is about 180 sest. per ann., Marquardt, *L'Org. fin.* p. 65. Cost of upkeep of *aquarius*, a superior type of slave who received wages, is 700 sest. Perhaps 400 sest. may be regarded as the normal cost of upkeep, which is then one-twentieth cost price.

ance of the slave cannot have been very great ; [1] in any case, it would not be represented by the figures 3 to 1 given for the ratio of efficiency.   The slave must be fed in sickness and old age, in slack seasons and busy seasons alike.[2]   And if individual slaves approach in trustworthiness or efficiency the free man, they have been encouraged by the right of acquiring profits and savings of their own, and rewarded by gifts in money or kind.   The more the slave is allowed to approach in status and rights and property the position of the free man, the more efficient he becomes ; the interesting history of the *peculium* is the best disproof of the cheapness of slave-labour.

' As far as slave nature allows '—the flaw in the solution which slave-labour was thought to offer has become apparent. For the moment slave-labour, being bound to the land, was thought to solve the problem of the shortage of free labour. But many who expended capital on slaves must have been disappointed.   True, labour was bound to the soil ; but the very act of binding it robbed it of incentive and efficiency, and the cost of binding swallowed up the meagre profits on motiveless and unintelligent work.   The whole implication of Columella's treatise seems to be that slave-labour is a second best in default of anything better.   For lands which need most care and skill the tenant is expressly reserved, and he might be a free man or a slave working with prospects of his own advancement.   If Columella does not explicitly say that he would employ free labour if he could get it, it is because it is so obvious a point ; [3] he is concerned to show how an estate may be made to pay by the utmost care and scientific handling ; but it is on the need for watchfulness that he lays emphasis.   Interested work, honesty, and ability are the desiderata of agriculture in his day, and slave-labour provided none of them.   Yet work had to be done, and any labour was better than none.   But it was a type

[1] See chapter xvii. of Tenney Frank, *Economic History*.

[2] In Varro, *R.R.* i. 18. 2, thirteen days in forty-five are given as the margin of waste.

[3] Cf. the statement that planters would prefer having work done by free negroes, if it could be done, to maintaining many women, children, and old men and invalids, and that it would be much cheaper, unless the price of free negroes' work were very exorbitant. *Summary of Evidence*, ii. 54.

of labour that paid best on one kind of farm—the grazing ranch.[1]

The very nature of the labour employable on *latifundia* tended to limit and localize them.

But it is doubtful whether the farm entirely given over to grazing was really common. The old conception of land as self-sufficient always haunted Roman agricultural theory, even though some specialization had been practised in the days of Cato. It lingered in sentiment for a long time ; the noble prided himself on his home-grown products, even though raised at a loss in a soil unadapted and a climate unfavourable. Perhaps it even received encouragement from those rich Stoics who could satisfy in their costly villas their caprices and their philosophy by a studied and expensive application to the practice of ' self-sufficiency.' What greater example of detachment ? But whether the self-sufficiency of the land is an economic fact or merely a pleasant hobby is a subject which must be delayed to a later section. In the meantime we may pause to consider the conditions of labour on a large estate ; and most of the information must be taken from the treatise of Columella, which was written from experience of the problem, and with the aim of showing how farming could be made to pay. Moreover, Columella's farm was typical of the farming methods of his day, and represented the prevailing type.[2]

III

It is notoriously difficult to reconstruct conditions upon the land in almost any period. The ancient historian, at any rate, had little to say upon the matter ; the poet shed over it a warm glow of sunlight and content, till his convert to rusticity learned that some day the shepherd's pipe must be exchanged for the hoe of the toiling husbandman. The kindly and sensitive gentleman who prefers that the accounts of his steward should not intrude upon the seclusion of his study is not likely to give much information about the life of his farm-hands. The satirists do little more than make fun of the stupidity of the hedger and ditcher—the *caprimulgus aut fossor* of Catullus. The rich quarry of inscriptional stones which

[1] Cf. Colum. vi. *prooem.* 4.   [2] Rostovtzeff, p. 193.

yields such valuable material for every other side of Roman life is here of little use. There remains the treatise of Columella, a counsel of perfection, perhaps : the steward whom Columella demanded never yet controlled any one's property ; no farm was ever so well laid out. But in default of other evidence the wishes of the idealist must be used as evidence of fact, and be brought to earth where possible by the witness of practice.

The word ' villa ' may equally well be applied to the Laurentine house of Pliny or the imaginary estate of Columella. The former is merely a house and garden, the latter includes the country-house, farm - buildings, farm-servants' quarters, and land with the farms of the *coloni*. Both would contain domestic slaves, perhaps brought out from town at each visit of the owner. This domestic staff has been dealt with in an earlier chapter ; it is the life of the resident farm-staff that concerns us here.

The villa is laid out with no economy of space. Due regard is paid to healthy position, and abundance of water, and beautiful outlook. The mistress is to be enticed from town to the country by a good view from her drawing-room window.[1] The sleeping-rooms of the slaves are to face due south.[2] The farm-buildings are divided into *pars rustica*, which includes the living and sleeping quarters of the slaves and the stables and cow-houses and pens, and *pars fructuaria*, granaries, barns, store-rooms, tool-sheds, and so on. As a general living-room a large kitchen is provided, lofty to prevent the risk of the beams and woodwork catching fire, and roomy enough to accommodate the whole staff at every season of the year—cool in summer and easily warmed in winter.[3] Food is prepared by *cellarii*, who presumably stay at home to cook for the gangs at work in the fields. For the slaves who may come and go at their pleasure—easily the majority under the Empire—*cellae* give sleeping quarters and perhaps some privacy ; the quarters of the cowherds and shepherds should be situated conveniently close to their animals, and all should be fairly central and easily visited by the bailiff ; on many a lowland Scottish farm the bothy boy still sleeps in the harness-room, and elsewhere stable-

[1] i. 4. 8.   [2] i. 6. 3.
[3] *Loc. cit.* ; so, too, Varro, i. 13. 2.

boys sleep in lofts above their horses.[1] Round all the farm-buildings ran a wall (*conseptum*), flung wide enough to enclose a yard. Close to the entrance the bailiff is to have his lodging; thus he can see everything that leaves or comes into the farm.[2] And to guard all, there should be watch-dogs trained to stay close to the villa; they should be black, for they are thus more terrifying to the thief, and in the darkness can approach an intruder unseen; they should not, however, be so fierce as to attack the domestic staff. In the fields the dogs should be white, for thus they are more easily distinguished from the wolf.[3]

Clothed in sleeved leather jerkins and hooded capes the slaves go out to their tasks in most weathers. Such clothing is for practical use rather than for show;[4] it is made on the estate. The bailiff's wife shows her worth by having wool ready prepared and combed for spinning, with which to occupy her slave-women on wet and frosty days, when a woman cannot work out of doors. They should make all the slaves' clothing to save expense. Once upon a time—up to our fathers' time, says Columella—such domestic labour was supervised by the woman of the house, who did not scorn to wear home-made clothing herself. Nowadays most are so corrupted by luxury that they never spin, and prefer silks of foreign weaving. The bailiff's wife therefore takes her place.[5]

Columella recommends specialization in work : anybody's work is nobody's, and responsibility cannot be fixed. And so the field-slaves go out under overseers, ' hardworking and thrifty,'[6] if they come up to the ideal; they must work as well as supervise. In the vineyards the slaves should not be dispersed in groups of twos and threes; gangs of ten are most easily supervised. This was highly skilled work, and here Columella, as has been seen, employs his ' rascally ' slaves—*improbi*—on the ground that they are possessed of quicker wits. The other workers make a long list, but it is doubtful

---

[1] Varro puts the poultry keeper close to the fowl-houses. In the villa excavated at Bosco Reale, near Pompeii, the slave quarters were between the rooms containing the vine and olive presses ; *v.* Stuart Jones, *Companion*, p. 172.

[2] Colum. i. 6. 6 ; so, too, Varro, *loc. cit.*

[3] vii. 12. 3.   [4] i. 8. 9.   [5] xii. *prooem.* 7–9.

[6] i. 9. 1, *magistri operibus.*

whether Columella really means his doctrine of specialization to hold good entirely. The ploughman—who must not be too tall, otherwise he grows tired too soon—could obviously be employed on another job when ploughing had finished. The ox-driver, whose enormous figure and voice should make him respected by the herds, must not bully his animals; he should use his stick as little as possible, and never a goad, which only makes his beasts sullen and obstinate.[1] The rules for the treatment of oxen after ploughing are set forth in detail, and must be learnt by the cowherd.[2] The qualifications of the goatherd are no less exacting; he must be hardy, active, patient of toil, nimble, venturesome, able to thread his way through rocks and thorns, leading his herd, not following as the shepherd.[3] The pig-man must know his pigs and their young separately; if he has not a good memory, he may mark them with letters, and so assign the right piglet to the right pig.[4]

Columella tends to speak too much of theory and too little of practice for our purpose. The same is the case with Varro, though he relieves much precept by a word or two on the life of shepherds, probably on a large grazing farm. Close to the farm, boys and even girls may look after a flock; to go out all day and to drive home the sheep does not need great physical endurance. But for pasturing in forest-clad mountains by tangled and rugged paths the strongest and most vigorous of shepherds are needed, and they go armed. They must be capable of dealing with wild beasts and robbers, and therefore fleet and skilled with the javelin. Not every race is fit for such work—the Bastulian and Turdulian are of little use; the Gauls are admirable. During the day they feed their flocks fairly close together, spending long lazy days in the sun, as Mowgli when he herded buffaloes. They take their food separately, and at dusk meet for a common meal and separate again to guard their flocks during the night. Food is sent up to them on pack-animals, horses or mules, and they prepare it in rude shelters thrown up to keep off the winds; here, too, they keep their implements and medicines for the flocks. Much the same life may be assumed for the rangers of herds of horses; but in this case the men are mounted, especially in Apulia and Lucania,

[1] i. 9. 2; ii. 2. 26, *calcitrosi.*   [2] ii. 2. 25, *bubulcus.*
[3] vii. 6. 9.   [4] vii. 9. 10, *porculator.*

where the mares are rounded up and driven to their stables at night.[1]

But even on Columella's farm all the labourers are not perfect. For those who behaved ill or earned the distrust of their overseers an *ergastulum* was provided. Built low in the ground, it was to be lit by as many narrow windows as possible, placed high enough to be out of reach.[2] From here the bailiff should have no power to loose any slave. If bad conduct makes it necessary for a slave to be condemned to the *ergastulum*, he may not be released without the master's knowledge. Its inhabitants call for special attention from the master; they are subject to so many overseers—the bailiff, the jobmasters, the warders—that injustice may easily be done them, and their natures thus permanently soured; cruelty on the part of their overseers only makes them more formidable. Their clothing and food should be examined frequently by the master himself; he should ask for complaints of neglect and ill-treatment, punishing those who merely wish to make trouble, and vindicating those who have a real complaint.[3]

No doubt few masters lived up to such a standard of conduct. But conditions under the Empire were different from conditions under the Republic. The *ergastulum* is more rarely met with, being reserved for insubordinate members of the country staff just as work on the farm is reserved for the punishment of unruly members of the town staff. Slaves working in chains are the exception. Pliny can write that no landowner in Transpadane Gaul ever works his slaves in chains.[4] Public feeling was against it; slaves could no longer be exploited as in the old days regardless of their health; they were growing dearer in price; *vernae* were constantly taking the places of imported slaves, and were apt to be privileged, even spoiled. There is a growing realization that cruelty is to be avoided, if only because it does not pay.[5]

---

[1] Varro, ii. 10. 5, 6, 10, and 11.

[2] Colum. i. 6. 3. The adjective is *subterraneum*, which can only mean, if there were to be windows, that the floor of the *ergastulum* was sunk a few feet below the level of the ground.

[3] Colum. i. 8. 18.

[4] Plin. *Ep.* iii. 19. 5. Mommsen maintained that under the Empire *vincti* no longer worked in the field; but Columella, as has been seen, recommends it in the case of his *improbi* working in the vineyards.

[5] Plin. *N.H.* xviii. 36; *v.* Marquardt, *Vie privée*, i. 226.

Nor are Columella's slaves immune from illness. If any of them fall ill, it is the duty of the bailiff's wife to look after them most attentively. For from such attention is born goodwill and obedience. Many a slave who has had every attention bestowed upon him when ill has been eager to show his gratitude by more trusty service.[1]   And so a sick-room or hospital is part of the regular equipment of a farm. The *vilica* must see that it is kept clean and aired whether in use or not. If any slave eludes work in the fields and returns home, she must find out the cause of his return—whether he is ill or merely idle. If she discovers that he is merely pretending weariness, she should put him into the sick-room. It is far better that a slave who is tired should rest a day or two rather than be urged beyond his strength, and so contract some real disease.[2]   It seems as though the *vilica* is herself to be responsible for the medical aid ; in Columella's last book, which is largely given up to recipes, a few formulae for medicines are to be found. But the slave-doctor is common among the numerous specialists in large staffs in the towns ; so, too, the slave veterinary surgeon ; and it would be an unnecessarily sinister view of Roman slavery to assume that while the mules had their *mulomedicus*, the horses their *medicus equarius*,[3] their ' fellow-slaves,' the slaves of the farm, went without medical help.[4]   In the staffs of the imperial family and of one or two noble families who have left many inscriptions, slave-doctors are common ; indeed, in one case there seem to have been many under the control of a *supra medicos* ;[5]   and the names are known of several slave-nurses attached permanently to the hospital.[6]   From the mention[7] of Apollonius, a slave-physician on a large estate in Greece, it may be inferred that, as is natural, the country staff were attended by slave-doctors on large farms. Varro, speaking of the smaller farms, says that local doctors were preferred on the ground that the death of so skilled a slave was too great a loss to be faced. Pliny was genuinely distressed by the ill-health of his slaves ;[8]

---

[1] Colum. xii. 1. 6.   [2] xii. 3. 7.   [3] Dess. 7813, 7814.

[4] For this use of *conservus*, cf., among other examples, Colum. vii. 12. 5 ; Apul. *Met.* vii. 27.

[5] *C.I.L.* vi. 3982.   [6] *C.I.L.* vi. 4475, 9084, 9085.

[7] Apul. *Met.* ix. 2.   [8] *Ep.* viii. 16.

in his household at least they were sure of every medical attention.

What is probably the most interesting part of Columella's work is devoted to the qualifications of the ideal bailiff and his wife. He played an important part in the management of land and industry, as is clear from incidental references to him in literature, and from the frequency of his name in inscriptions ; but little information is given as to his actual work. The description by Columella, therefore, is all the more valuable.

Choose a hardy slave, young but not too young, strong and skilled in agriculture, or he cannot direct work or win authority. Avoid a town slave, lazy and sleepy, long accustomed to the idleness of the circus and the theatre, taverns and gambling dens. Education may be dispensed with as long as he has a good memory.[1] To him must the secret of rule be disclosed, firmness which earns respect by tact and justice ; negligence and cruelty must alike be expelled by careful training in every excellence of mind. He should devote special attention and favour to the best of those under him, yet be sparing to the indifferent ; all should fear his sternness rather than learn to hate his cruelty.[2] And prevention is better than punishment ; it is better that he should see that his slaves do no wrong rather than by his own negligence make punishment necessary. In the good old days no bailiff would use a fellow-slave for any purpose but his master's interest ; he had his meals in the sight of the rest, and ate the same food, which led to efficiency and care in its preparation. But these days are over ; nowadays on holiday and festival he may invite a hard-working slave to a meal ' out of compliment,' but normally he lives apart from them. And no doubt such distinction between slave-bailiff and slave-farmhand was observed with all the rigidity peculiar to the humblest society, where the very minuteness of the difference demands more care for its preservation. The bailiff's duties lie out of doors ; supervision within the house falls upon other shoulders.

[1] Varro would like even the overseers to be able to read and write, i. 17. 4, and recommends that various rules of agriculture should be written out and hung well in view in the farmhouse ' that all, and especially the bailiff, may know them,' i. 36, and cf. ii. 2. 20.

[2] Varro says he should enforce his orders by words rather than by whip.

It seems to be an essential that he should be married ; there should be assigned to him—presumably he had some choice in the matter—a wife—*mulier contubernalis*—to help him in his work.[1] She, too, should possess high qualifications : she should have a good memory and a capacity for taking pains ; she should be young, but not too young ; sound in health, not too good-looking or her husband will never stir abroad, not too repulsive or he will never come home. Her main work is the guarding and preservation of every kind of produce, and for this end she is to relieve her husband of as much work in the house as she can ; yet to him she will render account, and on him final responsibility rests. She will send out slaves to work in the fields if she cannot find enough for them to do at home ; those whom she keeps indoors she must keep busy. She stores away the slaves' holiday clothing, the spindles and wool-working implements, she puts away all utensils (*instrumentum*)—*vasa ad cibum conficiendum, ad lavationem*, etc.—as tidily as did Ischomachus and his wife, on the principle that 'Carelessness is more trouble than carefulness.' She knows where to find everything at a moment's notice ; she knows how to keep moth and rust away. But Columella is not satisfied, 'for she must not be of sedentary occupation ' ; she must supervise the weaving of her slave-girls ; she must be responsible that the stables and pens and kitchens are cleaned out, the hospital kept aired ; at shearing time she must check the number of fleeces, at lambing time she should count the lambs ; she will inspect the produce brought into the farm and examine it to see that it is untasted and intact. She must supervise the storing of corn and wine and wool. She will store away all produce according to whether it is required for daily use or according to a month's or a year's estimated requirements, separating what is for immediate consumption from what is to be stored, ' that a year's supply may not be consumed in a month.' No wonder foresight is added to her other qualifications.[2] The storing of produce, however, for a year is interesting as showing that in some respects the self-sufficiency of the farm is taken for granted.

[1] If this is the meaning of the gerundive, ' assignanda est mulier,' i. 8. 5.

[2] Summarized from xii. *prooem.* 1, 2, 3.

Under so enlightened a master and so tactful and solicitous a *vilicus* and *vilica*, the life of the country slave might even be happy. At any rate a staff was grateful to one steward, Hippocrates; for they erected to him a memorial, 'his rule was gentle.'[1] Yet cruelty also leaves evidence. 'I was not able to live for more than thirty years,' reads the epitaph of a freedman shepherd overseer at Mainz, 'for a slave robbed me of life and then cast himself into the river Moenus; the river robbed him of that which he took from his master.' It may be an injustice to credit him with cruelty, or the slave with revenge, especially in view of an earlier line of the same epitaph,' Traveller, behold how unworthily I was snatched away that I utter my unavailing complaint';[2] but the pitiless treatment of farm slaves under the Republic cannot have given place at once to perfect conditions under the Empire. Faithful service on private and imperial estates is frequently recorded. A mistress is grateful to her *vilicus*, a good man and of the utmost fidelity;[3] at Atina a freedman and freedwoman discharged their duties well for fourteen years;[4] an under-steward of an imperial domain dedicates a monument to his own slave.[5] No doubt life on an imperial villa was more profitable and comfortable than on many a small farm. But even here a bailiff had a responsible and respected position, and if on a small estate like Martial's the chances of commissions and bonuses on sales were less frequent, the duties were less exacting, and a comfortable livelihood was assured. And there are many less interesting occupations than the management of land.

Nor was the condition of the subordinate staff to be altogether despised. Under the Empire family life was encouraged. Columella recommends a regular scale of reward to women of the estate who bear children; the rearing of three children entitles the mother to a holiday, while she may claim liberty if she bears more than this number.[6] For such justice and such care on the part of the master all help to increase his estate. But it seems no longer to be a question of the old callous encouragement of children with a view to sale. The home-grown slave under the Empire is a valuable member of the staff, and the inscriptions bear witness to the preservation of family life

[1] Dess. 7367.   [2] Dess. 8511.   [3] Dess. 7370.
[4] Dess. 7372.   [5] Dess. 7374.   [6] Colum. i. 8. 19.

and family unity to a surprising extent, at any rate in the towns ; and such family life is more easily encouraged and more profitable to the landowner, who would welcome a steady supply of labour born and bred on the place.   Even the shepherd, spending his time upon the upland pastures, is allowed by Varro to take a wife from among the slaves.   In hastily built huts, far from the farmhouse, she can prepare the food sent out by the bailiff ; when the shepherd drives his flocks to new pastures, she follows through the forest glades ; she must therefore be strong and healthy and not uncomely.   In many districts she is as good a worker as the shepherd himself ; in Illyricum, for example, she can equally well shepherd the flock or carry logs to the fire, or look after the farm implements in the huts.[1]   Even in backward Greece, where conditions seem to have been much behind the times, the humblest of slave-shepherds have their cottages ; [2] not only the bailiff has to wife a fellow-slave, but shepherds and cowherds speak of their wives and children,[3] and in at least one passage the shepherd's wife can call upon her husband as ' maritus.' [4]   The bailiff on a country estate who deserted his slave-wife to fall in love with a free woman was severely punished.   His wife burnt his account books, killed herself and her child ; and the bailiff met with a cruel death at the hands of his master, who bore ill the death of slave-woman and her child.[5]   If the *Metamorphoses* of Apuleius bears witness to a state of affairs in which brigandage and violence seem to be taken for granted, it none the less reveals an almost feudal system on the land.   The estate, which in some cases seems to be fairly extensive, if not very productive, is peopled by a vast staff of slaves, who live in their cottages close to their work.   They till a little land of their own, and sell the produce ; they own furniture and cattle ; [6] their prosperity is bound up with their masters'.   When the slaves of Tlepolemus and Charite heard of their deaths, they packed up their own furniture and departed with their goods and their animals ; they dreaded the unknown future which a change of master would bring,

---

[1] Varro, ii. 10. 6 and 7.   [2] Apul. *Met.* viii. 15.
[3] e.g. vii. 26.   [4] viii. 17.   [5] viii. 22.
[6] Varro recommends that slaves should graze a beast or two on the estate, i. 17. 7, and sheep and swine, that they may more easily maintain themselves and stick close to their work, i. 19. 3.

and they pitied the calamities which had befallen their master's house. The adventures which befell so numerous a troop— ' we lacked nothing but trumpets to be an army '—show the state of the country ; no indication is given, unfortunately, of the intentions of their vast migration.[1] Symptoms of devotion to the family of the master are not uncommon in the *Meta-morphoses*,[2] though it might be urged that self-interest plays some part ; this, then, would be the converse of the care of slaves by masters which the agricultural writers recommend, if only in the masters' own interest.   On an estate owned by a kindly master it was possible for a slave, happy in the posses-sion of family property and the goodwill of his master, to forget his slavery.[3]   Nor was the prospect of manumission entirely remote,[4] though on a well-managed estate it lost much of its value.

There is one detail in the villa of Columella which has hitherto escaped our attention.   Close to the villa should be an oven and mill, large enough to satisfy the needs of whatever number of tenants—*coloni*—the estate contains.[5] ' Be reason-able towards your *colonus* and ask for work on the home farm rather than for money-payments.   Make things easy for him ; for frequent letting is bad, still worse is the town-bred *colonus*.' As a rule the estate run by a bailiff is more paying to the master (nothing is said of the relative degree of efficiency in farming), but in distant farms the tenant is preferable, especially if those farms are corn-producing ; there supervision of a slave-bailiff is difficult and his temptations are great.[6]

The history of the colonate is interesting ; it is possible to trace the word from its original meaning of ' tiller of the ground ' to its later significance of ' predial serf.'   In Cicero's day [7] the

[1] Apul. *Met.* viii. 15.

[2] Cf., e.g., the joy of the servants at finding Lucius alive, xi. 18 ; the welcome given to Charite on her return, viii. 13 ; the uproar caused by the *faux pas* of the ' noseless ' man, ii. 26.

[3] Augustus sold a Roman knight into slavery for mutilating his sons to secure their exemption from military service.   Seeing the *publicani* eager to buy him, he gave him to a freedman of his own, ' ut relegatum in agros pro libero esse sineret ' ; in a town this would have been difficult. Suet. *Aug.* 24.

[4] *v. infra*, pp. 90 and 97.   [5] i. 6. 21.

[6] i. 7. 6.   [7] Heitland and Tenney Frank agree as to date.

colonus, in the sense of tenant farmer, whether free, freed, or slave, seems to be increasing in numbers, as the fallacy of slave-labour becomes clear ; in Augustus' time a great impetus was given to this method of land-management either by deliberate effort on the part of the Emperor, or by the growing scarcity of slaves.[1] Whatever the cause, the point of interest is that, though the tenant was often a free man, he was sometimes a freedman, or a slave.[2] Given a shortage of labour, it often becomes more convenient to let portions of a farm to tenants than to manage it by a bailiff. A small outlying farm was a convenient place in which to pension off a bailiff growing too old for his work, or a hard-working farmhand. Here he would spend his latter years, supervising the few slaves whom his master still entrusted to him, and using their labour to secure a profit on the year's working ; of this he would pay a portion to his master as rent, the rest he would keep as his own savings.[3] Sometimes he worked the farm with his own slaves, and doubt-less paid a smaller rent ; often he was granted his freedom ; [4] and in some cases the farm was bequeathed to him at his master's death.[5]

Such a plan was likely to work better than to put in a free *colonus*. The *servus quasi colonus* was still a slave, and within the power of his master ; but, more important, he knew the land. If he had been born on the estate, he knew every tree and every stone, and had perhaps grown to love it ; he had had experience in the handling of a slave staff ; he, if any one, would secure the best from land and worker alike. It has been said [6] that no other arrangement was so calculated to make Roman agriculture efficient on a basis of slavery.

On the colonate inscriptions help little, except for the imperial estates ; it is still possible, however, to read that when the wife of T. Alfenus Atticus, a *sevir* and freedman and *colonus*

---

[1] *v.* Heitland, *Agr.* p. 202.

[2] Attested for Augustus' reign by Alfenus Varus, *Dig.* xv. 3. 16.

[3] *Dig.* xxxiii. 7. 20 ; xxxiii. 7. 12. 3.

[4] xxxiv. 1. 18. 3. Heitland, p. 197, says ' manumission was a very rare event on country estates ' (of Cicero's evidence). On p. 291, speaking of Tiberius' time, he says ' practical farming seems to have been passing more and more into the hands of humbler persons, often freedmen.' The freedmen must often have been manumitted farm slaves.

[5] xxxii. 97.   [6] Heitland, p. 369.

on the Tironian estate, died, the whole staff joined in mourning her,[1] or that on the Marian farm a slave-tenant dedicated a stone to his six-year-old daughter ;[2] but for information on details the *Digest* is the fullest authority. There the position of the *colonus* at law is worked out in the fullest of detail ; here, however, it is only necessary to suggest that his constant recurrence and the variety of situations involving him on which the lawyers were asked to pronounce, is fair evidence of his frequent existence, though it gives no clue as to the comparative frequency at different periods. If later the *colonus* on a private estate, and perhaps more so on the imperial, was oppressed by rents beyond the capacity of his farm to pay, and was required to give time and labour in rendering services—*operae*—on the home farm, till he became bound by debt and later by law to the soil, still at an earlier date many slaves and freedmen made their farms give them a living in some security and tolerable comfort.

IV

In the first section of this chapter it was suggested that, in theory at any rate, the demand that the land should produce most of the food consumed on the estate was a favourite theme of poet and moralist ; in the second section it has been seen that the farm of Columella seems to presume that the same will be true in fact, if indeed the treatise is to be regarded as a practical guide. It may, however, only be a guide to the rich landowner, who can afford to run his farm uneconomically to gratify his whim. It remains to be seen how far Columella's precept corresponds with the general usage of practical farming. The slenderness of the evidence may be appreciated after a reading of Heitland's *Agricola*; it may, however, be possible to apply one or two general considerations—a dangerous method if entirely unbased on evidence, but permissible, perhaps, in default of any other, and justifiable if what evidence exists is used as a check on unrestrained imagination.

If it is true that foreign corn reached only a small part of Italy, if it is true that the nature of the country and the slow and primitive methods of transport made the carrying

[1] Dess. 7455.   [2] Dess. 7453.

of corn to any great distance economically impossible, then the majority of landowners must have been compelled to grow grain to provide for the needs of the household. Bread was, of course, the principal food of slaves and the poor free man alike in the country and in Rome. To buy corn carried from a distance to feed a large staff of slaves would have been to make a system already expensive too costly to be possible. No wonder Columella recommends the building of large granaries to store the grain from one harvest to another. Vines, however, may be grown if the soil is suitable, and the hanging crop sold to a contractor ; so, too, other produce depends upon the natural opportunities ; but a certain acreage of corn is a necessity on a farm of any size. For rigid specialization in any other produce implies two necessities—first, an accessible market where the demand is strong enough to absorb a large supply of one kind of produce ; secondly, a market whence a supply of produce, other than that raised on the farm, may be obtained in large enough quantities to feed a numerous staff. Varro gives the key to the situation, if it were not obvious. Raise lilies and violets if your land is close to Rome, where the demand is keen ; that is to say, specialization on any scale to the exclusion of corn is only possible near Rome, where foreign corn can be bought ; here luxuries might be raised—fieldfares and peacocks ; but elsewhere the limited demand does not justify such specialization, and the small available surplus of the corn which is necessary to life makes rigid specialization impossible. The available surplus was never likely to have been great, except in the famous corn-producing valley of the Po, where there were towns to consume it. Columella puts the average yield of corn at four times the sowing, and, even if any farm had devoted itself solely to corn-production, it would have been able to support few of its neighbours on such a yield in exchange for their specialized produce. If the surplus was limited, home production on the farm was necessary, and if most of the produce was consumed on the estate, the surplus was necessarily small ; a great surplus would have been an embarrassment, for there was little demand to absorb it.

Italy was a land of towns, and yet there was little demand. Though the small country towns have not left remains as plentifully as the more famous towns on the west coast or in the south, their nature can be reconstructed in outline. Their population was made up of owners of large and small estates and plots, skilled craftsmen and artisans, with a number of small shopkeepers. Craftsmen performing work which could not be done on the smaller farms worked in their shops, perhaps employing a slave or two, or travelled about working up the farmers' own material and being fed and housed on the farm for days.[1] The small villages and towns lived in such close connexion with the country that there was no large market for a large surplus, even if it had been forthcoming, and hence no keen competition. Round the few larger towns economic forces no doubt exerted greater play, but it would be a great mistake to read back into ancient times the elaborate specialization and distribution of modern days by which a farmer seldom eats of his own corn. Writing of Britain, Professor Haverfield explains that there the labourers lived in the town, and ' even those who provided for the town had their houses in the town and came out from thence and walked to their work perhaps a couple of miles away.' ' It was not the full town life of Italy, dominating the rural district which surrounds it and obeys it. It was rather the life of the country town which depends on its neighbourhood—is, as it were, the nucleus of it—the meeting-place of its farmers, the residence of those who conducted its trade and smaller industries, and even some of its gentry.' [2] But not every part of Italy was so dominated ; there were isolated valleys and uplands which were remote from the influence of a large town and yet flourished. Mr. Heitland, who could not be accused of undue optimism about agricultural conditions in Italy, takes it as ' certain that in these upland retreats there survived whatever was left of genuine Italian life.' [3] And not always in the uplands. In Pliny's time, on the banks of the Tiber, not far from the Apennines, it was still possible to find a settled country population ; ' you find the grandfathers and great-grandfathers of the young people still living ; you are constantly hearing old stories and tales of the past, so that, when you set foot there, you may fancy you have

---

[1] See, in particular, Varro, *R.R.* i. 17. 2 and 3, and the evidence collected in Heitland, *Agr.* pp. 176, 180, etc., *v.* index.

[2] *The Roman Occupation of Britain*, pp. 218–219.

[3] Heitland, p. 285, commenting on Pliny, *N.H.* xviii. 178.

been born in another century.' [1]   This sentence is worth many
pages of ranting from the rhetorical schools on the subject of
latifundia.

If this brief analysis of conditions holds good for a fair
portion of Italy with the exception of certain districts—the
Po Valley, the environs of Rome, and one or two neighbourhoods
where special economic conditions or natural resources brought
about a different play of forces—clearly the small farm must
have been a necessity.   Into the remoter districts the rich landowner would hardly penetrate ; to him easy access to some
centre was necessary.   On the other hand, the small producer
close to a limited market would be able to dispose of his small
surplus, and take in exchange the small quantity of those goods
which his farm did not produce and yet were necessary to him.
Here, then, is another cause tending to limit the absorption of
the Italian farm by large estates ; the nature of the markets
makes the large farm unprofitable except in certain exceptional
localities.

Yet we are told by Pliny the Elder that large estates ruined
Italy ; their evils were a commonplace in the schools of rhetoric,
and we are reminded of Pliny's *pulchritudo iungendi* and Trimalchio's insane wish to travel on his own estates from Rome
to the coast.

Pliny is describing a symptom when he means to diagnose a
cause.   The growth of slave-staffed estates was a sign of the
exhaustion, for whatever reason, of the country population,
and lasted only so long and in such places as the land could be
worked by no other methods.   If they ruined Italy, it was
because they bred not a sturdy free population but a race of
country slaves.   The rhetorical schools debated with a florid
vehemence a variety of themes, artificial, obsolete, imaginary ;
to deal with contemporary subjects was unsafe, for an unwary
statement or suggestion might give an opening to the omni-
present informer.   If the evils of the *latifundia* make their
appearance there, it is because they are disappearing from the
land.   Yet the splendid and flowing periods in which they were
decried still remained in the minds of those who had served
their apprenticeship in the schools, and were summoned forth
to do service again in histories and annals.   And Trimalchio's

[1] Plin. *Ep.* v. 6.

ambition, when stripped of exaggeration, may dwindle down
to Pliny's natural wish to round off a corner of his land. But
even if all these statements are taken at their face value, there
is at least one reason to prevent their being believed too im-
plicitly ; and that reason is the undoubted existence of the
small property.

V

To set out in full the evidence for the small property would
be to do again what has already been done by Heitland. The
desire to possess land is as strong under the Empire as earlier.
Ex-centurions, retired civil servants, freedmen enriched in
trade, turn their savings into land. The cases of Horace's father,
a freedman, Horace himself, Vergil, are too well known to need
repetition here. Suffice it to say that, when Horace sings of
the quiet and carefree life on a small farm,[1] he is singing not of
an unrealized dream, but of what he, in company with many,
actually enjoyed. Martial had his small property,[2] and Horace
and Vergil and Martial bear witness to the *colonus*,[3] and Horace
cites a case of a freedman buying a farm from his patron.[4]
The agriculturists know of the possessors of plots.[5] At the
beginning of the Empire land was not dear ; Augustus, indeed,
took measures to increase its value ; [6] a small holding could be
had easily. Imperial policy, too, always aimed at encouraging
a country population, whether by tariffs, credits, or decrease
in the city corn dole.[7] It has recently been urged that estates
of the size of Horace's were a characteristic feature of Central
Italy, and that the Campanian farms, about the same size,
were owned by men who lived upon them.[8] Even evidence
which shows the absorption of estates shows it to be a very
gradual process, often accounted for by exceptional circumstances. The evidence of the *tabula alimentaria* of Veleia shows
that in the first century A.D. the small property flourished in
this district and there was a keen struggle to secure even the

[1] *Od.* ii. 16. 37 ; *Ep.* i. 14. 1, i. 7. 1 ; *Sat.* ii. 6. 1.
[2] *Parvum rus.* See Friedländer's index, *s.* Nomentanus.
[3] *Od.* i. 35. 6 ; Mart. ii. 11, vii. 31.   [4] *Ep.* i. 7. 80.
[5] Varro, *R.R.* i. 17. 2 ; *agelli.*   [6] Suet. *Aug.* 41.
[7] Dio, li. 21 ; Suet. *Oct.* 41 ; *Tib.* 48 ; Tac. *Ann.* vi. 16, 17.
[8] Rostovtzeff, pp. 61 and 62.

smallest portion of land. At the beginning of the second century the small property still existed; in Trajan's time, the total area of land occupied by small owners had decreased much, but the number of properties was not seriously diminished.[1]

How was the small farm worked? Often by a slave or two under a slave-bailiff, especially when the owner only used his estate as a retreat from town. Horace's model farm was worked by eight slaves; the rest of his estate was let to five tenants.[2] The life of the slaves would be much like that described by Columella, except that they probably lived in much closer intimacy with their masters. Seneca, Pliny, Martial, Horace, all show themselves on friendly terms with their servants.

Meantime the free labourer still existed. Julius Caesar passed a law that one-third of farm labour should be free;[3] but, says Tenney Frank, he 'phrased a tendency already accepted.' Why, then, resort to law? Was it to secure the ready absorption of ex-soldiers on the land? Varro[4] says that farmers prefer to employ the doctors, fullers, carpenters, already in the neighbourhood rather than have their own on the farm; the same, too, holds good for important work, vintage and hay-cutting. We have already seen how Columella recommends free labour for cornlands. And so isolated hints may be collected to suggest the existence of free labour,[5] which will be further considered in the chapter on Industry.

But all this may be briefly put in certain conclusions of Rostovtzeff. 'We do not accept current views about the disappearance of the peasants in Italy.'[6] 'The largest part of Italy consisted not of vineyards, but of fields, and the fields were tilled with peasants.' 'The main labour on (Pliny's)

---

[1] About 300 properties reduced to 250. See de Pachtère, *La table hypothécaire de Veleia*, pp. 67, 68. The land offered as security for the loan was on the Apennines, and not in the rich valley of the Po; there is no question, therefore, of the land attracting capital, as some writers have said (e.g. Heitland, *Agr.* p. 296; Mommsen, *Die Italische Bodentheilung und die Alimentartafeln. Ges. Schrr.* v.). See de Pachtère, pp. 9 sqq.

[2] Rostovtzeff, p. 61.   [3] Suet. *Iul.* 42.   [4] i. 16. 4.

[5] See Heitland's indices.

[6] P. 191. Cf. Bury, *Later Roman Empire*, i. 309; the depopulation of Italy 'had probably reached its limit in the time of Augustus.'

estates was that of tenants.'[1] 'There was no period in the development of Italy when a peasant population did not exist.'[2] In the first century and the first half of the second century Italy was 'one of the best cultivated lands of the Empire.' Indeed, in the whole of his book there is no suggestion that slavery either drove out the country population or ruined agriculture. Other causes for the decline of both at certain periods are adduced—the development of the western provinces, the rise of a new aristocracy, the flight of industry and the consequent impoverishment of agriculture, and many others—but slavery is not attacked. There were changes in agricultural methods, in the size of estates, in the forms of land-tenure, and all these affected slave-labour on the land, but were not due to it. To mention one or two points from the volume which bear upon the previous argument of this chapter, the slave-ranches are confined to certain localities of Italy, Horace's farm is held to be typical for Central Italy, Columella's to be normal for his day. If, after this, there is a tendency for estates to increase and to be owned by absentee landlords, the owner-farmer still holds his own. The colonate grows in importance, especially in the second century, and the *coloni*, though often freedmen, are more often the peasants descended from generations of peasant ancestors. In the second century 'there was a large class of peasants mostly tenants,'[3] 'who were in a flourishing condition.'[4]

The contentions of this chapter have been :

I. That slave-labour was not responsible for the growth of *latifundia*, though it provided the labour which made them possible.

II. That free farmers of small estates still held their own.

III. That slavery did not kill free labour on the land.

IV. That slavery failed because it was expensive and inefficient, and was gradually realized to be so ; it could only be made a tolerable substitute for free labour by raising the status, prospects, and conditions of the slave to the level of those of the free man. A growing realization of this led to an improvement in the lot of the slave under the Empire.

[1] P. 191.   [2] P. 192.   [3] P. 192.   [4] P. 193.

CHAPTER IV

IN TRADE AND INDUSTRY

Nec enim quicquam ingenuum habere potest officina.

Cic. *de off.* i. 42, 150.

Ετεροι δ' εἰσιν ἐκ γένους δοῦλοι, τὰ τῶν ἐλευθέρων εὐμοιρίᾳ τύχης μετιόντες . . . ἀλλ' ὅμως εἰσὶ δοῦλοι, δανείζοντες, ὠνούμενοι, προσόδους ἐκλεγόμενοι, θεραπευόμενοι.

Philo, *Quod omnis probus liber*, 6.

T O discuss slavery in the realm of industry and commerce really presupposes a knowledge of the economic structure and history of the Empire; and there is no subject of ancient history more difficult to study and more beset with controversy and dispute. The archaeological material is of colossal bulk, and it is only lately that real attempts are being made to master it and weld a multiplicity of detail into an intelligible whole. And even then there are so many gaps in our knowledge—notably the absence of all statistics—that finality is impossible. The aim of this chapter must be very modest; it proposes to explain and illustrate the use of the *peculium*, without some knowledge of which it is impossible to understand the independent position occupied by slaves in commerce and industry, and, secondly, to indicate answers to the following questions: Are there any features in the commerce and industry of these centuries which can be said to be due to the fact of the presence of slavery? Did slavery, for example, dictate the method of organization or set limits to expansion, or prevent advance in technique or methods of production? Did the presence of slaves in industry ruin the prospects of free craftsmen? or was there no competition between the two types of labour?

Commercial and industrial enterprise includes many varied forms of activity; the hewer of stone and the digger of clay,

98

the dock porter and transport worker, the mason and the potter, the manager and overseer, the salesman and agent, the banker and private investor—all perform different services ; some provide mere physical strength, others skill of hand, others mental ability and experience, others ready capital. Yet the curious thing is that slaves are to be found rendering all these services. It is a far cry from the ' articulate instrument ' of Varro to the slave-manager of an enterprise representing large sums of money and widespread commercial interests ; and it is natural to ask why slaves should be so employed and how it was safe to entrust slaves with vast responsibilities. And the answer to both questions is the same—that the supply of the labour in demand, both crude and skilled, and the guarantees of hard and trustworthy effort were to be found in the institution of slavery and the conditions attached to it.

The age of Augustus was the beginning of a period of commercial and industrial expansion. The peace of the world was assured, so men thought ; the provinces were to be developed rather than exploited. The demand for raw material and manufactured goods was enormous. Slaves had, indeed, been engaged in such work before, but the sudden growth of trade compelled their employment in numbers that would otherwise have been unnecessary. The free craftsman still continued, and in the second century increased in numbers proportionately to the slave-craftsman. In the second place, trade had not yet lost its stigma ; the management of land was respectable enough, and along with it seems to go brickmaking on private estates, the only business which a Roman of noble birth cares to admit,[1] though, by degrees, he came to admit other forms of industrial enterprise ; as a rule, however, business was managed chiefly by slave-agents. At the same time, the Empire marks the beginning of a change in the prevalent attitude to business ; Augustus himself was descended from a rope-maker, a broker, a perfumer, and a baker,[2] and ' lucri bonus est odor ex re qualibet ' becomes a maxim more widely adopted ; Romans engage more freely and more openly in various forms of commercial and industrial venture. Yet, even so, the agent became more important, for commercial activities became more wide-

[1] See Tenney Frank, *Economic History*, p. 230.
[2] Suet. *Aug.* 2, 4 ; for Vitellius and Vespasian, see *Vit.* 2 ; *Vesp.* 1, 4, 16.

spread ; and such agents were almost necessarily slaves, partly because the Syrian or Hellenized Oriental showed a capacity for business and figures and languages which few Italians showed, even if they had been willing to serve in a subordinate position, partly because the bonds of slavery might at the same time be so relaxed as to offer an incentive to work by the prospect of wealth and freedom, so tightened as to provide a guarantee to the master against loss from the misconduct of his slave. The explanation of this paradox must be sought in an account of the peculium.

When Trimalchio brought back from Rome for his promising young slave some knives of Noric steel, he laid the foundation of the slave's peculium. From this humble beginning it might grow in a variety of ways till it equalled or exceeded the wealth of his master. Wages [1] or tips from the master or the master's friends were a normal source of income, and, carefully saved, no doubt amounted to considerable sums ; but larger presents were frequently given at the death of a master ; thus Petronius himself at his suicide gave to some of his slaves presents of money, to others a flogging. The master himself could only leave money by will to a slave if he gave him liberty at the same time. [2] Consideration for the heir was no doubt the explanation of this rule ; but his friends could leave legacies to his slaves. It was open to the master, however, to ask his heir to distribute money or other gifts to the slaves now passing into his possession. Voluntary economy on the part of the slave was another method of increasing the peculium ; if food was abundant, some of it could be saved and sold, 'cheating the stomach ' ; [3] or, again, the slave was often given an allowance on which to maintain himself. In other cases he was allowed to turn his leisure or, indeed, his whole time to profit, and hire himself out, either to a third person or to himself, paying his master a sum for the use of the time, and pocketing whatever he could make over and above. Farm-slaves were allowed to cultivate a plot or graze a beast or two, and the

---

[1] *e diariis*, Petr. 75, unless it means ' rations.'

[2] *Dig.* xxviii. 7. 21, 22 ; xxx. 34. 9.

[3] Sen. *Ep.* lxxx. 4, *fraudato ventre* ; so, perhaps, Petr. 75, ' ad hanc me fortunam frugalitas mea perduxit,' and certainly Apul. *Met.* x. 14, ' partes electiores surripere atque iis divenditis peculium latenter augere.'

profits were their own.[1] In business, contracts between slave and master or third person seem to have been common, and the work thus done, and no doubt the profits, were considerable. In A.D. 164 Flavius Secundinus recorded in writing at the request of Memmius, the slave of Asclepius, because he was unable to write, the terms of a contract by which the latter hired out his services in gold-working—*opere aurario*—for a period of about six months for seventy denarii. 'He must receive his pay at the stated times. He must render to the aforesaid hirer the full able-bodied services of a healthy man. If he wishes against the will of the hirer to leave his work or make holiday, he shall pay in cash five sesterces for each day.' But the contract is not one-sided : ' If at the conclusion of the period the hirer delays paying the wages due, he shall be liable to the same fine.' [2] The renting of land to a slave has already been noticed in an earlier chapter ; and in industry much the same system was used in various forms ; the master might lease a bank or a business or the use of a ship, the terms being a fixed return or the slave being paid on a commission basis. Opportunity to illustrate these cases will occur later.

Once the peculium was saved, it might be put to a variety of uses. Trimalchio, in singing the praises of one of his slave-boys, tells how he had bought a suit of Thracian armour, a round-backed chair and two ladles.[3] And no doubt in many cases this fund was expended in providing food or pleasure : the number of small eating-shops in Pompeii assume the existence of a poor population in which slaves must be included, and the *graffiti* make it clear that they had money to spend. But the peculium must not be regarded merely as petty savings, casually earned and idly spent. The slave who made his master's business yield profits, to his own profit too, very often, had a keen sense of the best use to make of his own money. Often he re-invested it in his master's business or in enterprises entirely unrelated to it. He could enter into business relations with his master, from whom he came to be regarded as entirely distinct, or he could make contracts with a third person. He could even have procurators to manage his own property and

[1] Varro, i. 17. 7.
[2] Bruns, *Fontes iuris Romani antiqui* (7th ed.), p. 370.
[3] Petr. 75.

interests.[1]   And so within the peculium may be found not only
land, houses, shops, but rights and claims ; though, if these were
to be enforced, the master's help would be needed, since the
slave, as a rule, had no power to initiate legal proceedings.

But the peculium could contain another type of property
—namely, slaves.   The number of inscriptions which refer to
the slave of a slave—*vicarius* or *vicaria*—is enormous, while
the literature, with the exception of the legal writings, says
practically nothing of them.   The number of *vicarii* varied :
sometimes it is obvious that only one was possessed ; on the
other hand, Musicus was a ' paymaster in the Gallic treasury of
the province of Lyons,' a slave official of some importance,
who died on a visit to Rome, whither he had been attended by
sixteen of his slaves ; one was his business agent, another a
sumptuarius ;   there were three secretaries, one doctor, two
cooks, two footmen, two chamberlains, two in charge of silver,
one valet, and one woman slave.[2]   The slaves of the Emperor
and ' public slaves ' frequently had *vicarii* ; thus a paymaster
in the department of public works had at least one, an overseer
of the Claudian aqueduct several, a *dispensator arce patrimonii*
five, a chief footman at least one.[3]   On the other hand, private
slaves possessed them no less, e.g. a head chef ; Faustus was
the slave of Eros, an accountant, and there are scores of other
cases.[4]   Some of the *vicarii* would be used, as in the case of
the Treasury official mentioned, as personal attendants, but
others were employed in the many ventures which a well-to-do
slave undertook.   Hipparchus, for example, is the slave of
the Statilian family.   But he has two slaves who are ware-
housemen.[5]   The *vicarius* called his owner by the title of
dominus or *magister*.[6]   A *vicaria* was often her owner's wife ;
therefore a slave's wife and his children might be part of his
peculium—a matter of great importance ; for, if on manumission the slave was given his peculium, then it was possible

[1] *Dig.* iii. 3. 33.
[2] Dess. 1514, ' dispensator ad fiscum Gallicum provinciae Lugdunensis.'
[3] Dess. 1604, 1612, 1659, 1821.
[4] Dess. 7468, 8418 ; e.g. 'supra cocos, Erotis dispensatoris vicarius.'
[5] Dess. 7440a and b, *horrearii*.
[6] e.g. 1771, Helius, ' vicarius eius, domino benemerenti.'   7888,
' [Th]amyris Liviae pediseq(uus) Cnismo Liviae ser(vo) magistr(o) suo dat
ollam.'

for him to free his wife and children ; whereas, if he married a
slave belonging to his master, it by no means followed that
on his own manumission his wife would also be manumitted ;
she and her children might remain the property of his former
master.[1] Many of the cases, therefore, to be referred to in a
later chapter, in which the title ' patron and husband ' occurs,
may denote, but not necessarily, that the wife was the *vicaria*
of a slave, who on manumission received her as part of the
peculium and in turn manumitted her ; on the other hand, she
may have been acquired as a slave after his manumission and
subsequently been manumitted.[2] One brief inscription may
be quoted to illustrate several of these points at once : ' L.
Calpurnius Urbanus, L. Calpurni Salviani l(ibertus), manu-
missus ex testamento, officio accepto nihil praeter optimum
praemium libertatis uxoris famulae suae (abstulit ex bonis
supra scriptis).' The situation is this : Urbanus has recently
been manumitted by will ; since his manumission was by will,
he had no right to take the peculium, unless the will contained
an express injunction to this effect, which in this case it did
not contain ; but unfortunately Urbanus' wife was part of the
peculium. Urbanus, therefore, approached the heirs of the
estate, and offered to return to them certain monetary benefits,
which he had received under the will and which may have
exceeded the (monetary) value of the peculium, in exchange
for the freedom of his wife who still remained their slave.[3]

Finally, besides being used in the ways mentioned, the
peculium might be surrendered in whole or part in return for
freedom. As a rule it must have been only a part that was
paid ; in trade and industry at any rate most slaves seem to
have taken with them into freedom some capital of their own.
There is no evidence that it was ever exhausted in paying for
freedom, which, on such terms, was by no means necessarily
preferable to slavery.

It was the existence of the peculium which made it safe
for a third person to deal with slaves, and therefore explains

[1] 7981a and b prove that a slave who has an *ancilla* in his *peculium*
calls her children *vernae*.

[2] A slave had no power to manumit his *vicarius* ; see ch. vii.

[3] *C.I.L.* ii. 2265, quoted Marquardt, *Vie privée*, i. 193, n. 3, but not
fully explained.

their rise to wealth and responsible position. In law it was the master's property,[1] but is often loosely spoken of as though belonging to the slave himself, and is indeed treated as such. For the business undertakings of the slave the master was liable to the extent of its value.[2] If the slave's independent enterprise failed, then the debts, if any, owed to the master could only rank in proportion with the claims of other creditors in assigning the assets.[3]

There existed no power to alienate this fund without the master's express command, unless a general permission of free administration—*libera administratio*—was given, which, however, did not include ' donation.'

While, then, a third person could rely on the good faith of the slave, since the safety of the peculium was the guarantee of it, it was to the interest of the slave to increase it, since, on manumission, he often received it entire. On manumission during the lifetime of his master, he received it unless it was expressly reserved ;[4] on manumission by will it did not pass to him unless there was a direct command in the will ;[5] so, too, on the sale or bequest of a slave the fund was not included unless it was expressly so stated.

Though the slave was given considerable latitude in the use of the peculium, ultimately his rights were derived from his master. The necessities of everyday business life may have made it increasingly convenient to give him considerable powers of initiative and agency, and by degrees he may have been treated in practice as a person distinct from his master. But in the background there were still the incapacities before the law which belonged to his condition. ' Ex contractu civiliter non obligantur, sed naturaliter obligant et obligantur.' No slave could be a witness or a *libripens* or a guardian ; he had no power of will-making, though he could receive a legacy ; he could not sue or be sued ; even criminal slaves were prosecuted through their masters, and after trial it was considered necessary to state most plainly that it was the slave and not the master who was condemned. In law, then, the slave suffers serious disabilities. But a recognition of him as a person creeps in ;

---

[1] Cf. Sen. *de ben.* vii. 4. 4.   [2] *Actio de peculio.*
[3] *Actio tributoria.*   [4] *Dig.* xv. 1. 53 (*manumissio inter vivos*).
[5] xxxiii. 8. 8. 7 (*manumissio ex testamento*).

for example, he is punishable if he buys knowingly a *res litigiosa,* though knowledge on the part of the master naturally throws the liability on to him; again, if anything is ordered to be given to A's slave by B, it is not enough to hand it to A.[1]

The activities of slaves in commerce are innumerable; the best way to discover them is to glance through the examples given by Dessau illustrating the employment of slaves—and of freedmen too, for as a rule the freedman practised after manumission the craft he had been taught as a slave. Numbers of them are shopkeepers, selling every variety of food—bread, meat, salt-fish, wine; vegetables, beans, lupine-seed, honey, lard, ham, ducks, and fresh fish; others deal in clothing— sandals, shoes, gowns, and mantles.[2] In many cases indication is given of the district in Rome where they plied their trade— in the neighbourhood of the Circus Maximus, or the Porticus Trigeminus; or the Esquiline Market, or the Great Mart (on the Caelian Hill), or the Suburra. Others are agents and factors buying or selling wholesale for their masters or patrons. Others, again, are dealers or merchants, and they generally, though not always, add the nature of their business—'negotiator suariae et pecuariae, negotiator aerarius et ferrarius, mercator vinarius, negotiatrix frumentaria et leguminaria.' But the fascination of these inscriptions and the detail which they contain must be resisted, and a few pages must be devoted to illustrating the degree of independence enjoyed by these agents.

Most of the retail shops seem to have been in the hands of freedmen conducting the business either solely in their own interest or on a commission basis, and many of them made considerable profit; Juvenal tells us that one of them had five shops and accumulated a knight's fortune.[3] But shops were leased to slaves also. It is possible that the shops which formed the front of the Pompeian houses were in some cases managed in this way, though the point is not certain.[4] The common term for a shopkeeper of this kind is *institor,* and inscriptions show a slave thus carrying on a bootmaker's

---

[1] xxxv. I. 44 pr.

[2] ' Pistor, lanius, salsamentarius et vinarius Maurarius, holitor, fabarius, lupinarius, mellarius, lardarius, pernarius, anatarius, piscatrix; crepidarius, calciator, vestiarius, sagarius.'

[3] Juv. i. 105.   [4] See Rostovtzeff, p. 515, n. 22.

shop, another the manager of a general store, another who was an *unguentarius*.[1] So, too, Pertinax is said to have carried on a wool-shop or factory by means of his slaves.[2] The term *institor* is held to embrace any one appointed to manage a business,[3] and covers all the pedlars to whom, in the words of the *Digest*, ' vestiarii vel lintearii dant vestem circumferendam et distrahendam, quos vulgo circitores appellamus ' ; [4] indeed, any slave acting as an agent connected with trade or business seems to come under this heading and so to expose his master to the *actio institoria*—a slave sent by a shopkeeper to fetch goods, an undertaker's assistant (*pollinctor*) who robs the dead ; a baker's traveller who has supplied bread to a district and has agreed to do so daily is considered to have bound the baker himself if the latter defaults. Various other cases may be found in the *Digest*, but the cases quoted have been chosen because they are taken from Labeo. Inns were frequently let to slaves in this way ; Varro advises that landowners should dispose of some of their surplus produce by building inns where their estates touched the main roads and placing slaves in them as managers.[5] Perhaps this helps to account for the sorry reputation of inns in ancient times. One such innkeeper has left an interesting record of himself. He is described as ' Vitalis, C. Lavi ser(vus) idem f(ilius), verna domo natus—institor tabernas (*sic for* -ae) Aprianas (*sic*).' He died at the age of sixteen years. ' I ask you, travellers,' the epitaph continues, ' to forgive me if I have ever given you short measure. It was to help my father. I beg you, by the gods above and the gods below, to let me commend my father and mother to you.' [6]

The extent to which slave secretaries and agents acted for their masters is shown very clearly in the receipts found in the

---

[1] Dess. 7546 ; ' sutori institori caligario,' 7607 ; ' seplasiari negotiantis ser(vo) institori,' 7608.

[2] Script. hist. aug. *Pertinax*, iii. 3. 4.

[3] ' Institor appellatus est ex eo, quod negotio gerendo instet, nec multum facit tabernae sit propositus an cuilibet alii negotiationi,' *Dig.* xiv. 3. 3.

[4] xiv. 3. 5. 4.   [5] i. 2. 23.

[6] Dess. 7479, found near Philippi ; for slaves adopted, see *supra*, p. 51 ; for the age of the boy, see Gaius, in *Dig.* xiv. 3. 8, ' nam et plerique pueros puellasque tabernis praeponunt ' ; for inns, *v.* Marquardt, *Vie privée*, ii. 99 ; and Friedländer, i. 289 sqq. (Eng. trans.)

house of Caecilius Jucundus at Pompeii. Jucundus was an auctioneer and broker and banker who seems to have transacted any business at all on a commission basis. A mule was sold for seventy sesterces ; Philadelphus, the slave of Caecilius Felix, gave a receipt for the sum to Jucundus, less his commission. ' I, Vestalis, the slave of Popidia, declare in writing that I have received . . .' begins another. Salvius *servus* signs another document.[1] A well-known advertisement found at Pompeii reads (or read, for it has now faded) as follows : ' To let, from the first of July next, the Arriana Polliana block of buildings, the property of Gnaeus Alleius Nigidius Maius, containing shops with the rooms over them, splendid chambers, and a house. An intending tenant should apply to Primus, the slave of Gn. Alleius Nigidius Maius.'[2] In the bronze tablet which records the ' alimentation ' established at Veleia, there are set out the details of the farms which served as security for the loans. The statement of their value is generally expressed in the same formula ; one, however, reads : ' C. Coelius Verus, acting through his slave, Onesimus, made a declaration that his farms . . .'[3] The slave is here making a statement of the value of the farm to the Government on behalf of his master. Another document, unfortunately mutilated at the critical point, shows the agreement between Cassius Frontinus and Julius Alexander to go shares in the profit or loss of a banking and moneylending business. Julius Alexander invested 500 denarii, and Secundus, the slave-agent of Cassius Palumbus, invested 267 denarii ; then follows a gap of many letters. It seems as if Secundus is advancing money of his own to Frontinus in order that the latter may invest it in this concern.[4] The so-called ' Baetic formula ' contains perhaps the clearest example of the slave acting for the master. It is a blank form of agreement drawn up for slave and free man, and pledging a farm as security for sums of money advanced. The relevant sentences read as follows : ' Dama, the slave of L. Titus, received the

---

[1] See Bruns, *Fontes*, pp. 355 sqq. ; Mommsen, *Ges. Schrr.* iii. 221.

[2] ' Splendid '=*equestria*, if Mau's explanation is correct. Dess. 6035 describes the word as *lectio corrupta* ; Bruns, p. 372.

[3] Dess. 6675, xvi.

[4] Bruns, p. 376. It is a *societas daneistariae*. The letters ' pr . . . tin ' occur in the gap ; the early editions of Bruns suggested *pro Frontino*.

Baian farm . . . from L. Baianius as security. It is stipulated and agreed between Dama, the slave of L. Titus, and L. Baianius that the above-mentioned farm and property shall be security up to the full sum which L. Titus has given or shall have given, has advanced or shall have advanced to L. Baianius. . . .'[1]

In sea-trading the need of a free hand, within limits, is excellently set forth in the opening words of the title on *exercitoria actio* in the *Digest*; ' owing to the conditions of sea-trading, we make contracts with ships' masters in complete ignorance of their status or character; therefore it has been thought just that he who appointed the ship's captain should be held liable in the same way as a man who puts an agent in charge of a shop or business is held liable; for there is greater need to contract with a ship's master than with an agent; circumstances allow us to inquire into an agent's status and to contract accordingly, but in dealing with a ship's captain this is not the case, for sometimes place and time do not allow ampler opportunities for consideration.'[2] To judge from inscriptions, *negotiatores* were generally free or freedmen, and they have left their traces over the whole of the Roman world. The two cases of slave *negotiatores* given by Dessau do not add very much information to their mere title; in one case Venustus is agent to the Treasury official mentioned above; in the other case Exinus is agent to L. Volusius Saturninus, consul suffectus A.U.C. 742, and probably both were business secretaries rather than traders.[3] But in the ports, and particularly at Ostia, crowds of slaves are to be found at the docks engaged in loading and unloading vessels, in warehouses storing and dispatching goods, in offices as bookkeepers and accountants. Perhaps the briefest illustration of the busy life of Ostia is to be found in a single inscription commemorating Cn. Sentius Cn. filius Cn. nepos Terentius Felix. He was an official or an honorary member of the following colleges or ' corporations '; the *curatores* of sea-going ships, the boatmen of the Adriatic, clerks *cerarii* and *librarii*, lictors and magistrates' attendants, criers and revenue-collectors, wine merchants, officials handling State corn, lightermen, carpenters, slaves and freedmen of the

---

[1] Bruns, *Fontes*, p. 334.   [2] *Dig.* xiv. 1. 1.
[3] Dess. 1514, 7389. Dessau quotes similar cases; *C.I.L.* vi. 9653, 4469, 4470, 7281.

township, oil merchants, cabmen, ex-army veterans, fishermen and fishmongers, and others ;[1] in other inscriptions occur bakers and builders, divers, shipwrights, and ballast-loaders.[2] The extent of the trade which passed through Ostia and Puteoli is revealed by the excavation of the enormous stores—*horrea*—used for the warehousing of goods ; and what is true of these cities may be guessed to be true in a minor degree of scores of others, while the career of Trimalchio and his speculations in sea-trade may serve as a type of many more. The thirteen-year-old Melior might have been equally successful, to judge by his epitaph. He was employed as an accountant—*calculator*—at Ostia, and 'such were his powers of memory, such his knowledge that he surpassed the praises of the epitaphs of all from earliest recorded time to the time of his death. The separate subjects which he knew could better be written in a volume than in an epitaph ' ; he would have gone far, ' if cruel fate had not grudged him to humanity.'[3]

It is a well-known puzzle in the study of the economic history of the ancient world that industry developed up to a certain point, but stopped short of making the progress which might have been expected. The small producer seems to have existed without feeling the competition of the capitalist ; the capitalist invested money in commercial enterprise, which he developed up to a certain point, yet commercial enterprise was always of a comparatively simple and direct nature, never reaching, as far as can be seen, the complex organization or the widespread interests and influence familiar to-day. Methods of production were improved somewhat ; there was progress in craftsmanship ; yet there was little attempt to discover labour-saving devices, or to simplify processes with a view to large scale production for an extended market. It might have been expected that some kind of machinery would have been invented, that an elementary science would have been applied to industrial methods. Agricultural implements, for example, were made in factories at the beginning of the first century ; yet very little, if any, progress in design is visible, and the same is true of industry as a whole, speaking generally. In other words, when thoroughness and capacity for organization on a large scale is shown by the Romans in other departments

[1] Dess. 6146.   [2] Dess. 6165, 6169, 6172, 6177.   [3] Dess. 7755.

—in the public services and the army—why should these characteristics be lacking in industry ? Many considerations have been offered to account for this ; some of them will be shortly considered in so far as they are relative to slavery, and more attention will then be paid to slavery itself as an alleged cause.

If slave-labour can be used for work upon the farm and in the household, it is a very easy extension to apply it to industry in the narrow sense. Cato recommends that in the winter the slaves should be kept busy in the making of implements—baskets and so forth—for use on the farm. It is traditional, too, that one of the functions of the *materfamilias* was to supervise the spinning of her slave-girls in whose midst she herself worked. Here is seen house-industry in its lowest and earliest form, by no means confined, of course, to Roman slavery, but familiar in most primitive societies. But long before the centuries of our study industry had become organized outside the home ; industry run on some considerable scale as a source of income to the rich man supplying home and foreign markets and using slave-labour was a feature of the Hellenistic age, and it has been claimed that in this period industry reached its highest level in the ancient world.[1] When the expansion of Roman rule took place so as to include the Greek world within the Roman Empire, vast numbers of trained slaves were swept into Italy, where Greek methods and tastes were copied ; Oriental traders established themselves in the ports, and commerce and industry became more organized and more extensive than they had ever been in Italy before. Under the early Empire goods were exported and, still more, imported ; pottery, lamps, jewellery, cloths, articles of use and luxury found their way even into distant markets. The seas were alive with trading vessels. What, then, became of our basketmaker and our spinning maid ? Yet, at the same time, villas have been found in Italy and the provinces where, to judge from remains, the household satisfied its chief wants from its own resources. Why, then, the need of a developed industry or commerce ? Was industrial slavery a specialized form of domestic slavery, or is it to be regarded as an entirely separate branch which reveals special conditions and separate organization ?

[1] Rostovtzeff, p. 303.

There are undoubtedly signs of house-economy in these two centuries, but such signs suggest that it was limited in form, in locality, and in time.   A certain amount of spinning and weaving was still carried on at home.   Propertius can ask his messenger whether Cynthia's handmaids seemed sad as they plied their task, and whether Cynthia sat working among them.[1]   In the Augustan age a son, praising the virtues of his dead mother, can write that she was ' modestia probitate pudicitia opsequio lanificio diligentia fide par similisque cetereis probeis feminis.' [2] If a Roman dame, whose family could afford that a very lengthy funeral panegyric should be inscribed on great slabs of marble, still worked at loom or distaff, the same is probably true of humbler folk, especially in the country.   In outlying farms more might be done than the preparation of cloth, but it is clear from Varro [3] and Columella that recourse was made to local craftsmen and shopkeepers for many necessaries.   The villas in remote provinces were sometimes more or less self-contained ; it would be to the interest of the landowner to produce as much as he could from the estate, for importation would be costly and uncertain.   Writing of the villas in Britain, Professor Haverfield described them as self-contained with traces of industry, like ' English country houses four or five generations ago ' ; and he quotes Cumont's verdict on Belgic Gaul : ' Les villas étaient des ruches actives où de nombreux esclaves ou journaliers exerçaient tous les métiers utiles a l'exploitation du domaine et parfois des industries d'exportation.' [4] And with rich landowners even in Italy it was often a matter of pride that the estate should be self-supporting, but no doubt they paid for their vanity.

That house-industry left traces of this kind cannot be denied, but such industry was limited either in the type of article produced or it was limited by conditions of locality or other circumstances.   And it was limited also in time ; for, as industry became decentralized, as the provinces developed industrial

---

[1] iii. 6. 15, iv. 7. 41 ; cf. Juv. ii. 57.

[2] Dess. 8394, Laudatio funebris Murdiae ; cf. 8402, ' lanifica pia pudica frugi casta domiseda ; 8403, ' domum servavit, lanam fecit.'

[3] Varro, i. 16. 4.

[4] Haverfield and MacDonald, *The Roman Occupation of Britain*, p. 230 ; e.g. Plin. *N.H.* xviii. 40.

undertakings of their own to the curtailment of imports from Italy, local industries supplied local needs, and the provincial markets contained cheap goods which made home production no longer necessary. The producer may still have been nearer the consumer than nowadays ;[1] but it would be a mistake to generalize from the few traces of house-economy which do exist that it was the prevailing form.[2] The brief review of selected evidence which follows will show the existence of industry and trade on a fairly large scale, and will illustrate the work of slaves in both.

The mismanagement[3] of the mines and quarries during the Republic led to their gradual appropriation by the Emperor. Most of them were outside Italy—in Dalmatia and Pannonia and Dacia, Noricum, Spain, and elsewhere ; there were quarries of marble in Greece and the islands, in Lydia and Phrygia and Egypt ; of porphyry between Myos Hormos and Koptos ; of emerald at Berenice. In Italy mining was not encouraged, the State even going so far as to limit the number of workmen allowed ; the reason, it has been suggested,[4] was the fear of concentrating large numbers of slaves so near home, while the use of free men would draw free labour away from the land. But the resources of the provinces were far richer, and the imperial fisc needed all the wealth it could muster. Though the State owned most of the mines, there was no monopoly,[5] and in spite of State-ownership methods employed in the working of them were varied ; but, however they were worked, slaves make their appearance in various capacities.

It is probable that a *procurator metallorum* or *marmorum* was in charge of the mines of a district, as seems to be the case in Lusitania.[6] He was an imperial civil servant whose duty was to supervise the working, if the mines were exploited

---

[1] For this, see Tenney Frank, *Economic History*, p. 220.

[2] As is done, e.g., by Salvioli ; for a criticism of this school, see Rostovtzeff, pp. 302 sqq. ; for Salvioli's arguments against big industry, see *infra*, p. 117.

[3] Cf. Livy, xlv. 18.   [4] Rostovtzeff, p. 294.

[5] The only monopoly of which Haverfield knows was the Spanish vermilion workings ; see ' The Administration of Roman Mines,' *Journal of the Chester Archaeol. and Hist. Soc.*, 1891.

[6] See the *Lex metalli Vipascensis* mentioned *infra*, and Marquardt, *L'Org. fin.* p. 331, n. 2.

direct by the State, or to let them out on lease to capitalists or companies who paid a rent for the whole undertaking, or to lease single workings to individual prospectors ; in other cases contractors received a commission proportionate to the metal or marble extracted, and imperial servants were present as supervisors.

If the State worked the mine direct, as was the tendency in the second century, an imperial slave or freedman was often in charge of the actual operations. Hymenaeus Thamyrianus was a slave in control of the marble quarries at Karystos ; similar slave superintendents are to be found at Chios and Paros.[1] Blocks of marble imported from Karystos and elsewhere and found in Rome are marked with the names of slaves connected with the various processes of its extraction. Thus one block shows that it was taken from a new mine belonging to the Emperor. Cerialis was the procurator ; Sergius Longus was the centurion in charge, for often, especially in the workings of precious stones, soldiers were stationed at quarries, though not necessarily connected with the operations ; Crescens, an imperial freedman, was the *probator* or expert who examined and passed the marble. Other inscriptions show that the block was hewn by a slave Epitynchanus, and transported by another.[2] It is very probable that slave-foremen in charge of different operations received some commission on the profits of the work done ; and this may account for the careful recording of their names.

Sometimes the mine or quarry was leased to a company or an individual taking the lease of the whole or of separate shafts. The vermilion mines of Sisapo in Baetica were leased to a company, and Epapra, a slave *vilicus* of the company, leaves his name and title to record the fact,[3] while a freedman, C. Miniarius Atimetus, who rose to be procurator of the company, had originally been a slave in its employ, and on manumission took the name Miniarius.[4] To illustrate most clearly the lease of a mine to individuals there remains the so-called *Lex metalli*

---

[1] Dess. 1600 ; Marquardt, *L'Org. fin.* pp. 331, n. 3, 332, n. 3.

[2] Dess. 8717, 8718, 8720.

[3] Plin. *N.H.* xxxiii. 118 ; Dess. 1875 ; cf. metallum Samariense and Antonianum in the same province ; Plin. *N.H.* xxxiv. 165.

[4] Dess. 1876, *minium* is vermilion.

Vipascensis, which contains the terms of the contract regulating the working of a copper mine in South Portugal.[1] It is an interesting document, for it controls to the most minute details the life of the mining village of free workers which sprang up round the mine. Besides insisting that the barber, to whom the monopoly had been given, should be without competitors—though slaves may shave their own masters and each other—it makes mention of the penalties inflicted on slaves for theft or damage done to the borings. ' Venae furem, si servus erit, procurator caedito ' ; further, the thief is to be sold into perpetual slavery, never to set foot in the mines or territory again ; the price of the slave so punished was paid to his master. If damage was done, the master was compelled to sell his slave with a condition that he should never return. Punishments for free men were almost as severe.

In one case at least the actual lessee of some mines in Egypt seems to have been an imperial slave, Ἐπαφρόδιτος Καίσαρος Σειγγριανός, μισθωτὴς τῶν μετάλλων,[2] but, as a rule, these slaves are to be found in responsible positions as foremen. There were also imperial slaves connected with the accounts of the undertaking, representing, no doubt, the imperial fisc. Thaumastus was a keeper of documents—*commentariensis*—of the gold mines in Dalmatia, and Felicissimus was *dispensator*, while freedmen served in various other capacities.[3]

Of the unskilled labour in the mines little is known. In some mines it was free labour hired by the contractor ; in other cases slaves were used either by the lessees or the State ; in others the State availed itself of the work of criminals condemned to labour for life or for a term of years in the quarries. Life must have been hard for many of them, and it is not surprising that they have left no record of themselves ; the account by Diodorus of conditions in the silver mines in Spain—one of the few cases in which mines remained the property of individuals —is not reassuring. Those who work in them, he says, bring

[1] Dess. 6891 gives part of it ; the remainder, discovered in 1906, may be found in Bruns, p. 293.

[2] *C.I.Gr.* 4713 (quoted Marquardt, *L'Org. fin.* 332, n. 7) = Ditt. *O.G.I.* 678 = *I.G.R.* i. 1255.

[3] See Dess. 1595 sqq. ; e.g. a *tabularius* in the Dacian gold mines, another in the marble quarries at Luna, in Italy.

their owners great profit ; but they themselves die in great numbers in the underground workings. Their bodies are wasted away ; they have no rest ; beneath the lashes of their overseers they frequently surrender up their lives. Some, with physical endurance and strength of will, endure for a long time in their misery, but death is preferable.[1]   But these were admittedly old mines in private ownership.   On the other hand, the quarry-men—*lapicidae*—of the State marble quarries at Luna, near Carrara, seem to have been better off, if the existence of their college is evidence.   The fragment contains merely the names of the decurions, but proves that the college had an unbroken life of seven years at least, and all those mentioned are slaves.[2]

In the brickyards and in the potteries large numbers of slaves were gathered.   Owners of land producing suitable clay developed on an extensive scale factories which they worked by their own slave-labour or leased to others to be similarly worked ; and this was a form of industry in which the imperial and noble families had great interests.   The Pansian factory—*officina Pansiana*—close to Ariminum,[3] passed through the hands of the Emperors from Tiberius to Nero, and the later Emperors owned potteries—*figlinae*—in numbers.[4]   Tiles from the Pansian factory have been found as far away as Istria and Dalmatia, besides in many places in Italy, and seem to have been produced not only for imperial needs but for commercial use as well.   So, too, the yards of Domitius Afer in the reign of Tiberius produced in such abundance that theirs is the predominant stamp on tiles in the buildings of the day at Rome.[5]   In these yards tile-makers—*tegularii*—and brickmakers—*laterarii*—were employed, but nothing certain can be gathered as to the conditions of their work.

The famous potteries at Arretium and Puteoli and Modena produced on a large scale during the period of their greatest activity—about 30 B.C. to A.D. 20—while hundreds of workmen must be assumed to account for the large output of ware from the Gallic potteries when they succeeded to the trade of the

[1] Diodorus, v. 38.
[2] Dess. 7228.   The record was made in A.D. 22.
[3] Mommsen, *D.P.R.* v. 301, n. 1.
[4] Marquardt, *Vie privée*, ii. 319 sqq.
[5] Tenney Frank, *Economic History*, pp. 229 sqq.

Arretine potteries.[1] At the same time, because fifty-eight slaves are known to have signed pieces from the pottery of P. Cornelius,[2] it does not follow that all these were employed at once. Such large-scale production, however, is exceptional in Roman industry, and is to be explained, it has been suggested, by the trade secret of the paste and the presence of a master-craftsman or designer. And perhaps the latter point is the more important, and might be one reason why the prosperity of some potteries lasted for so short a time.

In metal work, conditions varied. For gold and silver work there can have been no large-scale production, though many of the craftsmen were slaves. A master-craftsman worked in his own shop to the order of his customers, who frequently supplied the necessary material. Much the same kind of practice must be assumed in this work as existed in Benvenuto Cellini's day —the craftsman and his apprentices working in a shop open to the street. Relations between master and slave might be pleasant, as the following epitaph suggests :

> ' Shed for this lad, thou passer-by, a tear.
> Twelve years of boyhood's springtime he had lived,
> His master's joy, his parents' fondest hope,
> Whom cruel he has left to lasting pain.
> He knew to work with cunning craftsmanship
> At necklaces, and set in softened gold
> All kinds of jewels. Pagus was his name :
> But now, a bitter grief, within the grave
> As dust, a corpse without a name, he lies.' [3]

In iron work, small forges seem to have been the rule ; they were owned by *ferrarii*, *cultrarii*, and the rest, and here, too, a slave or two might be employed. But for work in bronze and copper, a real factory system has been claimed, which employed thousands of men. Capua seems to have been the chief centre of this industry, and the minute specialization of processes, more apparent in this work than in any other, is only intelligible on the assumption that there was organization on some scale.[4]

[1] Oswald and Pryce, *Terra Sigillata*, p. 4 ; see also Déchelette, *Les vases céramiques*, i. 91.

[2] Almost as many signatures are known for the pottery of Rasinius. See Gummerus in Pauly-Wissowa, ix. 1487.

[3] Dess. 7710.

[4] Tenney Frank, *Economic History*, p. 236, referring to Willers. See also Marquardt, *Vie privée*, ii. 368 sqq.

The funeral monument of M. Vergilius Eurysaces at Rome suggests that bakers frequently produced on a large scale. The reliefs on the tomb show the various operations in baking, and imply ' a big business concern in which scores and perhaps hundreds of working-men, both slave and free, were engaged.' [1] The loaves found at Pompeii bear the mark (C)eleris Q. Grani Veri ser, but there is no indication as to the size of the bakery.[2] On the other hand, the miller's and baker's shop in the third Insula of regio I. contains four mills, some of which were worked by animals, some by slaves. The dreadful picture of the slaves in the baker's mill given by Apuleius [3] can only refer to a village baker producing for a small demand. But there seems no reason to infer similarly appalling conditions of labour in Pompeii.

Even in the first two centuries some of the villas in Italy and elsewhere specialized in the production of goods for sale— e.g. a woollen factory in Britain, a factory of bronze articles attached to a villa in Belgium, while lamps were made in Africa in this way.[4] The villas at Pompeii were owned often by producers of oil and wine. The Vettii, for example, owned many vineyards in the neighbourhood, and seem to have made various brands of wine in some quantity. The frescoes found in their house illustrate well the nature of their business, and, if slaves are substituted for some of the Cupids, a fair idea of the occupations of the staff can be gathered.[5]

Besides the theory of the prevalence of house-economy, other reasons have been adduced to account for the failure of industry to develop. Lack of stability in general conditions, it is urged, and the fear of proscriptions and confiscations made capitalists shy of investing money in industrial enterprise ; there were only two attractive investments—land and usury— beyond which capital had not the confidence to move. Local supplies satisfied local demands ; there was no big market to absorb production on any scale, and in any case transport was poor and costly. Most of these points were brought forward by

[1] Rostovtzeff, plate iv. ; Dess. 7460.   [2] Mau-Kelsey, p. 498.
[3] Met. ix. 12.   [4] See Rostovtzeff, p. 166.
[5] Mau-Kelsey, p. 326. For the inscriptions on the amphorae showing varieties of wine, see Dess. 8590, 8591, 'xv K. Ian. de Arriano dol. xv,' and 'Idibus Ian. de Asiniano racemat. dol. i.'

Salvioli.[1]   In all of them there is some truth, and in so far as they apply to agriculture, some judgment has been passed on them in the previous chapter ; they may not, however, apply with the same validity to agriculture and industry.   All these statements, true up to a point, must be modified, and in their modified form may not account, even though the causes may be cumulative in effect, for the phenomenon which they seek to explain.

Lack of confidence in the general situation may perhaps be attributed to the early years of the Empire, but cannot be held to last very long in view of the trade built upon the seas, which no less than industry needed security.   Attractive estates were more likely to provoke the unwelcome attentions of a Caligula or Nero ; an industrial concern might pass unnoticed, yet be more profitable than was apparent.   Money certainly was invested in speculative trade, and the growing export of manufactured articles from Italy presumes that money was invested elsewhere than in land or usury.   To say that local supplies satisfied local demands gives as misleading an impression as most generalizations ; there is enough evidence of widespread export to disprove the statement.   The pottery of Arretium, of Le Graufesenque and Lezoux and Rheinzabern, spread in great quantities over the western provinces ; Gallic pieces were found in their original packing at Pompeii.[2]   There was export of lamps, of oil, and wine, and of metal work.   At the same time, it is true that transport was a difficulty, but only transport by land.   The brick-trade, for example, was only able to secure limited markets for this reason ; where the same stamp is found in comparatively distant places, it is generally a stamp from the imperial yards.[3]   But transport by water was easy and cheap, comparatively ; and it was by sea and river that the pottery of Gaul was conveyed—by the Rhone, the Saône, the Moselle, and the trade-routes of the Mediterranean.   The colleges of the watermen on the rivers of South France have left abundant record of themselves.[4]   Whenever, then, there is production for export, there is generally easy access to water-routes.   And the farther away a district is from water-routes, the

[1] P. 153 sq. e.g.   [2] Cf. D. Atkinson in *J.R.S.* iv. 27.
[3] See Tenney Frank, *Economic History*, pp. 229–230.
[4] Cf. a fascinating study on *Arles Antique*, by L. A. Constans.

more it is compelled to rely on its own resources. The evidence which at first sight seems to contradict this is the presence of imported wares in or near the camps. But the army possessed the means and the money to carry by road goods which otherwise, by the ordinary channels of trade, would not have penetrated so far or so frequently.

The latest explanation of the failure to develop big industry has been advanced by Rostovtzeff,[1] who finds it in the lack of competition depending on the character, number, and buying capacity of the customers. After the restoration of peace by Augustus, industrial centres revived, but the very peace which was responsible for their new life automatically limited the market, which was now confined to the population of the Empire ; whereas the expansion of Hellenistic industry was due to the inexhaustible demand of non-Greek peoples. As long as Roman civilization advanced territorially, Roman industry flourished. When a halt was called, there was no need of further development ; the provinces created industries of their own, large enough to supply their own markets. The purchasing power of the town population grew, but their numbers were few in proportion to the country population, whose lot remained much the same as before ; if demand was feeble, there was no chance of building up a capitalistic industry.

It is impossible not to think that the positions represented by Salvioli and Rostovtzeff are nearer than seems apparent at first sight. The theory of house-economy is not tenable ; but demolish the walls of the house and the boundaries of the estate, and set up rather the vague limit of district or area or province, and many of the arguments advanced seem acceptable to both. Though the stress laid upon the degree of commerce or the scale of production varies, for both writers the demand is limited, purchasing power low, local industries are sufficient often for local needs, the free craftsman flourishes by the side of the slave, transport is difficult, slave-labour expensive, large-scale production non-existent.

The results of this brief sketch of evidence and arguments are twofold : it has been contended (i) that there are many causes which operated to prevent the development of industry ; (ii) that slavery was consistent with the most advanced methods

[1] Pp. 302 sqq.

of organization known in the Roman Empire. The position reached, therefore, is that the charge against Roman slavery so far is not proved. It remains to consider certain other arguments sometimes brought forward by those who would place the whole blame upon slavery.

It is said that slave-labour was cheap and abundant, and therefore prevented development. On this point some considerations have already been offered in connexion with agriculture ; but the fallacy of the statement is seen even more clearly in industry.

It must be repeated that imported slaves were becoming less numerous during the Empire, and even those imported were of a less intelligent type. It became increasingly difficult to enslave an already trained craftsman, as was done in the heyday of Roman expansion. The skilled craftsman of the East was free to ply his craft as a protected and sometimes privileged provincial ; life and freedom were assured ; the campaigns of Pompey were over, never to recur again ; Eastern industries revived and flourished, and, slave or free, the craftsman remained there unmolested. If he came west, he came, when free, at his own wish, induced by attractive openings ; if a slave, then he would be bought to supervise a workshop and train *vernae*, but he would be bought at a high price. The most skilled of M. Perennius' artists in his pottery at Arretium were Tigranes and Bargates, and their date is about the Augustan age.[1] They are obviously Orientals, and their names are not common among slaves or freedmen. But the impression gathered, though a thorough test has not been made, is that the names of slave-artists stamped upon the pottery become increasingly Latin in form as they are later in time, and the Latin name is not so likely to be given to a slave from the East as to one born in Italy.[2] It became increasingly necessary, then, to train *vernae* who had been maintained since birth, or to buy slaves and train them. The period of training was naturally unproductive. The initial training and the need of

[1] It is possible that the name of the *owner* is M. Perennius Tigranes or Tigranus. For the reasons for the doubt, see Chase, *Boston Catalogue of Arretine Pottery*, p. 18. H. Gummerus, art. ' Industrie-Handel,' in Pauly-Wissowa, identifies Tigranes and Perennius.

[2] The argument obviously is not decisive ; see *infra*, chapter viii.

an incentive made industrial slavery, in its more skilled branches at any rate, by no means cheap. The exertion of skill is a voluntary effort, and the best work cannot be extracted by the motive of fear. A regular wage, a share in profits, commission on output or sales, were all recognized methods of stimulating the interest of the worker ; it was only by virtue of the incentive of the peculium that craftsmanship was consistent with slavery.

It would be interesting not only to have some indication of the contents of individual peculia, but to know to how many slaves the fund was permitted. In the case of industrial slaves it is natural to suppose that its frequency and value increased as labour ascended in the scale of manual skill or mental ability. It is tempting to try to prove its frequency from the frequency of manumission, but, as will be seen, there are too many loopholes for such proof to be positive. The inscriptions show freedman artisans and traders in profusion ; they are more numerous than slaves, but that does not prove that they were so in fact. Three-quarters of the ships' carpenters known to us are ex-slaves ; this might suggest that very considerable slave-labour was thus employed, for probably a freedman more often left a record of himself than a slave. But the inference is by no means certain ; it is quite possible that at any given moment more freedmen were actually employed than slaves. A similar inference has been drawn with regard to potters. The stamp of the potter is notoriously vague ; and it has been disputed in many cases whether it refers to a free man, a freedman, or a slave. One solution pronounces in favour of a slave-craftsman on the ground that, if all who use the stamp are freed, then the number of slaves employed must be so enormous as to be impossible. But the inference again is by no means positive ; there is no certain evidence to prove that slave-potters must bear any given ratio to freed. To this problem we shall return later. Again, the freedmen whom we do know through inscriptions had been freed either on the death of their master or during his lifetime ; in the former case they took their peculium, in the latter case they did not, unless in both cases there was provision to the contrary. It has been held that four out of five manumissions took place by will, a statement difficult to prove, and at the least doubtful ; but, even so, our surviving wills generally bequeath the peculium to *some* slaves at any rate, though the proportion is quite obscure. In the case of those manumitted during the lifetime of the master it is quite obscure whether they carried over the peculium into freedom, or whether they surrendered it in payment for freedom, or whether they were manumitted gratis. It is impossible to prove, therefore, from the frequency of the fact of manumission in our inscriptions either the ratio of manumitted to non-manumitted or the ratio of those who received their peculium on manumission to those who did not. But other considerations make it probable that the fund was extremely common, and therefore made slavery an expensive system. It is only necessary to remember, as will be done in later chapters, the pocket-money which the slave spent in cookshop and tavern, the subscriptions which he paid to his college, the offerings dedicated to god or to town, the funeral monuments which he erected, the property which the humblest of his class possessed, to realize that the peculium in some form or other was common enough ; it is only necessary to glance at similar offerings dedicated by freedmen, to read of their wealth in the literature and their prosperity so obvious in the inscriptions, to realize that the majority of them must have carried over into freedom some capital, small or large but generally adequate, to start them in their new ventures.   And the intricacy of the law of the peculium is an argument which should be given its due weight.

It is said that slavery prevents the discovery or the elaboration of mechanical methods. Vast resources of man-power make machinery unnecessary ; given cheap labour, there is no incentive to the owner to invent or to employ when invented any mechanical contrivance which will save labour or increase output. He is content to exact the utmost possible from slaves who can be easily replaced, while in ancient times at any rate he was not inclined to increase his output to any great extent, since demand was neither keen nor steady enough.

Such a line of argument may be true enough elsewhere, but it does not seem to be entirely valid, as applied to Roman conditions, for there was no lack of incentive to discover mechanical methods, and the plea of limited demand is not as cogent as appears at first sight. No weight need be attached to the argument that, just as a country is said to obtain the government it deserves, so an age evolves the scientific or economic devices which it needs ; and some even go so far as to claim the non-discovery of machinery as a proof of the prevalence of house-economy. But no age ever needed mechanical transport, for example, more than the Roman Empire.

In Roman industry the brains existed both to see and to use the advantages of machinery. Seneca admits [1] the inventions due to slaves, and from the point of view of the employer the motive was not lacking to use such inventions. Slavery was an expensive system of providing crude labour, and, still more, skilled labour. The baker in Apuleius, though he treated his slaves abominably, would have found it cheaper to turn his mill by mechanical power, and in the case of skilled slaves the economy of machinery is more obvious ; cost of upkeep, cost of training, cost of peculium would be automatically abolished. It was not slavery that hindered the application of machinery to industry, but rather the absence of cheap and good fuel. The ancients knew of many more mechanical devices than often we admit. Steam was successfully used as a motive power to work ingenious contrivances ; coal was known, but was very little used ; and if machinery remained the plaything of the scientist, it was because there was no abundant supply of coal available close at hand.[2] As for the plea that demand was not great enough, to produce the same at a less cost is surely sufficient motive ; there is no need to assume that output need necessarily be increased. In short, whatever the arguments which can be adduced to suggest that cheap labour retards progress, and whatever cogency they may have, they must collapse when the expensiveness of slave-labour is realized.

Slavery has been accused of destroying advance of technique. But the charge is quite imaginary. The day is past when Roman art can be universally condemned as a lifeless imitation

[1] *Ep.* xc. 25 and 26 : ' Speculariorum usum perlucente testa clarum transmittentium lumen—suspensuras balneorum et impressos parietibus tubos, per quos circumfunderetur calor—marmora—lapideas moles in rotundum ac leve formatas, quibus porticus et capacia populorum tecta suscipimus—verborum notas quibus quamvis citata excipitur oratio et celeritatem linguae manus sequitur.'

[2] Steam : see, e.g., article on Heron of Alexandria, by T. L. Heath, in *Ency. Brit.* Coal : Theophr. *de lap.* 12–16 ; Pliny, *N.H.* xxxvi. 141 ff., if *gagates lapis* is coal ; Solinus, p. 102 (Mommsen), use of coal in the temple of Minerva at Bath.

of the Greek—devoid of originality or inspiration, overlaid with florid and vulgar ornament. Much of the best work was done by slave-artists, and there is no sign of stagnation. In sculpture there is progress, and in portraiture ; in pottery the early types are improved upon, new motifs are introduced. It is only necessary to follow carefully the plates in such comprehensive works as have now been written on Terra Sigillata to realize that there was still creative talent, and that it was consistent with slavery.[1] If later there is a marked tendency to standardization, other reasons must be sought ;[2] for some of the triumphs of Roman art occur when slave-labour was abundant, possibly preponderant, in industry.

Finally, the conditions of Roman industry cannot be attributed solely to slavery in view of the fact that a considerable proportion of those engaged in trade and industry were freeborn.

There is no reference in the literature to any conflict between the two types of labour ; though many charges are brought against slavery by the ancients, there is no mention of any complaint of this nature. Many of the other charges are not lacking in discernment, and the absence of any reference to rivalry between the two raises a presumption that it did not exist. At the same time, the indifference of ancient historians to economic phenomena should be remembered ; hence the silence of the literature must be regarded merely as corroborative proof of a position which must be established by other methods, if at all.

The main argument must be found in the general economic and social conditions of the times. In our survey of agriculture the same question was raised with regard to slavery on the land ; and much the same considerations were used then as must now be held to account for conditions in industry. In agriculture, it was contended, slavery was introduced on a large scale, and maintained because the economic fallacy contained

---

[1] Cf. Oswald and Pryce, *Terra Sigillata* ; Déchelette, *Les Vases Céramiques*. A useful introduction to the arts and crafts is to be found in Stuart Jones, *Companion to Roman History*, and, if the bibliography is followed up, progress becomes apparent.

[2] Rostovtzeff, p. 167 sq., finds the reasons in (i) the decentralizing of industry ; (ii) local production of cheap copies for a provincial population whose purchasing power was limited.

in it was not realized till later, and labour of any sort was imperative in view of the tendency of free labour to be attracted elsewhere in spite of a moderate revival of agricultural prosperity. In industry the facts are much the same ; in the Republic industry had employed a considerable proportion of slave-labour ; the restoration of peace opened up prospects of expansion ; in the first half of the first century A.D. Italy was the chief country to export manufactured goods. The sudden demand for labour was satisfied in the most obvious way— by slaves, who were still plentiful. But in this there is nothing to prove that the free artisan, who still flourished, was squeezed out ; there was still room for him. His output went to satisfy the large and sudden demand, and, since industry was still craftsmanship, his existence was still economically possible. If he needed crude labour, he employed a slave or two, whose condition of life was probably happier than that of slaves employed in a factory ; but there was no question of his elimination, for his standard of life was not much higher than that of the skilled slave.

Towards the end of the first century Italian industry declined ; Italy no longer held the predominant place as an exporting country of manufactured goods. Provincial workshops sprang up and flourished. What, then, happened to free labour in Italy ? Was the falling off of the export trade the ruin of the free craftsman in Italy ?

Simultaneous with this decline influences occurred which tended to preserve the equilibrium between free and slave labour. The price of skilled slaves increased ; they became more difficult to procure ; they had to be trained, and had to be treated with increasing humanity. It was the growing expensiveness of skilled slave-labour which not only preserved the balance but actually increased the free element which became more numerous in the second century. The revival of provincial industry had the same effect. It is true that slaves were employed here also, but the whole tendency of local production for a limited market was to destroy the advantages offered to slave-labour by mass production and to encourage the free craftsman.

If precise statements are asked for to prove these general statements, the reply must be disappointing ; the evidence for economic conditions is scattered, disjointed, fragmentary ; it is capable of varied interpretation. In one respect it is entirely deficient—namely, statistics. Further it is often difficult of access and still more difficult to summarize. We must, however, indicate its nature.

The references in the literature are isolated and tantalizingly vague. But their value cannot therefore be minimized. We have already seen that the agricultural writers presuppose the existence of smiths, carpenters, doctors, and masons who could be hired to visit estates. For vintage, too, and harvest special hands were employed as occasion demanded. The reliance thus placed on local free labour presumes that its supply, if not large in any district, was at any rate constant. Such allusions, if worked out in their implications, not only justify the statement that ' a surprisingly large part of the farm-work was done by paid labour from outside,' [1] but, taken in conjunction with other considerations, justify a belief that in the country towns and villages free labour flourished in a small way more than inscriptions would lead us to suppose. And if the agricultural nature of the provinces is borne in mind,[2] the existence of the free shopkeeper and trader and craftsman in considerable numbers becomes increasingly probable. He may not have made a fortune ; the smith in Apuleius,[3] a free man earning wages at a neighbouring forge, seems to have lived meagrely enough, but Greece was easily the poorest of the provinces. But if it is true, as we believe the evidence and probability demand, that in most places, with the exception of the big producing and distributing centres, trade and industry were on a small scale, then small workshops and retail shops owned and worked to a considerable extent by free men must be assumed. And this view is reinforced to a certain degree by the inscriptional evidence. There are many signs of free traders and free craftsmen.[4] Of these free men, it is true, very many bear names which suggest that their descent is to be traced back to slavery ; but, even so, that does not take away from their value as evidence that free labour existed by the side of slave-labour. The membership rolls of the colleges of craftsmen (*collegia fabrum*)

---

[1] M. E. Park, *The Plebs Urbana in Cicero's Day*, p. 52.
[2] Rostovtzeff stresses this point.   [3] *Met.* ix. 5.
[4] The evidence is given by Gummerus in Pauly-Wissowa, ix. 1496 sqq.

show no slave-members, probably because they did not admit slaves ; yet these colleges often contained many members in comparatively small townships.

It is tempting to try to work out from inscriptions, apparently so precise, the statistics which are missing in the literature. It is possible, for example, to spend considerable time and trouble classifying types of labour in various industries and balancing one group against another on a numerical basis. But there is always something unknown which makes any conclusions drawn only tentative. The stamps of potters make this clear : the form, Cn. Atei Hilarus, can be interpreted to refer to a slave or freedman ; P. Corn. Poti., a common type, might refer to Potus, the slave of Cornelius, or to P. Cornelius Potus, a freedman or free man.[1] Kühn has attempted to draw up lists showing the proportion of slave and freed and free, but he relies solely on inscriptions on stones and does not distinguish between employer and employed. For the whole of Italy he reckons 75 per cent. freedmen.[2] Gummerus regards this figure as too high, and produces the following table : [3]

	Freeborn.	Freed.	Slave.
Rome . . .	27 per cent.	66·75 per cent.	6·25 per cent.
The rest of Italy .	46·25 per cent.	52 per cent.	1·75 per cent.

It is reasonable that the proportion of the free element should be greater in Italy than in Rome, if, as has been urged in this chapter, village industries were often in the hands of free men. Such figures probably give as near an indication as is possible. At the same time the selective nature of the evidence must be

[1] See M. E. Park, *op. cit.* p. 81, for a summary of views. Dressel says *liberti* ; Oxé says proprietor on early vases, probably freedman on later ; Chase says slave, *op. cit.* p. 17. The conclusions drawn by Park are (i) no indication of free labour, (ii) the free man appears as owner and is often a working potter, (iii) manumission frequent : (i) seems uncertain if (ii) is true. See Gummerus in Pauly-Wissowa, ix. 1498 ; Frank, *Amer. Hist. Rev.*, 1916, p. 693.

[2] *De opificum Romanorum condicione privata quaestiones.*

[3] *Op. cit.* ix. 1501.

remembered. Most inscriptions come from big towns, and
many of the references to workmen come from the lists of
members of *collegia* there; the free craftsman took less pride
in his craft, or at any rate did not advertise it as much in his
epitaph, while the freedman not only admitted it but sometimes derived a cognomen from his trade,[1] though the farther
away a man's family receded from a slave origin, the less willing
he was to admit a trade.   Again, funeral reliefs, showing the
craft or profession of the dead man, might be expected to help,
but unfortunately, though they give often invaluable information about the technical details of Roman industry, they give
no indication of the status of the man commemorated.   And
the spirit of the reliefs themselves may be variously interpreted :
one interpreter sees in them the ostentation of the new-rich
parading the methods by which he has made a fortune—they
would, therefore, be evidence of slaves and ex-slaves in industry ; another sees in them an honest pride in humble work
well done, which might be felt equally by free or freedmen.[2]
No examination, it seems, which concentrates on one particular
field of evidence is likely to produce acceptable results ; it is
only by surveying the archaeological evidence in its relation
to the general history of the Empire that valid conclusions can
be reached.   What seemed to each individual investigator of
supreme importance is then seen to be of only relative value in
the light of the whole.   And the first comprehensive treatment
of this kind has been undertaken by Rostovtzeff in his *Social
and Economic History*.   It is interesting to find this scholar,
whose command of the archaeological evidence and all that
has been written about it is second to none, summing up as
cautiously as he does.   Writing of the townships of the Flavian
and Antonine age, he says : ' One step below on the social
ladder stood the petty bourgeoisie, the shop-owners, the retail-
traders, the money-changers, the artisans, the representatives of
liberal professions, such as teachers, doctors, and the like.   Of
them we know but little . . . we shall never be able to say

[1] See Gummerus, ' Cognomen und Beruf,' in *Commentationes philo-
logicae in honorem I. A. Heikel* (Helsingfors, 1926), pp. 48 sqq.
[2] For Rostovtzeff's opinion, see *op. cit.* p. 506, n. 34, and for the
reliefs, S. Reinach, *Répertoire de reliefs grecs et romains*, and Espérandieu,
Recueil général des bas reliefs, etc., *de la Gaule romaine*.

how many shops were owned by this petty bourgeoisie and how many were run by slaves and freedmen (*institores*) for the members of the municipal aristocracy. . . . On a lower plane stood the city proletariate, the free wage-earners and the slaves employed in the shops and in the household. We have no means of defining their numerical strength or their material conditions. Our sources very rarely speak of them, and the ruins of the excavated cities do not yield statistics.' [1]

The contention of this chapter has been that slavery does not deserve to be accused of preventing advance in organization or technique. Put generally, the grounds of this statement are two. First, if Roman slavery had been of the same nature as American, then the charge might stand; but given the peculiar conditions of Roman slavery in industry, what can be predicated of slavery elsewhere is not valid in this case. Secondly, there are other causes, social and economic, which will go far to account for the phenomenon to be explained.

[1] P. 178.

CHAPTER V

IN THE SERVICE OF STATE AND TOWN

Admiranda tibi levium spectacula rerum.

Vergil, *Georgics*, iv. 3.

Tu quoque, legiferis mundum complexa triumphis,

Foedere communi vivere cuncta facis.

Rutilius Namatianus, *De Reditu Suo*, i. 77.

T HAT the State should possess slaves is not surprising; war, after all, was the affair of the State, and the captives might well be State property. What is surprising is the remarkable use made of public slaves under the Empire and the extraordinary social position occupied by them.

Before the Empire all ' public slaves '—*servi publici*—were the property of the State and were controlled by the magistrates as the servants of the Senate. When, however, the Emperor used his own slaves and slaves bought by the fisc to staff an imperial civil service, ' public slaves,' though often performing similar duties, were technically distinct, each class belonging to each element in the diarchy. If the ' public slaves ' tend to become obsolete [1] or to mean merely ' slaves of the Emperor '— *servi Caesaris*—or slaves of a municipality, it is only in accordance with the general drift of things from diarchy to the supreme control of the Emperor. Two further distinctions must be made. ' Public slave ' came to mean before the Empire a slave of the State employed in its many offices, and the term implied a given occupation and often social position ; a captive of war held by the State prior to sale, or a freedman becoming the property of the State under the *Lex Aelia Sentia*, A.D. 4,[2] was not a ' public slave ' unless the State decided to employ

[1] Mommsen can find no trace of *servi publici* outside the capital after the foundation of the Empire, *D.P.R.* i. 362.

[2] Cf. Gaius, i. 27.

130

him in some capacity or other. Secondly, 'public slaves' belonged strictly to the State, i.e. the Senate and People of Rome. But it was common[1] for towns to possess slaves of their own, just as any 'universitas' could possess slaves ; but these slaves of towns differ in certain important points from the slaves of the State, and need separate consideration.

The methods by which the State acquired these slaves varied. Conquest provided some, though always fewer ; early in the first century proscriptions and confiscations provided others ; at other times the *actor publicus* (himself a slave) was commissioned to buy from the market or from private owners ;[2] occasionally a gift was made by individuals : Augustus, for example, thus gave up the slaves whom he had inherited from Agrippa.[3] One method of recruiting this class is conspicuously absent—that of birth—and for the good reason that the State possessed no women slaves, and therefore no slave children,[4] since the child took the status of the mother.

That the social and legal status of these slaves was superior to that of private slaves is clear from the evidence.[5] It is probable that they frequently married freed or free women ;[6] for example, Epagathus was a *servus publicus ad Juturna*, i.e. he was employed on the aqueducts ; he married Attia Felicitas, a free woman ; their daughter was called Attia Epagatho.[7] They enjoyed a salary,[8] and seem to have had a special right to possess half their *peculium* as their own, with the power of disposing of this half by will.[9] They frequently rejoiced

---

[1] Lex col. Gen. xcviii. allows the aediles to exact five days' labour from all males for public works. This would include slaves. Probably this regulation was made because the town was a new foundation, and would not yet possess public slaves of its own.

[2] Tac. *Ann.* ii. 30, iii. 67.

[3] Frontin. *de aq.* 98 ; *v. infra*, p. 137.

[4] Neither women nor children appear in the inscriptions ; contrast with the slaves of the townships, *infra*, p. 132.

[5] Cf. Mommsen, *D.P.R.* v. 107.

[6] *v.* Halkin, *Les esclaves publics*, though there was probably no right in the matter, as Halkin seems to imply, pp. 130 and 135 ; the rest of their privileges would account for it. Mommsen, *D.P.R.* i. 367, says they never married *ancillae*.

[7] Dess. 9050.   [8] Cf. Frontin. *de aq.* 118, for details.

[9] Ulp. *fr.* xx. 16, 'servus populi Romani pro peculii parte dimidia testamenti faciendi habet ius.'

in two names, the second denoting their previous owner, e.g. Fortunatus Publicus Sulpicianus,[1] and it is possible that they wore the toga.[2]

The slaves of the townships were acquired frequently by gift in the will of a rich and devoted citizen. But the township possessed women-slaves, *ancillae*,[3] and their children became slaves of the townships. Thus one inscription shows the death of a public slave aged fifteen months, another of a child seven years, ten months.[4] This is the chief distinction between slaves of the townships and *servi publici* in the strict sense. In other respects the position is very similar, and indeed the old ' public slaves ' seem to have served as a model for the townships. There seems to be some right of testament;[5] a salary in kind was given;[6] and the peculium seems to be assured by right at emancipation.[7] These slaves frequently married free women, the children as usual taking the status of the mother. Besides these rights they enjoyed that of wearing the toga, and frequently possessed wealth and esteem.[8]

And it was with good reason that they enjoyed some consideration, which, together with their rights, placed them in a position far more secure and comfortable than that of many free citizens ; for their work was both important and responsible.

The work of slaves of the State, slaves of the townships, and slaves of Caesar comprises much of what would now fall to parts of the higher and the whole of the lower branches of the civil service and of the servants of municipal corporations, working

---

[1] Dess. 4990a ;   cf. 4983 sqq., Domitianus Modianus Maecianus Julianus Cornelianus. Some have only one, e.g. ' Soter servos publicus,' *C.I.L.* vi. 2344. Lehman, quoted by Halkin, says, ' brevitate totius tituli probabiliter excusatur.' Halkin suggests that they were bought from dealers, whose name need not be recorded.

[2] *Limocincti.* Mommsen, *D.P.R.* i. 371, n. 1, says that they did not, in spite of Dess. 1965, an inscription of a *servus publicus*, with a relief of a man, clothed in a toga, with a woman and child = *C.I.L.* vi. 2365.

[3] e.g. Dess. 8053, Junoni Tyches Iuliae Augustae Vener. (Pompeii), though Dessau's explanation differs from Mau's—slave of colonia Veneriae (Pompeianae), slave of Julia, priestess of Venus.

[4] *C.I.L.* x. 163, xi. 2556.

[5] No text of law shows this, but *C.I.L.* x. 4687 shows the fact.

[6] Plin. *Ep.* x. 31.   [7] *Dig.* xl. 3. 3.

[8] Dess. 6511, for possession of a vicarius ; *C.I.L.* ix. 4112, 5177, for wealth.

both with head and hands. Since each municipality was in fact a miniature of Rome, the work of the *servi municipiorum* was very similar to that of the *servi publici populi Romani*; on the other hand, the duties of *servi Caesaris* were much wider; e.g. in one whole department at least they performed a work which was not undertaken by public slaves.[1] Under the Empire taxes were more and more collected by agents of the Emperor, while under the Republic they were farmed to collectors, who might use the services of their own slaves, but not of those of the State.

Both the State and the townships found it convenient to use the help of a public slave in at least ' three cases in which security may be taken by a public slave in what is essentially private business.'[2] To omit all technicalities, security may be given to a public slave by a person adopting a minor, since it would be no security if given to the minor himself. The goods of a person in captivity with the enemy may be placed in the custody of one who gives security to a public slave; thirdly, an intended guardian—*tutor*—can give security that the property of a ward—*pupillus*—shall be preserved intact to him. Of the first of these cases Professor Buckland writes: ' The solution found was to give security to a public slave, perhaps with an incorrect idea that those entitled were part owners of the slave as members of the public. . . . It is perhaps rather the public than the " common " quality of the slave which accounts for his use.'[3] The State is thus availing itself of the impersonal nature of the slave, an idea which has already been observed to be of importance in the legal position of slaves in business and commerce. Hence in Rome and the townships the *actor publicus* was an important official; through him the community acted whenever it had to enter into contracts, stipulations, and similar legal relations.[4] When Pliny endowed education in his native town of Comum, he transferred land to the State agent, receiving it back as tenant from him after he had determined a rent for it.[5] It has already been noticed that the *actor publicus* bought slaves for the State or town. But it may be

---

[1] For a minor exception *v. infra*, p. 134.
[2] Buckland, *Slavery*, p. 322.   [3] *Id. Textbook*, 126 sq.
[4] Halkin, *op. cit.* p. 43 ; cf. Mommsen, *D.P.R.* i. 212.
[5] Plin. *Ep.* vii. 18.

worth while to quote for illustration the actual text of a receipt given by one of these slave-agents : ' On June 18, in the duum-virate of L. Veranius Hypsaeus and L. Albucius Justus, I, Privatus, slave of the colony of Pompeii, declared in writing that I had received from L. Caecilius Jucundus 1675 sesterces, and previous to this day, on June 6, I received 1000 sesterces as rent for the public pasture.   Done at Pompeii in the consul-ship of Gnaeus Fonteius and Gaius Vipstanus.' [1]

Many of the servants of State and town were employed in financial work.   The college of priests thus employed them ; to others the quaestors entrusted the transcription of their accounts.   Taxes became under the Empire a concern of the Emperor's staff, but it is possible that the *vicesima libertatis* [2] and, for a time,[3] the *quinta et vicesima venalium mancipiorum*—the first a tax on manumission, the second a tax on sales of slaves created by Augustus—were paid into the senatorial treasury ;   these taxes would then be administered by public slaves.   A department for gathering arrears owed to the Senate is suggested by an inscription to ' Narcissus, publicus Cilnianus a reliquis populi Romani.' [4]   Again, a good reason may be found for the use of slaves in these positions ; there was always the possibility of torture, and, since the owner—that is, the com-munity—owned what the slave owned, the risks of embezzlement were less likely, and embezzlement did no harm.   A few public slaves seem to have been attached to consuls,[5] who certainly used them for correspondence ;   but more were assigned to aediles, naturally.[6]   Some were even used by the censors as clerks.[7]   In the townships also public slaves were attached to magistrates.[8]

In the ceremonial of religion these slaves figured largely in Rome under the Republic, and continued to do so under the Empire.   They helped with the sacrifices offered by the *curiones*,

[1] The Latin and the above translation are given in Mau-Kelsey, *Pompeii*, p. 494. For other of Jucundus' documents, see Bruns, pp. 355 sqq.

[2] The point is disputed ; see Mommsen, *D.P.R.* i. 375, n. 4.   Contrast Dess. 1863, which suggests that the collecting was in the hands of *socii*, with 1868, which mentions a *publicus*.

[3] Afterwards absorbed by the fisc.   [4] Dess. 9049.

[5] Plut. *Galba*, 8 ; see Juv. x. 41, for the slave riding in the consul's car.

[6] Mommsen, *D.P.R.* i. 374.   [7] *C.I.L.* vi. 2333.

[8] Apul. *Met.* i. 24 ; Lex col. Gen. lxii.

the priests of the *curiae*, and served as assistants in some capacity to the pontifices, to the augurs, the xv viri sacris faciundis, the vii viri epulonum, the sodales Titii, and the sodales Augustales and Flaviales.[1] Of their duties little is known ; one at least was an apparitor—*viator*—and another in charge of documents —*a commentariis*—another a treasurer—*arcarius*. Of those attached to the Arval Brothers a little more can be gathered from the surviving minutes of the college. In the year A.D. 87 Narcissus is entered as having been chosen assistant ;[2] in A.D. 155 Epictetus Cuspianus was appointed in the place of Carpus Cornelianus, who had been promoted to the quaestors' department.[3] In the month of May the festival of Dea Dia was held, and in the detailed minutes which survive of the sacrifices made in her honour the following entry often occurs : ' the sons of senators . . . together with public slaves carried to the altar ' certain offerings of incense and wine.[4] The entry for the year A.D. 218 contains more details : a solemn cleansing and feast shared in by the members of the brotherhood assembled and sitting upon thrones ; an offering carried by sons of senators and by public slaves ; more ceremony and a procession ; the sacrifice of a lamb ; the dispatch of two members with the public slaves ' ad fruges petendas.' The priests then enter the temple alone, and chant the ancient hymn ' Enos Lases iuvate ' ; after which, upon a sign, the public slaves enter and receive from them the books containing the litany.[5] At other times they assist in the ceremony of cleansing ; if a tree fell through age or through lightning in the grove of Dea Dia, the ceremony was performed *per calatorem et publicos*.[6]

Apart from the actual ceremonies, public slaves were em-ployed as temple-keepers, though the inscriptions show that they give way here, too, to slaves of Caesar.[7] Thus Successus Valerianus is a *publicus a sacrario divi Augusti*—that is, he is a keeper of a shrine of the *sodales* in the imperial house ;[8] but from later examples keepers even of the public temples, for example,

---

[1] Dess. 4978 sqq. [2] Dess. 5029. [3] Dess. 5030.
[4] e.g. 5038 ; A.D. 145 ; ' pueri patrimi et matrimi senatorum fili praetextati cum publicis at aram rettulerunt.'
[5] Dess. 5039. [6] Dess. 5043 sqq.
[7] For slave *aeditui* in the literature, see, e.g., Tac. *Hist.* i. 43, iii. 74.
[8] Dess. 4993a.

of Vesta, are slaves and freedmen of Caesar. The townships, again imitating the imperial city, employed public slaves for religious purposes.[1]

Various other kinds of work performed by these slaves are clear enough under the Republic, but the organizing genius of Augustus introduced many changes and improvements, which tended to replace these slaves by other persons, whether slave, freed, or free. Thus the fire-brigade of Rome, previously manned by public slaves, was reconstituted in 6 B.C. and again in A.D. 6, when seven *cohortes vigilum* of a thousand men each were enrolled chiefly from freedmen and Junian Latins.[2] So, too, in the customs houses, the personnel becomes more and more imperial.[3] Public slaves were employed in the prisons under the Republic, but there is no evidence for this under the Empire ; the townships employed them thus, as is clear from Pliny. ' It is customary to guard prisons by public slaves. Shall I use slaves or soldiers or both ? ' ' Slaves,' writes back the enduring Trajan.[4] But in Bithynia there was much slackness : ' I find criminals sentenced to the mines actually performing the duties of public slaves and being paid as such.' ' All sentenced within the last ten years must serve their sentence ; the rest must work in the baths, must clean sewers, and mend roads.'[5] In the townships firemen were probably slaves, such as those who put an end to the Cena Trimalchionis.[6] At Rome the department of the corn-supply—*cura annonae*—was in the hands of imperial slaves, as will be seen presently ; but in some townships store-keepers—*horrearii*—who were also public slaves, were employed. The administrators of the ' alimenta ' had public slaves to help them in their administration of the funds of each district in Italy. At Sipontum, for example, Liberalis was an *arcarius* who formerly was in the department of the alimentations for thirty-two years.[7] His son was

---

[1] *C.I.L.* x. 3941, ' Soter colon(orum) (servus) [a] sacris.'

[2] See Dio, liii. 24, for Egnatius Rufus using his own slaves as a fire-brigade when aedile, 26 B.C. ; lv. 8, for the aedile's fire-slaves ; lv. 26, for Augustus' reorganization. See also P. K. B. Reynolds, *The Vigiles of Imperial Rome*, Oxford, 1926. For Junian Latins, *v. infra*, p. 184.

[3] See Marquardt, *L'Org. fin.* 346 sqq., and, e.g., Dess. 1855, 1856.

[4] Plin. *Ep.* x. 19, 20.   [5] x. 31, 32.   [6] Petr. 78.

[7] ' Egit rationem praefectorum ' (i.e. ' praefectorum alimentorum '), Dess. 6476 ; 6519 gives an *alimentarius* of Saepinum.

Augurinus, a *verna* of the same State, and a ' measurer '—*mensor*. *Arcarii* are common in many towns ; *dispensatores* occur less often.   At Placentia a public slave was overseer of the market— *vilicus macelli*—while *tabularii* serve in municipal record offices.[1]

But of another department [2] more is known, and here the tendency for the ' slaves of Caesar ' to supersede the ' public slaves ' is excellently shown.   Further, the actual working of a department can be seen better here than anywhere else, and it is proposed to treat it at greater length.   The water-supply of the city of Rome had from early times exercised the attention of magistrates.   One by one the springs of the Sabine and Alban hills were tapped, and the vast aqueducts arose built of solid masonry, to be a memorial of that solidity of Roman character which always sought to check the extravagance of art by the limits of the useful.   By the end of the Republic four aqueducts had been built, carrying water in open or closed channels from the valley of the Anio, and the springs by Frascati, to supply the needs of the growing city.   The system of water-supply, the work of, roughly, one hundred and eighty years, had been under the administration of the aediles and censors, and sometimes of special commissioners.   The lifetime of Augustus saw four more aqueducts built and a change made in the method of administration.   In 33 B.C. Agrippa, most efficient of ministers, took over as aedile the control of the system and added to it the Aqua Julia and the Aqua Virgo. On his appointment he organized a gang of two hundred and forty of his own slaves and trained them to undertake the maintenance and repair of the fabric of the aqueducts, retaining control even after he had ceased to be aedile.   On his death in 12 B.C. he bequeathed this staff to Augustus, who, not to be outdone, handed it over to the State as a body of trained ' public slaves,' and created a *cura aquarum*, first under the control of Messalla Corvinus.   Under Claudius the Anio Novus, and the greatest of the aqueducts, the Aqua Claudia, were added, and the length of channel, now increased by one hundred and twenty miles, called for a larger permanent staff.   Hitherto,

[1] *C.I.L.* v. 8850.
[2] On this section, *v.* Herschel, *The two books of Sextus Julius Frontinus on the water-supply of the city of Rome*, 1899 ; H. Stuart Jones, *Companion to Roman History*, and bibliography given there.

the care of the system had remained nominally with the Senate ; but Claudius, taking the opportunity to bring one of the essential services still closer under imperial control, appointed a freedman to be ' procurator aquarum.' Either he hoped to secure more efficient service under imperial administration or he was influenced by his powerful freedmen to create a new office for them to fill—if, indeed, the stories of his subservience to his freedmen are to be credited. At any rate, a freedman as procurator is to be found certainly under Vespasian, Domitian, and Trajan.[1] Under the charge of his procurator Claudius placed a new body of permanent officials, four hundred and sixty in number. There was, therefore, a twofold control [2]—a senatorial curator with a staff of two hundred slaves, an imperial procurator with a staff of four hundred and sixty slaves ; between them they managed roughly two hundred and eighty miles of channel, of which about seven-eighths was subterranean or enclosed. The whole system is calculated to have carried each day thirty-eight gallons of water per head of the population of Rome.[3]

Such was the condition when Frontinus was appointed curator by Nerva. From his office in the enclosure of Juturna close to the forum he directed the operations of his officials. He found them organized according to craft—foremen and paviors, levellers and masons, fitters, cleaners, and the rest. Most of them lived inside Rome ; it was necessary, however, that some should be stationed along the course of the aqueducts to deal with emergencies which needed skilled labour at once.[4] Their work was the maintenance of the aqueducts, a work which Frontinus describes with all the pride of the head of a department ' as worthy of the most painstaking care, for it is the chief evidence of the greatness of the Roman power.' Of the capacities of mind requisite for his own office he has a high opinion ; [5] and it may be counted to him as a qualification that he brings to his new work a firm determination ' nosse quod suscepi.' But it is the nature of the work of his subordinates which is our concern.

---

[1] Dess. 8678, 8679 ; *C.I.L.* xv. 7295.

[2] *v.* Greenidge, *Roman Public Life*, p. 413.

[3] Herschel. Stuart Jones regards it as an underestimate, *Companion to Roman History*, p. 150.

[4] Frontin. 117.   [5] Frontin. 119.

The ravages of time,[1] the resourcelessness of occupiers of land, storms and hurricanes, bad workmanship in the original building (common in the later aqueducts)—all these keep his watermen ready to go out at a moment's notice. Sometimes the whole of the water of one channel must be held up or diverted till the deposits of lime have been cleaned away; sometimes the roof falls in, causing floods which damage the sides of the channel and the structure below. The repairs must generally be done in winter, when water is less in demand; never must two channels be closed at the same time.[2] For extensive or structural alterations it was within the discretion of the commissioner to call in the help of contractors.[3] There was also some clerical work to be done in the office of the commissioner; some of it fell to freedmen,[4] some to the *vilici*, whose duty it was to be familiar with the grants made by the Emperor through his procurator, and the conditions on which they were issued. The *familia Caesaris* also seems to have undertaken the manufacture and stamping of lead pipes, for their stamp is still to be seen on numbers of lead water-pipes—*fistulae plumbeae aquariae*.[5]

If the water-commissioner was conscientious and painstaking, the same cannot be said for his underlings. But the new broom was determined to sweep clean, and he found many abuses to remove; indeed, the fraud and malpractices of the watermen seem to have become notorious.[6] We may trace their malpractices from the country to the very doors of the houses in Rome. 'Lapsed' waters, which had leaked away from the channel, or from the tanks, were subject to grants, but such grants were seldom made. These waters were frequently stolen by the watermen—*aquarii*[7]—who authorized unofficially their use to owners of the adjacent land. Yet a decree expressly forbade the carrying away of such waters;[8] for the constant flushing of drains conduced to the health of the city. To avoid frequent cutting of the pipes,[9] all water carried into Rome was drawn from delivery tanks, whence it was drawn off by outlet pipes of specified and approved size to private lands; it was in these delivery tanks that the *castellarii* found the widest scope

---

[1] Frontin. 120 sq.   [2] Frontin. 122.   [3] Frontin. 119.
[4] Cf. Dess. 1607.   [5] Cf. Dess. 8680, 8681.
[6] Frontin. 114, ' adhuc illa aquariorum intolerabilis fraus est.'
[7] Frontin. 110.   [8] Frontin. 111.   [9] Frontin. 106.

for their ingenuity, which met with a due reward from the grantee of the water-right. In some cases Frontinus found outlet pipes of larger diameter than granted, others he found unmarked with the official stamp, others he found variable at the will of the watermen.[1] But more subtle forms of fraud also occurred ; the lower the outlet the greater the pressure, though rule insisted that all depths of outlets should be the same ; or the outlet pipe inserted in the tank was of correct diameter, but the same diameter was not maintained for 50 feet as required by law.[2] After the water had left one tank, it was still liable to theft during its passage to the next ; with the connivance of the watermen these mains were tapped by small pipes carried under the city pavement to private houses. There seems to have been a special inspector to detect such pilfering ; [3] Frontinus says he collected quite a quantity of lead by removing these pipes.

Scattered over so many miles of channel and performing a skilled work, it was easy for the watermen to avoid detection if the curator or procurator brought less energy to bear upon his work than Frontinus. In numbers the staff was big enough, perhaps too big ; for Frontinus found many of them used for private work, and he determined to reduce them to order by issuing a daily programme of work, and keeping a record of work done.[4] The conditions of work, then, do not seem to have been too severe ; wages in kind were issued by the treasury for the ' public ' staff, by the fisc for the imperial staff,[5] and there are records which prove that watermen enjoyed that superior social position which, as has been seen, was granted to public servants. Sabbio, *vilicus* of the Aqua Claudia, married a wife who was not a slave, and dedicated a monument to himself and to her and to his wife's freedmen and freedwomen and to his own *vicarii*. So, too, Sporus, *vilicus* of the same aqueduct.[6] Nor were prospects entirely lacking : it is possible that Moschus, Aug. libertus, who served in the Record Office of the Water Department, *a commentariis*, had been promoted from slavery as a waterman ; it is probable that Abascantus Atimetianus, whose name appears as maker on a lead pipe found at Frascati,[7] had originally been the slave of an

[1] Frontin. 113.   [2] Frontin. 112.   [3] Frontin. 115.
[4] Frontin. 117.   [5] Frontin. 118.   [6] Dess. 1612.   [7] Dess. 8681.

unknown Atimetus before he passed into the imperial service ; later he is to be found in Rome dedicating as a freedman a shrine adorned with mosaic in the Greek style—*pavimentum Graecanicum*—and statues of Silvanus, Jupiter, and others.[1] Another maker of a pipe who worked under the procuratorship of Alypus in the time of Domitian later rose to be *procurator aquarum* himself.[2]

The townships, too, had their watermen ; they have left their names on one or two lead pipes, but, otherwise, little is known of them.

' The Princeps, since he is not a king, has neither magistrates nor ministers subject to his will.'[3] Yet the imperial civil service is worthy of the wonder of all who love sound and careful administration, for by it the world was ordered. In part the civil service was developed from institutions of the Republic ; other elements were taken from the economy of a Roman household, and therefore many posts were held by slaves or freedmen. The master of that house was the Emperor ; his servants, therefore, were the servants of the Empire, for the house was nothing less than the Empire. But, as the servants of a private household may be divided into those who attend to the near and personal wants of the master and those who have charge of his estates, so the Emperor's servants fall into those who are domestic and those who deal with the affairs of the world in what we should call the departments of the civil service. Yet all are *servi Caesaris*, alike the clerk in the imperial treasury and the valet of the imperial wardrobe.

The main outlines of imperial administration are tolerably clear, thanks to the wealth of inscriptions available. At the same time, in the lower branches of the service in particular, there is not much evidence as to the type of work, conditions of life, or chances of promotion ; in many cases many officials are known, but the titles of their offices often convey little, being mere labels which give little more than a general indication of their duties. There is no Frontinus for each branch of the service.

The three important secretaryships of the early Empire would first claim attention, and of these the most important

---

[1] Dess. 3536.   [2] *C.I.L.* xv. 7296.
[3] Greenidge, *Roman Public Life*, p. 405.

was the so-called *a rationibus*, originally held by freedmen of the Emperor and after Hadrian's reforms by a knight.[1] But to deal with each secretaryship would be to multiply detail of very similar kind ; and here it is proposed to deal only with the *a rationibus* as fairly representative of the other two. The department corresponded to the Treasury, under a chief official corresponding to the Chancellor of the Exchequer, and it rose in importance as the imperial fisc absorbed all the revenues of the State at the expense of the senatorial treasury. In the subordinate levels there worked numbers of clerks and financial officers, all freedmen and slaves. The business dealt with must have been of vast range ;[2] throughout the Empire wherever the imperial treasury was concerned—and, as will be seen, its claims were ubiquitous—there was to be found a local agent of the fisc, who was in touch with the central office. The titles of the subordinate officials[3] do not convey much in themselves —*tabularii*,[4] who received moneys and issued receipts ; *dispensatores*,[5] who are paymasters ; *arcarii*, cashiers ; *commentarienses*, who file and classify documents and reports ; *tabellarii*, who are postmen. These titles (and others) are not peculiar to the fisc at Rome, but may be found in the provincial branches, in other departments of the service, in business firms, and in private households. But, if the titles do not give much information, they suggest a diversity of duties, and they may be supplemented by a passage to be found in Statius, of all places. In a consolatory poem addressed to Claudius Etruscus, son of a freedman who was *a rationibus* from the time of Nero to that of Domitian, Statius gives a poetical description of the work of the central treasury.[6] When the poetry is cut away,[7] it is discovered that the functions of the office fall into estimates,

[1] Friedländer, vol. iv. p. 31 (Eng. trans.), gives a list of these officials as far as they are known.

[2] ὁ ἐπὶ τῶν καθόλου λόγων τῶν μεγίστων is the Greek title.

[3] Given by Hirschfeld, *VG.* 32 sqq., and many in Dess. 1479 sqq.

[4] According to Mattingly, *The Imperial Civil Service of Rome*, p. 109, always freedmen.

[5] According to Mattingly, *loc. cit.*, always slaves ; and superior to *arcarii*. Mommsen, *D.P.R.* v. 110.

[6] Stat. *Silvae*, iii. 3. 86 sqq. The name of the father is not known. See Hirschfeld, *Kleine Schriften*, p. 839.

[7] As, e.g., by Mommsen, *D.P.R.* v. 297, n. 1. See also Marquardt, *L'Org. fin.* p. 390.

disbursements, receipts according to the various magistracies and departments, and include the finances of the armies of the proconsuls and legates, the corn-supply, the department in charge of temples and public works,[1] the water-supply, the upkeep of roads, the Emperor's palaces, the Mint, the administration of such taxes as were paid to the fisc as opposed to the military and senatorial chests. The correspondence must have been colossal, and it is a pity that more has not been preserved. One example, about quite a trivial affair, may be quoted in condensed form :

I. *From Septimianus, freedman and assistant official in the fisc, to Cosmus, freedman, chief fiscal minister.*

The men who have leased the imperial estates complain that they are not receiving fair treatment from the magistrates and 'stationarii' of Saepinum and Bovianum, who detain flocks and shepherds as they pass through, on the ground that the men are runaway slaves, and the beasts stolen. As a result, the sheep on the estates die. We have written again and again, insisting that the imperial interest should suffer no loss. But they persist, saying that they will take no notice of my letters or yours. I ask you therefore to inform Bassaeus Rufus and Vindex Macrinius, the praetorian prefects, that they may write to them.

II. *From Cosmus, freedman and chief fiscal minister, to Bassaeus Rufus and Macrinius Vindex, praetorian prefects.*

I send a copy of a letter I have received from Septimianus, a fellow-freedman and my assistant. I ask you to prevent this injury and loss to the treasury.

III. *From Bassaeus Rufus and Macrinius Vindex, praetorian prefects, to the Magistrates of Saepinum.*

We send a copy of a letter received from Cosmus. We warn you to stop injuring the men who have leased these estates, and thus inflicting loss on the treasury ; otherwise we shall inquire and punish.[2]

Tact and firmness—and what more need we ask of a Government department ?

---

[1] Temples, mines, and quarries.

[2] Bruns, p. 242 ; Friedländer, vol. iv. p. 34 (Eng. trans.).

In the provinces the work of the fiscal servants was the same. In each province, senatorial and imperial, there was a procurator—in the imperial provinces often a freedman till Hadrian [1]—in charge of all the departments concerned with revenues due to the fisc, though in senatorial provinces his work would be less important. In the chief town of each province there was a central bureau where records and valuations of property were kept,[2] and in all probability there was a provincial treasury [3] into which all taxes and revenues payable to the fisc were paid, except those dues administered by a special agent of the Emperor and paid direct to Rome. Taxes [4] due to the provincial treasury were collected by imperial slaves, working sometimes under a *conductor*,[5] who was not now left to extort what he could but was paid a fixed salary, sometimes under the procurator himself. [6] Special procurators with special staffs of imperial slaves in some places administered the *patrimonium Caesaris*, which included Egypt, and estates, mines, quarries, and factories throughout the Empire ; in other places it was administered by the ordinary officials of the fisc.

To follow the slaves into the various sub-departments would again be to multiply details which do not so much bear upon the duties and activities of the slaves themselves as contribute to our amazement at the vastness and precision of the whole system. But two sub-departments of the *a rationibus* are worth attention for a moment—the Mint and the corn-supply.

The Mint was under the supreme nominal control of the

---

[1] For Trajan's procurators, freedmen, and their powers, see Plin. *Ep.* x. 28 Maximus, 84 and 85 Epimachus.

[2] See Marquardt, *L'Org. fin.* 397, where a list of places where these *tabularia* existed is given, e.g. Tarraco, Salma (Dalmatia), Poetovio, Ancyra, etc.

[3] Such provincial fisc is known for provincia Lugdunensis, Dess. 1514 ; there was a ' fiscus Asiaticus,' which was probably at Rome, Dess. 1515 sq. The titles are 'dispensator ad fiscum Gallicum prov. Lugd. ': 'adjutor tabulariorum fisci Asiatici,' and ' a commentariis fisci Asiatici.'

[4] For example, ' vicesima hereditatum ' (Dess. 1557, ' vilicus et arcarius xx. hered.') ; 203, ' vicesima quinta venalium mancipiorum ' ; 1855 sq., ' portoria.'

[5] Occasionally the *conductor* used his own slaves, e.g. Dess. 1861.

[6] Dess. 1855 shows the ' portorium Illyrici ' administered by *conductores* and *servi* ; 1856, dated A.D. 182, shows it administered by procurator and *servi*. The tendency was for *conductores* to disappear.

Emperor's minister *a rationibus*, but the immediate head—from the time of Trajan at any rate—was a *procurator monetae*, a knight. In charge of the minting processes an *exactor auri argenti et aeris*, a freedman, was placed ; under him served freedmen and slaves. The titles of the various specialists are known, and specialization seems to be as minute and rigid as in other departments. The *scalptores* engraved the dies ; *flaturarii* prepared the flans ; *aequatores* trimmed them to secure accuracy in size and weight ; *suppostores* placed the flans in position ; *malleatores* struck the upper die ; *signatores* supervised the striking, and were responsible for good impressions. Attached to the office of the Mint were the inevitable *dispensatores* ; there were also *nummularii*, who put the new money into circulation by State payments and by exchange.[1] Occasionally private slaves are found at the Mint ; these belonged to the *conductor monetae*, for till the third century the work seems to have been leased to a contractor, though the exact scope of his control of the work is uncertain.[2] About all the slaves and freedmen employed in this department there is little of interest to add ; it may, however, be noted that the *fourré* denarii of the first century—copper denarii coated with a film of silver—may owe their existence, not to State economy, but to calculated frauds on the part of the Mint officials.

Sometime between A.D. 8 and 14 the office of *praefectus annonae*, always occupied by a knight, was created, with the object of ensuring an adequate supply of corn for the city ; the importance of this department made the position of *praefectus* one of the most distinguished in Rome. Beneath him he had multitudes of slave and freedmen officials in Rome and in the ports of Puteoli and Ostia ; *vilici ex horreis* and *horrearii* were in charge of the granaries ; *actores a frumento* and *dispensatores a frumento*[3] received and distributed the grain ; *mensores*

---

[1] *v.* Mattingly and Sydenham, *The Roman Imperial Coinage*, vol. i. p. 16. Dess. 1633 sqq. give examples of most of the above titles ; also a dedication by a dispensator to the Genius of the Mint.

[2] Mattingly and Sydenham suggest he is responsible for the whole process of minting. Stuart Jones, *Companion to Roman History*, p. 348, suggests that only the preparation of the flans was leased.

[3] Dess. 344. The latter may have been under the ' praefecti frumenti dandi.' See Marquardt, *L'Org. fin.* p. 164 ; Hirschfeld, *Verwaltungsbeamten*[2], p. 233 ; and cf. Sen. *de brev. vit.* 18 and 19.

measured it ; *saccarii* transported it in bags from the docks to the porticus Minuciae, where it was distributed.   The office [1] of the department was peopled with *tabularii* and others.[2] Special slave-officials were in charge of the corn, which was put on the market at a reduced price ; others supervised the carrying of the grain to such of the Emperor's troops and servants as were entitled to it.[3] Of the work of these officials little more can be added than is contained in their title, but for the *horrearii* there remains a document which must be quoted for its modern ring.   In these State granaries—such is the wish of the Government to encourage the importation of grain—bins and floorspace were leased to corn merchants.   The terms of the lease stipulate that merchants shall give due notice when a cargo is expected ; there is to be no subletting of space allotted ; no responsibility is undertaken for the safe keeping of goods brought in ; [4] if the rent-charges are not paid, goods may be confiscated ; the warehouseman is acquitted from all blame if goods are left in store without being committed to the care of a watchman.

From one branch of State service, at any rate, slaves were rigorously excluded, except on one or two occasions of exceptional stress.   They were not allowed to fight in the army because not thought worthy of the honour.   Doubtless other motives were present also ; it would be a dangerous experiment to train too many slaves systematically in the use of arms, though it was done on a small scale in the gladiatorial schools ; [5] and even if trained, they would make poor soldiers.   Twice Augustus availed himself of this source of recruits, compelling rich owners to give up their slaves, whom he freed, at a price. Suetonius says he kept them in special companies apart from free men and armed distinctively, but the sequel shows him to be wrong.   In one case the purpose was the protection of the colonies on the borders of Illyricum ; in the other, the protection

---

[1] ' Officium,' *C.I.L.* vi. 8473.

[2] Dess. 1536 sqq.

[3] ' Dispensator frumenti mancipalis,' Dess. 1536 ; ' servi a frumento ministratorum,' Dess. 1808.

[4] ' [invectorum in haec horrea cu]stodia non praestabitur,' as restored in Bruns, p. 372. Dess. 5914 is less bold.

[5] These made good soldiers ; cf. the gladiators in the civil wars at the bridge-building on the Po, Tac. *Hist.* ii. 34–36.

of the bank of the Rhine after the defeat of Varus.[1] But it was a dangerous experiment, for the very slaves who had been enrolled in A.D. 10 were the leaders in the revolt of the German armies a few years later. But, after all, they were a ' city rabble, accustomed to rioting and impatient of work.'[2] The same expedient was tried with possibly similar results at other times, by Nero, for example, after the declaration of war by Galba,[3] and by Marcus Aurelius after pestilence had thinned the ranks of his armies.[4] But normally slaves and freedmen were excluded. Domitian had restored Claudius Pacatus, though an ex-centurion, to his master because he had been proved to be a slave.[5] Pliny had discovered two slaves in the army in Bithynia ; they had already taken the oath, but had not yet been assigned to any army. What must be done ? We must find out, answers Trajan, whether they deserve capital punishment. If they were picked out for service, then the mistake lies with the recruiting officer ; if they were offered as substitutes, those who offered them made the mistake ; if they came voluntarily, knowing their status as slaves, they must be punished. But, he adds, all this should have been found out when they were passed for service.[6]

To the rule that slaves do not serve in the army, there is an apparent exception. We have already seen Germans, Batavians, and others carried off to form an Emperor's bodyguard. But this force was never part of the army ; it is true that it was organized on a military basis, but the members bear only a cognomen, and so are slaves, and, in addition, were under the control of a *curator Germanorum*, which suggests that the force was regarded as a department of the Emperor's household rather than a military detachment. It was replaced probably under Trajan by a regular military guard.[7]

If, however, slaves served rarely in the fighting line, they are regularly to be found in great numbers behind it, employed

---

[1] Suet. *Aug.* 25 ; Dio, lvi. 23, freedmen ?

[2] Tac. *Ann.* i. 31. ἀστικὸς ὄχλος in Dio, lvii. 5.   [3] Suet. *Nero*, 44.

[4] Script. hist. aug. *M. Aur.* xxi. 6, 7 ; he called them *voluntarii*, ' after the example of the *volones.*'

[5] Dio, lxvii. 13.   [6] Plin. *Ep.* x. 29, 30.

[7] *Supra*, p. 18. See Mommsen, *D.P.R.* v. 74 and 75. The Germans were organized in *decuriae*, a term as applicable to the *familia* as to the army. See Dess. 1717–30, which show the *decuriae* ; cf. 1745.

as servants, and in the commissariat and transport;[1] *dis-pensatores*, as paymasters, served in the *fiscus castrensis* as representative of the fisc at Rome.[2]   Here, too, their loyalty was a doubtful quantity.   When the army of Civilis advanced against Vetera, it was hoped that the slaves within the walls would provoke a mutiny: *fluxa servitiorum fides*.[3]   It was the servants of the camp who exposed Galba's head on a pike,[4] and a slave of Verginius, found by the soldiers in Vitellius' camp, was said to be there to assassinate their general.[5]   That slaves acted as spies is only to be expected.   On more than one occasion a Roman general menaced by his mutinous legions was forced to take refuge in the tunic of the slave ; thus Vocula escaped on the Rhine.[6]

In the fleet slaves were common enough.   Augustus had freed 20,000 slaves, and put them to the oar,[7] and upon this basis he built up the navy, which remained always a depart-ment organized and controlled by the Emperor rather than a public service.   Once the fleet was established, slaves and freedmen served in many capacities, though the tendency after Claudius was to recruit the fleet from foreigners—*peregrini*.[8] But slaves are to be found as captains of vessels—*trierarchi* ; as marines—*milites* ; as helmsmen—*gubernatores* ; and as *proretae* and *celeustae* ; and at several dates a freedman is found in command as *praefectus classis*.[9]   The representatives of the fisc may again be found in the *dispensatores* attached to the fleet.[10]

Of the activities of slaves in the service of State only a hint

---

[1] *Calones* is the common term.   Dess. 2157 gives *cacus*, i.e. *servus militis*, according to Paulus ; cf. Plautus' word, *cacula*.   The number of *calones* and *lixae* who entered Cremona with the army was 40,000 and over !   Tac. *Hist.* iii. 33.   Hadrian received Cappadocian slaves for service in the camps, Script. hist. aug. *Hadr.* xiii. 7.

[2] e.g. Dess. 1651, ' adiutor tabularior(um) fisci castrensis.'

[3] Tac. *Hist.* iv. 23 ; cf. iv. 60.

[4] i. 49.   [5] ii. 68.   [6] iv. 36.

[7] Suet. *Aug.* 16.

[8] Marquardt, *L'Org. mil.* p. 242, n. 2, gives a list of nationalities in the fleet at Ravenna.   Pannonians and Dalmatians were very common.

[9] Optatus under Claudius ; Anicetus under Nero ; Moschus under Otho ; Hermogenes under Hadrian.   But no doubt a freedman in this position is exceptional.   Dess. 2820 sqq. give the various specialists.

[10] e.g. Dess. 2906.

has been given ; but enough may have been said to prompt two questions :

First, why should slaves have been so employed ?

The answer must be found in several causes which operate at once.

The circumstances of the origin of the State services must be held chiefly accountable. Republican tradition insisted that voluntary State service was the highest form of occupation for the free man of leisure, and Republican practice demanded that the high administrative posts should be held by men of military training. There was little distinction, if any, between civil and military service in the higher branches of State service under the Republic. The organization of the provinces by Augustus, with a view to sound administration rather than reckless exploitation, created a multitude of posts both in Italy and abroad. As has been seen already, in the slave-staffs of any Roman of wealth there would be men of ability performing similar administrative duties on a small scale. Augustus created a civil service by enlarging his own household, and asking the co-operation of the knights.

But there were other elements in the Roman tradition. The work of the clerk was despised. Yet Latin is full of metaphors drawn from bookkeeping. Such terminology is really derived from the accounts necessary in the management of an estate ; the accounts of the landlord or the director of a company are different in dignity from the figures of the ledger-clerk. This tradition of independence, of managing one's own business instead of an employer's, spread from higher circles to the best type of poorer citizen ; we have already seen it in the land and in industry. The love of one's own plot of land, or the independent status of craftsman, were always powerful motives in Italy. If men wished to enlist in the service of the State, there was always the army, which needed recruits and offered an honourable career worthy of a Roman.

Further, the growing number of townships offered frequent opportunity of public service rewarded by a local glory and esteem which none of the minor civil service posts could offer. To make such posts attractive it would have been necessary to exalt them beyond their worth ; and if they could have been filled without some attraction in the way of prestige or pay, then the army would have been starved.   And, after all, it is probable that the Government did actually secure the most efficient servants available ; the Greek and Syrian slave had a capacity for business and languages far greater than that of the Italian.   And any Government deserves all credit for efficiency in its permanent staff, no matter from what source that staff is recruited.

Secondly, what must have been the effect on the slaves so employed ?

The effect can only have been Romanization, with all that it implies.   To be taken from the now despised countries of Syria and Greece, to be set to do often responsible work in the service of the Empire, to be trained in Roman methods of organization and to appropriate Roman ideals can have brought nothing but good to these servants themselves.   The consciousness of helping forward the work of the Empire was undoubtedly an inspiration to many who record quite gratuitously their devotion to Rome and Augustus in the lands, however distant, to which their duties had summoned them.   The cementing of Empire was wrought by many means, and Rome gathered in of the nations only to send them forth as her missioners.

CHAPTER VI

THE SLAVE AS MAN

Et servi homines sunt.

Petr. 71.

Quid est enim eques Romanus aut libertinus aut servus ? nomina
ex ambitione aut ex iniuria nata ; exsilire in caelum ex angulo licet.

Sen. *Ep*. xxxi. 11.

THE relation between law and opinion is a commonplace
of discussion. Both have been found to react differently
upon each other under different circumstances, law often
guiding and educating opinion, but generally crystallizing with
hard and clear-cut precision upon a long seething opinion which
is often vague and shapeless, but on the whole generally held,
if not clearly conceived. In our review of slaves in industry and
commerce it has been seen how the compulsion of convenience
and self-interest drove slave-owners into a practical recognition
of the slave as a person in the narrow field of agency and contract.
It was a slow process, and law naturally lagged behind opinion,
though very probably in this sphere its tardy progress was
speeded up by the urgent pressure of practical need upon those
who were most able to influence and amplify the commercial
law. Yet, even so, law withheld much, though custom bestowed
more than it was compelled.

Much the same is true of the relationship between practice
and theory as regards the family life of slaves.[1] While law
recognized the slave merely as a *res*, classed with movable pro-

---

[1] As, indeed, in the family life of free men. Cf. Greenidge, *Roman
Public Life*, p. 20 : '. . . it would be very misleading to fill up the
context of Roman private life by analogy with this harsh outline (of law).
Like most of the theory of Roman law, it had little correspondence with
the facts ; and this non-correspondence of fact and theory is the strength
and beauty of Roman family life.'

perty, while Varro regarded him' as an articulate implement
as opposed to wagons and the like, which were 'voiceless
implements,' both law and agriculture are compelled eventually
to take into account the constantly self-asserting humanity of
the slave.   Varro himself, in the age of Augustus, is forced to
write that the farmer should encourage family life among his
slaves, who then become more attached to the estate ; [1] Ulpian,
in the age of Severus, writes that, if a farm and its *instrumentum* are bequeathed, the wives and children of its slaves
are included, on the ground that it must not be supposed that
the testator commanded so cruel a separation.[2]   Indeed, epitaphs
suggest that an unbroken family life was securely counted on ;
thus, Lais, a slave, put up a monument to her dead husband,
and to herself and their children.[3]   The will of Trimalchio
contains a clause promising a property and his *contubernalis*
to Philargyrus, whom he declares free.[4]   Though the scene of
the reading of the will is ridiculously foolish, the fact attested
is a sober fact of truth.   The so-called ' Testamentum Dasumii '
contains a precisely similar bequest.[5]   Even if the will contained no such provision, the case was not beyond hope.   A
case occurs of a freedman, who had been left a legacy by the
will of his master, surrendering all claim to it, and asking in
return that the heir to the estate should manumit his *contubernalis*.[6]   Over two centuries separate Varro and Ulpian,
and in that period a growing tendency to respect the family

[1] Varro, i. 17. 5.

[2] *Dig.* xxxiii. 7. 12. 7. ' As a token of gratitude, a feeble and infirm
old woman placed an amber ring on Mr. Barnard's hand. Her chief joy
was that she and her family were able to live free of the thought that at
any moment separation might be effected by the sudden sale of one
member to another master' ; from a report in *The Times* of April 30,
1926, on the Emancipation of Slaves in Burma.

[3] Dess. 1618.   The erection of monuments for the living also was
common ; cf. 4993a, 1710 quoted p. 169, *infra* ; 7724 gives a reason :
'. . . sibi fecit dedicavit et titulavit ; fecimus quot fili nostri non faciunt.'

[4] Petr. 71.

[5] Bruns, p. 304 : '. . . et Sabinum notarium et . . . rationibus
redditis cum contubernalibus suis liberos esse iubeo. Cf. Scaev. *Dig.*
xxxii. 41. 2 : ' omnibus autem libertis meis . . . contubernales suas, item
filios filias lego.'

[6] *C.I.L.* ii. 2265 ; quoted in full, Marquardt, *Vie privée*, i. 193, n. 3, and
supra, p. 103.

relationships of slaves makes itself apparent. But, though such tendency is everywhere attested, in strict theory the position of the slave as regards family rights remains much where it had been under the Republic. Yet even the law adopts the language of usage ; though the union of slaves can strictly be only *contubernium*, the jurists are as ready as the slaves themselves to speak of *maritus, uxor, filius, parentes, pater* within the boundaries of slavery.[1] The *ius gentium* is triumphing over the *ius civile*, the claim of common humanity over arbitrary convention ; and the moralist may find it interesting that the highest of human relationships, the bond of the family, used in part the self-interest of the master as the means of establishing its claim even upon the low level of slavery and amid a system antagonistic to it at that level. Thus spiritual values broke through the artificial disabilities which society in its initial blindness to those values was led to impose.

If a reason is sought for this humane tendency of the law, it must be found, in part at least, in the influence of Stoicism on Roman jurisprudence. The theme is familiar and has been often handled ; but it is worth while here briefly to indicate and account for this alliance, and suggest the result for slavery.

Ius gentium originally meant 'the usage of the world, of all mankind,' 'such customs or usages as the Romans found in the experience which they would pick up away from Italy in war or commerce or travel, or in their intercourse with *peregrini* in Italy itself to be universally observed,' and this is the meaning of the word throughout its history. To the jurists of the second century B.C. *ius gentium* was 'formally distinguished from *ius civile* as universal, informal, often unwritten usage to special, formal, recorded enactments.'[2] But in the two centuries in which we are interested the *ius gentium* had acquired even greater significance. It had come to be regarded as the model, not yet perfect, which all actual law attempts to imitate. For

---

[1] For law, see *Dig. loc. cit.* and elsewhere. For slaves themselves, see Dess. *passim*, but for examples, *contubernalis*, 1611, 1786, 1950, 7400 ; *coniunx* (wife), 1539, 2906, 7392, 7402, 7864 ; (husband), 1759 ; *maritus*, 1510 ; *mater*, 7401, 7430 ; *pater*, 1517, 7430, 8438 ; *filius*, 1515, 1516, 1657, 4381, 7864, 8082 ; *soror*, 7430 ; *filia*, 3507 ; *frater*, 1809. So, too, the literature, e.g. *uxor* Colum. xii. 1 ; Apul. *Met.* viii. 22. Dess. 8438 gives 'pater carissimus et conservus' ; cf. 7887.

[2] Henry Nettleship, *Journal of Philology*, vol. xiii. p. 179.

this there were two chief reasons. The historic Greek controversy of φύσις and νόμος had drawn attention to the arbitrary nature of human regulations, and had set in distinction to
imperfect and localized rules the conception of a universal code
established by nature, simple and easy, but smothered by man-
made convention, surrendered by man long ago, but still
capable of recovery. On this distinction Greek Stoicism had
fastened ; and ' to live according to nature ' sums up the same
ideal as it was transferred to Roman soil, where it found, foreign
as it was, a ready reception in conservative circles anxious to
retain simple Italian manners in the face of foreign influences.
Further, Rome had come into contact with civilizations and
legal codes more highly developed than her own ; the diversity
of law and custom had been forced upon her notice as she tried
to govern province after province. The edict of the praetor
was, therefore, compelled more and more to enlarge its scope
so as to include within it practices long established elsewhere
but new to Rome.

    And so, in conservative and legal circles under the Empire,
the belief was established that the formerly despised *ius gentium*,
now so much enlarged, was really an approximation to the *ius
naturale*, which mankind had lost sight of. It was the fate,
therefore, of civil law to be gradually superseded by *ius gentium*
as more of the *ius naturale* was recovered ; and so the conception
of natural law, as in philosophy, so in jurisprudence, had a
simplifying, a unifying, and a levelling effect. The ground
common to the lawyer and the philosopher is obvious ; at the
same time, the alliance is one of growth ; the change in the
lawyers' attitude to *ius gentium* was not instantaneous ; Stoicism
did not make an immediate convert, nor can philosophy claim
the whole credit, for experience in world-government was a
profound teacher. Nor, as Maine points out, is it wise ' to
measure the influence of Stoicism on Roman law by counting
up the number of legal rules which can confidently be affiliated
on Stoical dogmas. . . . The influence on jurisprudence of the
Greek theories which had their most distinct expression in
Stoicism consisted not in the number of specific positions which
they contributed to Roman law, but in the single fundamental
assumption which they lent to it.' Further, it must be remembered that the body of Roman law was not evolved theo-

retically from a few Stoic first principles ; Stoicism merely
influenced the growth of a body born long before Stoicism was
thought of, and still developing on its own lines. Therefore,
when the Roman lawyer asserts that ' all men are equal,' he
means, in Maine's words, ' that under the hypothetical law of
Nature and in so far as positive law approximates to it, the
arbitrary distinctions which the Roman civil law maintained
between classes of persons cease to have a legal existence.'
' The jurists who thus expressed themselves most certainly
never intended to censure the social arrangements under which
civil law fell somewhat short of its speculative type.' Obviously
they did not, for they define most clearly the barriers separating
men. The main influence of Stoicism on law, therefore, is to
be found not so much in special enactments of Stoic Emperors
—and there it is clear—as in a certain broad spirit of interpretation by which older law, ambiguously expressed in the
first instance or modified by later rule so as to become ambiguous, and cases unprovided for by rule, or hard and oppressive
because of special circumstances, are dealt with in a sympathetic
way which is biased in favour of humanity and liberty, because
these are in accordance with the ideal *ius naturale*. Several
cases of *favor libertatis* have been mentioned in the foregoing
chapters ; most occur in rather technical legal processes where
Stoicism was able to insert itself between the chinks of the legal
armour. Thus, under the *lex Iunia Petronia*, when the votes
of the jury were equal in a *causa liberalis*, freedom was to be
given. The child of a slave-woman is to be free if the mother
is freed between conception and birth.[1] The unborn child is
to be regarded as born if it is to be for his good, as unborn if for
his disadvantage. So, too, Hadrian abolished the rule under
the SC. Claudianum, by which in special circumstances the
mother might be free, but the child a slave.[2] The disinclina-
tion of the lawyers to assume that a testator intended that the
families of slaves should be broken up, has already been noticed,
and the growing tendency to recognize slave-relationships as
valid and permanent has also been observed. It is possible
that here, in particular, the influence of Stoicism is to be traced,

---

[1] Paul, ii. 24. 3 : ' Media tempora libertati prodesse, non nocere
possunt.'

[2] *v. supra*, p. 14.

for Stoicism set the utmost value upon the unit of the family. The old law remained, however, in essentials ; the slave was still a *res* ; but whenever new law had to be made, or old law revised, the humane spirit of Stoicism crept in.

Such is the irony of the fate determining what of ancient literature and art shall perish, what shall survive, that, in order to discover how slaves lived, recourse must be had to the inscriptions commemorating their deaths. It may be that, if all literature had survived, little would have been discovered therein to reveal intimately the hopes and feelings and affections of slaves ; possibly, however, some autobiography, some brilliant sketch revealing as clearly life in the *familia* as Petronius depicts the society of freedmen, possibly the musings of some slave-philosopher or the novel of a realist writer, another Apuleius, would be in our hands to give guidance in the interpretation of the bare statements of the monuments, and to add homely details and graphic touches which else must be left to the varying guesses of our imaginations. For to write a character-sketch of any slave who lived is impossible ; individuals are known, some brief details of their life or character are recorded, but, until in a relatively few cases they emerge into freedom and notoriety, they remain shadowy types rather than persons. Any full-length portrait, if it had to be attempted, would necessarily be composite, like Apelles' statue, unless, indeed, Apuleius' fiction may be taken as founded on fact. Fotis is no reputable character—so much may be said at once—but she alone of all the slave-women whom we know really lives. Strong and buxom, she is a real maid of all work ; kitchen-maid and waitress, she receives the guest visiting her master, carries up his luggage, brings oil and towels, guides him to the nearest baths, sees to the stabling of his horse, for which she buys oats and hay. Her comeliness is irresistible ; her white apron and crimson girdle serve only to set off her crowning glory, her hair ; ' but in my Fotis not her studied care thereof but rather its disorderliness did increase her beauty ; her rich tresses hung gently about her shoulders, and were dispersed abroad upon every part of her neck, hanging from the nape, and fell fairly down enwound in a kerchief, until at last they were trussed up upon her crown in a knot.' Indeed, so glorious was her hair that it inspired a page of excellent writing on women's hair in general. 'Behold it encountereth with the beams of the sun like swift lightning, or doth swiftly reflect them back again, or changeth clean contrary.' 'Finally, there is such dignity in the hair that whatsoever she be, though she be never so bravely attired with gold, silks, precious stones, and other rich and gorgeous ornaments, yet if her hair be not curiously set forth, she cannot seem fair.'[1] To such an attraction Fotis added vivacity and wit ; her replies are quick and clever ; her penitence after leading her lover into danger and her impulsiveness are admirably rendered. The pity of it is that Apuleius does not set her in a context that may be quoted.

From mixed motives of vanity and kindliness the rich and noble families of the Statilii and Volusii and others,[2] not to mention the imperial families, built for their slaves and freedmen elaborate monuments to contain the ashes and record the names and duties of their dependants. These might give a misleading picture of the relation of slaves to one another and to their masters ; for the rich can afford to gratify their whims, and sometimes the whims even of the rich are benevolent. But luckily these *columbaria* are not the sole material ; single stones, single tablets in public monuments, humble epitaphs, roughly carved and badly spelt, testify that the poor master who owned in some cases merely one slave, the patron who had freed his one slave at cost to himself, the wife, the husband and child, the betrothed, the brother—all were anxious from the motive of affection to record their sorrow and pride in the death and character of some one whom they had loved.

'De mortuis nil nisi bonum ' may be required of our piety and our anxiety to meet with a similar leniency, but history demands the good with the bad, and, in being more scrupulously exact, is more callous of feeling. But luckily the exaggeration from which most epitaphs tend to suffer is of less importance in slave inscriptions, and is more easily discounted, if the cynic demands such adjustment ; for it applies not to exploits or conquests magnified or misrepresented, but merely to the strength of human feeling. If we doubt the statement[3] that

[1] Apul. *Met.* ii. 8, 9, 10 ; W. Adlington's translation (1566), reprinted in the Loeb Classical Texts.

[2] Dess. 7407, 7863, etc.

[3] Dess. 1807, of a freedman, ' sine ulla querella.'

a wife lived with her husband for thirty years without a complaint, we may discount it as much as we please, especially as
the husband's view is unrecorded; but the statement remains
to prove at any rate a stable and lasting family life.   If we are
told that ' Papus as long as he lived was dear to his fellow-
slaves,' [1] there seems no reason to suppose that they were led
to write this inscription from any other motive than that of
affection.

Within slavery is to be found as close and affectionate a
family life as in the households of the great—certainly closer
than in imperial circles at many dates.   Of husband and wife
the conventional epithets are used—' incomparabilis, bene-
merens, cara, amans'; [2] of father, ' piissimus, indulgentissimus,
carissimus'; [3] of son, ' dulcissimus, desiderantissimus.' [4]   Long
periods of married life are frequently mentioned; [5]   there is
one delightful couple at Carthage who live to the ages of one
hundred and two, and eighty years.[6]   Generally, but not
always, slaves of the same household marry.   The advantages
are obvious : in the Statilian house Scaeva, a courier, marries
Italia, a spinning-maid ; Pyrrhe, a secretary of Rubria Helvia,
marries P. Rubrius Optatus.[7]   Filial devotion is not lacking.
An assistant accountant in a Government office returns after
long lapse of years to gather together the ashes of ' a most
duteous father.'   ' I have built to you a tomb to be an eternal
abode, that it may be well and worthily believed that you
begot a son.' [8]   So, too, another imperial servant, a freedman,
restores the tomb of his parents who had still remained slaves.[9]
Jucundus, her father, Phyllis, her mother, Chrone, her sister,
bewail the loss of Jucunda, aged fourteen, a laundress—vesti-
plica.[10]   Hilarion pammusus died at the age of fifteen ; yet no
wonder, ' for the gods desired him.' [11]   The death of the son of
a public slave of Beneventum ' left everlasting tears to Carpus,
his father.' [12]   Time has spared the epitaphs even of little
children, who, if they lived but a few months, after nineteen

[1] Dess. 8413.   [2] e.g. 1509.   [3] 1517, 8438.
[4] 1515, 1516.   [5] e.g. thirty-two years, 9049.
[6] 1680.   [7] 7432c, 7400.   [8] 8082a.
[9] 1680.   [10] 7430.
[11] 8482, 'quem di appetiverunt.'
[12] 7671, ' aeternasq(ue) lacrimas reliquit Carpo parenti.'

centuries are still remembered : ' To Eucopion, who lived six months and three days, the sweetest and most charming babe, who, though he could not yet speak, was our joy. L. Curio Terminalis, and Verna and Sosipatra his parents, wrought this monument.'[1] ' Spude, poor wee girl, she lived two years, three months, twenty days.'[2] Epagathus, a public slave, commemorates his three-year-old daughter.[3] A mother and father bewail in six lines of verse their son 'rising four' (' in quartum surgens annum '), who had been carried off by a witch just at the age when he could be a joy to them. The child pathetically warns other parents to guard their children carefully if they would keep their happiness.[4] That such little lives were valued seems to be suggested by the precisely accurate record of another inscription. The small son of Blastus lived six years, nine months, fourteen days, and one hour ; he was born at twelve o'clock on Monday, five days before the Kalends of September, and died at seven o'clock on Saturday, the third day before the Ides of June.[5] And the simplicity of the Latin increases the pathos of the epitaph of Calliste, aged sixteen—'nuptura idibus Oc[t.] moritur IIII idus Oct. Pa[nathen]ais mater pia kar(ae) fil(iae) fec(it).'[6]

Fellow-slaves can write affectionately of one another—' Here lies one whose death proved how true and loyal a friend he was to his friend.'[7] ' We were made slaves at the same time, we served in the same house, we were freed together, and this day which takes you from me is the first which separates us '[8]—and were willing to spend of their savings to honour in death those who were dear to them : ' with his own money ' often reads as a proud boast of loving self-denial ; ' of his poverty ' is the fine admission of Acastus, who dedicates a memorial to Italia, a sempstress and perhaps his betrothed.[9] Hygia, the slave of Flavia Antiochis, perhaps once a slave herself, can afford to put up a *columbarium* with urns and an inscription to her husband and infant daughter ; and she herself is provided with

[1] Dess. 8487.   [2] 8493 'pusinna miserina.'
[3] 9050. He was ' servus publicus ad Iuturna, a statio aquarum,' Dessau says.
[4] 8522.   [5] 8528.   [6] 8529a.   [7] 8418.
[8] 8432 ; cf. Dess. 7354, ' Hilara minor viva rogavit ut ossa sua in olla Midaes conicerentur cum mortua esset.' They were.
[9] 7428.

a memorial after her death by Aulena Nebris, perhaps another ex-slave.[1]

If there was a possibility of such family life for a slave as can be recognized as that of a human being, perhaps there were other elements in that life which gave him something to live for, which suggested to him a sense of his own dignity, however his superiors might humble him, which raised him in his own respect, though he received none elsewhere, and created in him the consciousness that, though he was on the lowest plane of a society minutely differentiated, yet in spite of it life was not so barren as to be impossible.

On the whole it may be said that Roman religion was never hostile to the slave. It did not close the temple doors against him; it did not banish him from its festivals.[2] If slaves were excluded from certain ceremonies,[3] the same may be said of free men and women—men being excluded from the rites of Bona Dea, Vesta, and Ceres, women from those of Hercules at the Ara Maxima. In the days when the old Roman divinities counted for something, the slave came to be informally included in the family, and could consider himself under the protection of the gods of the household. The old festival of the Saturnalia, though it may have been modified under Greek influence, even in its primitive form probably commanded that reversal of the positions of slave and free which was its most marked characteristic later.[4] The Matronalia on March 1 similarly commanded that mistresses should wait on their slaves, while the thirteenth of August was a slaves' holiday.[5] There is tolerable evidence that slaves were sometimes manumitted in the temple of

[1] Dess. 7919.   [2] Boissier, *Rel. rom.* ii. 318.

[3] Cf. Min. Fel. 22. Slaves were forbidden to set foot in the temple of Leucothea, Plut. *Aet. Rom.* 267D, where more details are given. When Claudius offered *obsecratio*, 'summota operariorum servorumque turba,' Suet. *Claud.* 22. On the other hand, the whole populace took part in a *supplicatio*.

[4] See Warde Fowler, *Social Life*, p. 290. For this feature of the Saturnalia, see the reff. given, Marquardt, *Le Culte*, ii. 384, and add Sen. *Ep.* xviii. 1, complaining that the whole year is now December; Petr. 58; Script. hist. aug. *Ver.* vii. 5.

[5] Marquardt, *Le Culte*, ii. 373 (and add Plut. *Aet. Rom.* 287E). The day was sacred to Diana in Aventino, and it was a slaves' holiday because, according to Festus, Servius Tullius dedicated a temple on that day; according to Plutarch, he was born on that day.

Feronia—an ancient Italian goddess.[1] Augustus ordered that freedwomen should be eligible as priestesses of Vesta.[2] The law insisted that a slave's grave should be regarded as sacred,[3] and for his soul Roman mythology provided no special heaven and no particular hell. Even Juvenal agrees that the slave, soul and body, is made of the same stuff as his master,[4] and Statius is willing to transport a favourite slave belonging to his friend from slavery to Elysium in two hundred and thirty-four lines, while an imperial freedman accomplishes the same journey in one hundred and six lines.[5]

This does not carry us far in determining whether religion meant anything to the individual slave. Once more the evidence comes from inscriptions ; and here the ancient gods of Rome are far to seek. Jupiter, Juno, Silvanus, and the rest occur, but often with strange titles, which show that the Italian deity has been identified with an Eastern counterpart. But most slave inscriptions are dedicated to gods who are patently foreign, and since slaves were generally of foreign race, this is only to be expected.[6] It cannot be said that the State was opposed to the practice of these religions ; during the course of these two centuries it had to broaden its policy considerably ; provided that a cult was not dangerous socially or morally or politically, and reciprocated 'the State toleration with an equal toleration of its own,'[7] then no obstacle was offered. And, as the State granted licences more and more freely to colleges and was especially indulgent to the colleges of the poor—*collegia tenuiorum*—the slave found no difficulty in the practice of whatever cult he had brought from the East or learnt from parent or friend or college.

It is impossible not to be struck by the simple piety of many of the inscriptions. From Rome to distant frontiers

[1] Serv. *Aen.* viii. 564. See Warde Fowler, *Roman Festivals*, pp. 199, 253.

[2] Dio, lv. 22.

[3] *Dig.* xi. 7. 2 ; but contrast the dreadful picture in Hor. *Sat.* i. 8. 8, *eiecta cadavera*.

[4] xiv. 16.

[5] *Silvae*, ii. 1, iii. 4 ; cf. ii. 6 ; cf. the immortality promised to Polybius' brother by Seneca, *ad Polyb.* ix. 8.

[6] For the spread of Oriental religions by slaves, *v. infra*, p. 223.

[7] Hardy, *Christianity and the Roman Government*, p. 13.

prayers rise to a variety of gods, and thanks are offered for prayers answered. In Rome a slave of Caesar, together with his wife and daughter, offer a gift to Bona Dea.[1] In Dacia Callistus *Aug. n. dispensator* prays to Jupiter Dolichenus for the safety of himself and his family.[2] To Silvanus a freedman and a slave pray for the welfare of themselves and their master in seventeen lines of verse which bear resemblance to Ovid and Vergil.[3] In some cases the god has visited his suppliant in a vision, and commanded certain offerings to be made in return for special benefit. Mercurialis, at the command of the divinity itself, set up a marble statue to Mars Augustus, the saviour of his body. He was an official engaged in collecting taxes near Brixen, and perhaps had been compelled at some time to fight for his life.[4] Callistus records a vision granted by Bona Dea,[5] while Sextius Attius Dionysius dedicates a statue complete with base to Sanctus Silvanus at the god's command ; he had prayed for freedom, and the god had granted it.[6] Another slave makes a bargain with Bona Dea for his freedom, ' ser(vus) vovit, leiber solvit.' [7] To the same goddess Felix, a public slave, fulfils his vow upon the restoration of his sight ; the doctors had given him up, but after ten months he had been healed.[8]

In some cases the god chosen is appropriate to the trade or occupation of the worshipper, fishermen praying to Neptune,[9] a head gardener—*vilicus hortorum*—and a forest-ranger— *saltuarius*—to Silvanus,[10] but there is little such specialization, since many of the gods, in taking over new characteristics, have lost the significance of the old.[11] If the cost of the offerings is any indication of piety, then slaves ' in proportion to their poverty ' were pious indeed. Statues, shrines, temples are dedicated and restored by slaves providing the money singly or together ; at Aequiculi a shrine to Serapis and Isis, at Nepete five altars to Feronia, at Asisium a temple to Jupiter Paganicus ; [12]

---

[1] Dess. 3507. [2] 3014.
[3] 3530 ; for prayers for masters, cf. 3197, ' Mercur(io) invic(to) sacr. pro salute Praesentis n. [S]agaris act. e[ius]' ; 3645, 3663.
[4] 3160. [5] 3503. [6] 3526. [7] 3491.
[8] 3513 : '. . . ob luminibus restitutis derelictus a medicis.'
[9] 3287. [10] 3521 sq.
[11] e.g. the titles of Silvanus include *sanctus, castrensis, domesticus, erbarius, felix, invictus, Pantheus, conservator, custos, silvestris.*
[12] 4381 (A.D. 172), 3481, 3039.

to Mithras marble altars are regularly erected by slaves,[1] and in one or two cases even the completely furnished chapel—*spelaeum cum omni apparatu*—is due to their generosity.[2] The marble group representing the *tauroctonia*, and now in the British Museum, was dedicated by Alcimus *servus vilicus* about A.D. 102 ; at Nersae in Aequiculis Apronianus *arcarius reipublicae* restored a chapel 'on behalf of the welfare of the Council and the people.'[3]

Though Eastern deities broke down opposition in Rome and Italy so successfully that they were enthroned beside the ancient Italian gods, the same cannot be said of Judaism and its offshoot Christianity. Into the reasons for the feud between Rome and Judaism, it is impossible to enter here. That there were many slaves among the adherents of Judaism is only to be expected, and is proved by the periodical expulsion from Rome of freedmen and others who practised Jewish customs.[4] But though Judaism made some converts, especially in circles where it was fashionable to gain some amusement from dabbling in new superstitions, it leaves little intimate record of itself in the literature or the inscriptions.[5] Christianity, however, was notoriously spread by slaves ; it is alike the reproach of its persecutors, and the glory of its apologists. In the *Octavius* of Minucius Felix, Caecilius the pagan taunts Christianity with having collected the dregs of the people, mere ignorant men and women, paupers ; but the charge of poverty is caught up by Octavius: 'This is not a reproach but a glory ; can he be poor who is rich in God ? '[6] Indeed, the early churches contributed to a fund from which grants may have been made to ransom

[1] e.g. Cumont, *Les monuments relatifs aux mystères de Mithras*, Inscr. Nos. 48, 53, 67, 68, 144, 202, 204, 245, 538a.

[2] Cumont, 175, 312a.

[3] *Op. cit.* 69=Dess. 4199 : 153, c. A.D. 172.

[4] Tiberius expelled 4000 freedmen, Tac. *Ann.* ii. 85 ; cf. Suet. *Claud.* 25, for a similar expulsion ; cf. the story of Clemens and Domitilla under Domitian.

[5] e.g. Waltzing, *Etude historique sur les corporations professionelles*, iv. 236, gives only two examples of *communautés juives*—one at Rome, one at Brixia. At Pompeii a wine-jar was found with the name M. Valerius Abinnericus—Jewish or Syrian, according to Mau-Kelsey, *Pompeii*, p. 18. Maria and Martha appear on wall-inscriptions, though 'Maria' as a name is not conclusive evidence of Jewish blood.

[6] cc. 8 and 36.

slaves who were Christians.[1] The proper names mentioned in the Pauline epistles would by themselves be sufficient evidence,[2] and the roll of martyrs contained the names of the slave-girls Blandina and Felicitas, ' who were celebrated in the festivals of the Church with honours denied to the most powerful and noblest born of mankind.'

The secret of the maintenance and spread of these Oriental religions is to be found in the institution of the *collegia*, which are of great importance for the private life of the slave ; for they extend their services beyond the province of religion, and in many cases must have furnished most of what made life worth living for him.   Though strictly all colleges were required to be licensed, in practice the growth of ' colleges of the poor ' was tolerated by the State ; indeed, it may be said that their rapid increase left no alternative.   Before joining a college a slave was compelled to obtain his master's leave, which seems   to   have   been   granted   readily.[3]   Slave-rebellions, therefore,   cannot   have   constituted   a   real   menace ;   the very   liberty   of   association   suggests   both   the   comparative contentment of the slave and the realization, first by the master, then by the State, that slaves must be tolerably well treated.[4]

It is not easy to differentiate the functions of a college. With the cult of a god there are generally combined opportunities for social meeting and dinners, while in many cases the college made provision for the funerals of its members.   It joined, therefore, the functions of a church, a social club, a craft-guild, and a funeral society.   Thus, it is in these inscriptions that most of our information about the private life of the slave may be found.   Unfortunately for this essay, the subject is of singular attraction ; but here all that can be done is to

[1] Tert. *Apol.* 39 ; for Christianity in every grade of society, see Tert. *Apol.* 1 and 37 ; *Ad Scap.* 5.

[2] Cf. Lightfoot on *Philippians*, p. 172.   Clement was probably a freedman or slave of the Flavian family.

[3] *Dig.* xlvii. 22. 3. 2.

[4] For these *collegia*, see Boissier, *Rel. rom.* ii. 238 sqq. ; de Marchi, *Il culto privato di Roma antica*, vol. ii. ; T. Schiess, *Die römischen collegia funeraticia* ; and see Hardy, *Christianity and the Roman Government*, for the law concerning them, and their influence in the spread of Christianity.

pick out a few examples which will give some indication of what the college meant to the slave.

True to Roman conservatism and Roman love of the collegiate system of control, the college modelled its organization upon that of the township, just as the township took Rome as its pattern. Some colleges were confined to free men, others to freedmen and slaves, others to slaves alone ; but it is possible to find all classes blended together. Wherever slaves are to be found in the same college as free men, they suffer no disability ; in a college election their vote is of equal worth, and they rise to office, frequently taking precedence over free men. They serve as *magistri* and *ministri,* as *curatores, decuriones,* and *praefecti,* and so on.[1] They were hardly likely to become *patroni,* for the duties of patron—and the list of patrons of one college is often long—involved considerable outlay of money in return for the honour ; in colleges of slaves and freedmen rich freedmen like Trimalchio were frequently invited to stand, and in many cases accepted the office in more than one college. The functions of the other officials were not very arduous ; the *curator* in some cases was responsible for the admission of new members, for the distribution of surplus funds and the execution of decrees ; the *magister* offered sacrifice,[2] convened the meeting and presided ; he took an oath before entering office and rendered accounts on leaving it, and was liable to a fine for mismanagement.[3] All very trivial ; but the slave most certainly derived some satisfaction from holding office in a society where free men were his subordinates, and, being debarred from politics or local affairs, he enjoyed the management of his college's business, and gained some sense of his own dignity and importance. Particularly in the cult of Mithras the equality of slave and free is apparent ; here master and slave join in offering to the deity a tablet or a shrine, and the names of both are recorded together.[4] Here, too, slaves may be found occupying exalted position in the hierarchy, being initiated

---

[1] Cf. Waltzing, *op. cit.* iv. 251 sqq., 356, etc. Occasionally women are found holding office, e.g. Dess. 7882d.

[2] Cf. lex coll. Dianae et Antinoi, Bruns, p. 388.

[3] Cf. lex coll. Aesculap., Bruns, p. 391.

[4] Cf. Cumont, No. 464, ' in honorem domus divinae deo invicto Mithrae Axius Verus Q. Vetius et Probinus Veri votum solverunt libentes merito.

into mysteries for which the rich and the noble might not be considered worthy.[1]

But the majority of slaves seem to have belonged to colleges which were composed of freedmen and slaves only, and drew their membership from many quarters or from one large household only.   The slaves and freedmen of Caesar naturally group themselves together into colleges : slaves and freedmen working in mines or quarries, on imperial domains, as personal attendants of the Emperor, couriers, gladiators, clerks, and accountants—wherever in Rome or the provinces the imperial servants are to be found, there traces may be found of associations which provided social reunion, common worship, and a fitting monument at death.   At Rome the slaves of the great families were numerous enough to make their own colleges ; the household of Scribonia, of Livia, Octavia, Marcella minor,[2] of the Statilii, and the Volusii are the most conspicuous cases, but inscriptions show that scores of lesser households scattered over the Empire contained similar associations.   Even in them, small as they often are, the same orderliness and love of organization appear ; a Charter is drawn up, patrons elected, officers chosen,[3] funds administered, fines imposed, lands bought, shrines and monuments erected, complimentary decrees carved in lasting stone. Of these humble colleges there is ample evidence, fragmentary indeed, but yielding rich results to patient study.   In some cases, however, lengthy portions of the Charter have been preserved, and one of these—the *Lex collegii funeraticii Lanuvini* [4]—will furnish illustration of the rest, though the college is not confined to slaves.   The college was founded in A.D. 133, and in 136 its meeting-place was the temple of Diana and Antinous at Lanuvium.   The preamble opens with the record of a gift, followed by a quotation from a decree of the Senate which authorizes burial clubs, prayers for the safety of the Emperor, and an exhortation to members to pay their subscriptions regularly that the club may fulfil its purpose, and may flourish for long

[1] e.g. Cum. 28 (A.D. 184)=Dess. 4203 ; Cum. 157=Dess. 4215, *pater eonum.*   Cum. 157 gives a case of a public slave of Sentinum in a college otherwise containing no slaves.

[2] Dess. 7879 sqq. e.g.

[3] The epitaphs of slaves show their pride in these offices; e.g. 7353, 7354.

[4] Dess. 7212. Bruns, p. 388.

years. New members are advised to read the rules carefully, that later there may be no ground for complaint.[1] Soon, however, the language changes to the solemn formulae of Roman law. *Placuit universis*, that new members shall pay an entrance fee and a flagon of good wine and contribute five asses each month, that any member whose subscription is in arrears for two months be not entitled to the benefits of the college, that three hundred sesterces be paid to the heir on the death of a member, that fifty sesterces be divided among those who attend the funeral. If a member died within twenty miles of Lanuvium, three members, who received a fee for their service, arranged for the burial. If the death occurred beyond this radius, the person arranging the funeral received this grant. Whenever a member who was a slave died and his body was withheld by master or mistress, then he was to have the honour of a *funus imaginarium*. Every slave-member on manumission was to present to the college a flagon of good wine. The president, appointed in turn as his name was entered on the roll, paid a fine if he failed to provide a dinner for the club. Then follow rules as to the fare to be provided, the honours [2] to be paid to ex-presidents who have served the college well. Further it is resolved that any complaint or business should be brought forward at a business meeting, that on holy days the feast may go forward quietly and merrily.[3] At this feast no member may quit his place to make a disturbance nor cause uproar or insult a fellow-member under penalty of a fine of twelve sesterces ; an insult to the president cost twenty sesterces.

Such are the rules governing the poorest of colleges, too poor to erect a *columbarium* or to buy ground for burial ; hence the grant of funeral expenses. But many even of the slave colleges were richer and built *columbaria* or bought land, and slave-members either gave complete shrines or bought an urn to contain the ashes of their relations. Thus a *verna* gives a complete *columbarium*, another has built for himself and his posterity a shrine enclosed by railings, adorned with brass

[1] ' Et sic intra ne postmodum queraris.'

[2] Which included ' ex omnibus divisionibus partes duplas.'

[3] ' Item placuit si quis quid queri aut referre volet, in conventu referant, ut quieti e[t] hilares diebus sollemnibus epulemur.'

ornaments and containing a burial urn of onyx.[1] When another college dedicated its sepulchre, Tata, who was the first *curator*, provided a miniature gladiatorial show, besides furnishing the interior equipment of the *columbarium*.[2] For the whole staff Eumaeus, a *dispensator*, erects a sepulchre; Ianuarius *Augusti servus* and Atilia Eustasia restore the fabric of another which had fallen into decay.[3] To such quotation there is no end.

Thus the college provided means for good fellowship in life, and the certainty of a decent burial and the crowning glory of an epitaph ; and in this last the slave found a melancholy pleasure. It is not so much the fear of death which seems to haunt these obscure people as the thought that from being obscure they should pass away leaving no trace that they have existed. More than one benefaction was made to ensure that money should be provided in the form of interest on a capital sum to maintain a tomb and keep alive the memory of the benefactor for all time.[4] It is on respect to the tomb that the legends insist ; as to what the future holds they show no curiosity. ' Whosoever has placed a lighted lamp on this tomb, him may golden earth cover.'[5] ' May whosoever removes this epitaph meet with the anger of the shades of those who lie here.'[6] As for the future, ' May the earth lie lightly upon thee,' is the commonest wish ; ' Non fueram non sum ; nescio, non ad me pertinet,' is the confession of another slave ;[7] another complains, ' Fortune makes many promises to many; she fulfils them to none. Live for the day, live for the hour, for nothing is thine own ' ;[8] while ' Superi vivite, valete ! inferi, havete, recipite Nicenem '[9] contains more hope than most. A club of the members of the Statilian house called themselves by the mournful name of ' Comrades in death.'[10] One epitaph[11] may be quoted in full :

---

[1] Dess. 7886, 7930.   [2] 7884.

[3] 7853 and 7856 ; cf. sqq.

[4] Cf. Petr. 71, where Trimalchio appoints a freedman to take care of his tomb. *Custos monumenti* occurs in the inscriptions.

[5] Dess. 8132.   [6] 8199.   [7] 8165.

[8] 7976.   [9] 8129b.

[10] 7360, *commorientes*.

[11] 1710 ; and see *Hermes*, i. 344, and *Revue de Philologie*, 1879, pp. 88–90, for a discussion of the very interesting Latin.

SACRED TO THE SHADES

of	of
FLAVIA ANTIGONA, who is alive, and may her life long be spared to me.	VITALIS, our Emperor's courier, who is alive, and may his life be long with her.

While still Vitalis and enjoying vitality, I built myself a tomb, and every time I pass I read with these two eyes my epitaph. I have ranged the whole countryside on foot as courier ; with hounds I have hunted hares and foxes withal, and afterwards drained welcome tankards of drink. Much that youth does I have done ; for some day I shall die. Do you, young man, if you are wise, build a tomb for yourself while you still live.

But not every sepulchral inscription is such cheerful reading. Some record tragedies sad enough : a small boy drowned in a fish-pond, another bitten by a viper, a freedman returning to a burning building and crushed by a falling wall, a *verna* trampled to death in a crowd.[1]

Besides the recreation offered by his college, the slave was at liberty to go to the theatre and the games.[2] There he followed the success of a school of gladiators and joined in demanding the death of those who disappointed him. He knew a good gladiator and could size up his points ; one of the freedmen at Trimalchio's banquet complains that a magistrate produced some feeble twopenny-halfpenny gladiators whom you could have blown over.[3] In the circus he followed the fortunes of the rival factions, and clamoured for the manumission of slave charioteers who pleased him ;[4] he knew the names, ages, and pedigrees of the horses,[5] scribbled their names on the walls of shop or room with prayers for their victory, as at Pompeii, or made bets on the prospects at the next games.[6] Inns and cookshops were a favourite resort ; the decadent noble is said by Juvenal to keep company there with runaway slaves and others of less reputable character, while Eumolpus in quest of a runaway is on the point of searching the cookshops for him.[7]

---

[1] Dess. 8518, 8521, 8520, 8524.

[2] Colum. i. 8. 2.   [3] Petr. 45.   [4] Dio, lxix. 16.

[5] Marquardt, *Le Culte*, ii. 297, n. 5.

[6] Cf. Petr. 70, where a slave invites Trimalchio to make a bet ' si prasinus proximis circensibus primam palmam.'

[7] Juv. viii. 172 ; cf. xi. 81. Petr. 98.

The freedman, and no doubt the slave, could criticize his township's magistrates, and deplore the passing of the good old days when men were men ; the graffiti of Pompeii record his love affairs, and lengthy *tabulae defixionum* his hates, which were not confined to personal enemies. A public slave of Tuder had written up imprecations on the tombs of decurions, local senators, and a solemn supplication and thanksgiving was made to Jupiter Optimus Maximus Custos Conservator for preserving the city and the order from destruction.[1]

Meantime the slave was still a slave. Nevertheless, it is possible to exaggerate the gulf separating him from the rest of society. In outward appearance he did not differ from the free man ; neither colour nor clothing revealed his condition ; he witnessed the same games as the free man; he shared in the life of the municipal towns, even contributing what he was allowed, and sometimes at least sharing equally in bequests made to it,[2] even though the bequest was only a gift of nuts to be scrambled for by the children of the town, slave and free.[3] And often apparent equality in outward things counts for more to the individual than actual identity of rights before the law. Between the slave and the free there seems often to have been little social barrier. Pallas, it is true, a freedman himself, signifies his wishes by a nod or a gesture to his slaves that he might not degrade his voice in the presence of such ;[4] but not every freedman was imperial, nor every imperial freedman a Pallas. On the contrary, we have seen slaves and freedmen working together in factory and office, sitting as fellow-members of the same college, and sharing the expenses of offering or tomb.[5] The truth is that any real gulf between slave and freed would have divided families. Marriage between slave and freed[6] and even free was very common, and relationship between these grades was too manifest to be ignored. Some of these cases are remarkable, especially that of Oriens, a public slave of Saepinum. Oriens, together with his wife Thalia, his

[1] Dess. 3001, ' . . . sceleratissimi servi publici infando latrocinio. . . .'
[2] e.g. Dess. 5672, 5673.
[3] 6271, ' sparsio . . . pueris plebeis sine distinctione libertatis.'
[4] Tac. *Ann.* xiii. 23.   [5] Cf., e.g., 1623, 1634.
[6] e.g. Dess. 7392, ' Prepon et Minucia ☊ lib. Caletyche ' ; 1787, ' Secunda lib.' and ' Epigonus Caesaris Aug. sutor.'

fellow-slave, dedicate a monument to L. Saepinius Oriens, a *sevir Augustalis*, his father, and to L. Saepinius Orestes, a *quattuorvir* of the town, his brother. Thus, while Oriens and his wife are slaves, his father is a dignitary of the same town, and his brother is a magistrate.[1] Nor were slaves thought unworthy of a place in the same vault with their master's family ; L. Arruntius Stachyus erected a tomb for his wife and son and Hygia, a *verna*. A freedman of the Emperor dedicated in A.D. 149 an elaborate monument to Yacinthus his *verna*, himself, his children, and freedmen and freedwomen and their posterity.[2] Such inscriptions, and they are by no means isolated cases, suggest that the literature presents on the whole a somewhat one-sided view of the relations between slave and freed ; if it refers chiefly to Rome, its witness is not true of the country towns.

We have seen that the prospects before the slave offer sometimes misery and poverty, sometimes happiness ; his life may be empty or full, and in the distance lay the hope of manumission. It is possible, however, that often manumission made life harder ; independence must often have been bought dearly. ' You don't realize the cares of a master,' says Martial to Condylus, ' or the advantages of a slave's life. You sleep well on a rug ; your master lies awake on a bed of down. You salute no one—not even your master ; he salutes in fear and trembling a number of patrons. You have no debts; he is burdened with them. Do you fear the torturer ? he is a martyr to gout.'[3] And though no author more often refers to the brandmarks on the forehead of a slave than Martial, there is something in this point of view ; given a tolerable master, the slave could be sure of a living, enjoying the pleasures of the moment, careless of the future, leaving responsibility to others. Yet then, as now, a struggling independence was generally preferred : relying upon his *peculium*, the slave started out upon some enterprise of his own ; he succeeded, or he lived, or he drew free corn in Rome. If he prospered, he could sometimes thank the system of slavery, as the freedman in Petronius ; if he failed, he could

---

[1] Dess. 6519. The solution is that Oriens' father was freed by the town ; the brother was born after the father's freedom ; therefore office was open to him. 1480, father a freedman, son Caesaris *verna* ; 1497, father a slave, son freed.

[2] 8138, 8364.   [3] Mart. ix. 93.

blame it, quoting, if he liked, Dio Chrysostom : ' It is characteristic of slaves to be quite incapable of helping themselves.' [1]
Philosophers might discuss the nature of true liberty, proving
that the slave could enjoy greater freedom than the powerful
monarch ; that such precepts fell upon unheeding ears is shown
by the history of Manumission.

[1] xxxiv. 53R : τὸ μὲν γὰρ ἐφ' ἅπαν ἀποστῆναι τοῦ βοηθεῖν αὐτοῖς ἀνδραπόδων
ἐστίν.

CHAPTER VI1

MANUMISSION

ἢ τοὺς μὲν δούλους δι' αὐτὸ τοῦτο μάλιστα ἐλευθεροῦμεν, ὅπως ὡς πλείστους ἐξ αὐτῶν πολίτας ποιώμεθα;

Dio Cass. lvi. 7. 6.

'GAIUS JULIUS MYGDONIUS, a Parthian by race, born free, but captured in the age of youth; he was handed over into Roman territory and was made a Roman citizen.'[1] Yet Gaius' Parthian kinsmen were still in arms against the Empire.

Not many years before, loyal Italians had turned against Rome to wrest from her the rights of citizenship. Under the Empire, auxiliaries had to endure long military service, and the leading men of municipal towns spent their fortunes in works of public use to obtain local magistracies,[2] and obtained those same Roman rights. Pliny, wishing to reward his physician, can think of no higher gift, but he had to beg it of an Emperor's generosity.[3] Yet a master can bestow full membership of the State upon a foreign slave.

Was it good for the slave suddenly to emerge from bondage into citizenship, for the master to have the power of citizen-making, for the State to be forced to receive these new members ?

If the early republican legislators could have foreseen the problems of the future, perhaps they would have curtailed the right of the master to confer high status on his manumitted slave. But the right, once given, is difficult to recall ; the rights

[1] Dess. 1980.
[2] For exx. v. Dess. 1982, 'c(iuitatem) R(omanam) per h[ono]rem ii. vir. consecuti'; 6680, 'per aedilitatis gradum in curiam nostram admitterentur et per hoc civitatem Romanam apiscerentur'; cf. Lex. Salpens., cap. xxi.
[3] Plin. *Ep.* x. 6, 7, 11, 106, 107.

173

of the paterfamilias are involved. And if the State were to claim the sole right to manumit into citizenship, it could only be guided in the last resort by the judgment of the owner as to the slave's fitness. But, as slaves increased and were more often freed, the political bearing of manumission became evident; the Republic saw long struggles on the subject of the libertine vote in the tribes, and attempts were made to diminish its influence. But no modification of the principle that manumission gave citizenship was ever made till the evils of too lavish a bestowal of it had long made themselves apparent. By that time the tribes had ceased to be of any political importance, and, even though an inroad was being made upon the authority of the head of the family, many of those heads agreed with the measures of the Emperor when he sought to limit the gift of citizenship and to strengthen the control of the patron over his freedman.

The motives for manumission are not far to seek. At one end may be put the farcically elaborate scene in Petronius, where a slave-acrobat falls and jars Trimalchio's arm. Fortunata, Trimalchio's wife, rushes up in a terror of alarm; doctors hurry to the place. 'My suspicion was not far wrong': it was all a plot that the wounded hero might magnanimously forgo punishment and free the fellow on the spot. It must never be said that so great a man was injured by a slave![1] Midway come other reasons: slaves were expensive to keep; an impoverished family manumitted to avoid the expense of maintenance, while at the same time retaining some service from their freedmen. Scaevinus, when trying to justify the events of the night of the plot against Nero, urged that he freed his slaves not because that night might be his last if the plot failed, but because his poverty was unable to keep them, and he was afraid that his will, which gave his slaves liberty, would become invalid.[2] Or, dying slaves were freed; scant consolation to be given on their death-beds the freedom denied to them through life! Yet it was valued. Martial freed Demetrius, his *amanuensis*, as he lay dying at the age of nineteen. 'Even as he was sinking he was conscious of his reward, and called me patron,

[1] Petr. 54; cf. 41, where Trimalchio frees a slave impersonating Bacchus, with the words, 'Dionyse, liber esto.' Trimalchio valued his slaves cheap or his jests dear.
[2] Tac. *Ann.* xv. 54.

he who was soon to travel a free man to the waters of the underworld.'[1] Did manumission, then, alter his lot after life ? Perhaps ; but it often affected the fate of his kin on earth. At the other end are countless cases of real gratitude to slaves for long service or signal achievement. Or slaves were freed with a view to marriage—'Flavia Aphrodisia patrono et conjugi benemerenti,' reads a typical epitaph [2]—and very often by time-expired soldiers.[3]

That such gratitude was shown need provoke no cynical surprise. Even Aristotle had to surrender logic, and manumitted in his death the slaves whom he had once classed as a race apart. The Roman was even less likely to feel the claim of consistency. If he had little of logic in his theory of slavery, he, too, no less than Aristotle, sometimes had a heart. Yet he was no sentimentalist ; a certain grasp of the main point kept him sane. And therefore manumission was often given by will, or as a trust to be carried out by the heir on coming into the property.

Manumission by will had advantages : [4] it retained the services of slaves to the very last moment in which their owner could use them ; it kept the slave in a suspense of good conduct to the end. Trimalchio made no secret of the provisions of his will. ' My object in making them known is simply that my household may love me as if I were dead.' [5] The manumitter departed from life in a comfortable glow of self-righteousness, which he may have earned by this one deed ; he could rely on the grudging gratitude of those who may have hated him, and could trust that a suitable gathering of mourners would lend more than mere respectability to his funeral. ' He was well mourned ; he had freed a few slaves, you see, though his

---

[1] ' Sensit deficiens sua praemia, meque patronum Dixit ad infernas liber iturus aquas,' Mart. i. 102. Dess. 7842 gives a case of manumission on the day of death ; cf. Petr. 65.

[2] 1519 ; cf. 1552.

[3] Cf. Dess. 2049, 2110. For such marriage, cf. Philostr. *Vit. Ap.* viii. 30 ; and Orelli, 6404, quoted by Boissier, *Rel. rom.* ii. 347 : ' I freed her for nothing ; she has gone off with a lover ; she has deceived her master.'

[4] Professor Buckland believes that nine-tenths of manumissions were by will.

[5] Petr. 71. Trimalchio was cut out of his foresters' wills *cum elogio*, 53.

wife's tears flowed rather grudgingly.'[1]   We need not grudge Chrysanthus his mourning, or his slaves their freedom ; Petronius, the author of this brilliant farce, was true to the spirit of it on his death-bed; to some slaves he gave money, to others a flogging.[2]

The frivolity of Petronius or the Trimalchio of his creation is hardly substantial enough for a treatment of manumission by will.   Look rather at the solid fragments of marble still recording the elaborate provisions drawn up by Dasumius[3] in the year A.D. 108.   It is a lengthy document, full of the repetitions of the law.   The quotations given represent a mere fraction of the whole.   After legacies to many friends, including Pliny and Tacitus, the will reads: ' If Eros my valet shall have rendered a satisfactory statement of his office to my heir, let him be free ; so, too, let X and Y be free, unless by any later writing I shall forbid any of them to be free.   Whomsoever I shall so forbid, he shall not be free, nor shall my heir give to him anything to account of the *vicesima* tax,[4] nor pay to the collector of that tax any sum on his behalf.   As for all the rest whom I have ordered to be free, I wish to reserve from my estate what they will owe to the tax-collector on that account ; I leave it as a trust to my heir or heirs to give, assign, and bestow that sum to each separately without any dispute.'

There follow long bequests of money, jewellery, mules, plate, property to freedmen, freedwomen, and others.   The property is tightly tied up so as to produce revenue for Dasumius' freedmen and their issue together or in turn.[5]   ' Further, I ask my heirs and leave it as a trust to all my heirs, but chiefly do I beg it of your goodwill to me, my good friend Servianus, not to allow after my death any of those whom you manumit by will or codicil or any of your freedmen to be laid in my sepulchre, or any of my own freedmen, save Eucolpus and Harmastus and Anatellon.   I wish, however, that all should have right to approach, walk round, and draw close to my monument, all

---

[1] Petr. 42.   [2] Tac. *Ann*. xvi. 19.

[3] Consul about A.D. 103.

[4] Five per cent. on legacies, paid by Roman citizens.

[5] Cf. Buckland, *Textbook*, p. 359 : ' It gives lands to *liberti* with no power to sell or pledge them with a right of accrual or survivorship, and a direction that on the death of the last survivor the lands are to go to *posteri* on the same terms,' etc.

save you, Hymnus, who, though you know that I have done
much for you, have nevertheless shown yourself so thankless,
that as a punishment for what I have suffered or feared at your
hands I order your removal if you trespass upon my sepulchre.' [1]

Manumission by will was easy; it was only necessary to
name or describe the slave, and to assert in some such formula
as ' liber esto ' that he should be free.   If a legacy was to be
bequeathed, then liberty must go with it, if the slave belonged
to the testator; if he was the property of another, a legacy must
stand by itself.[2]   Slaves so freed became *liberti orcini*, the
freedmen of the dead man.

If, however, certain legal restrictions connected with the
validity of a Roman will [3] interfered with the wishes of the
testator, or if a codicil were added after the will were made,
then he had a wider range of powers given to him by the ' trusts '
—*fideicommissa*—which Augustus had made valid.   A trust
was an injunction to the heir; if it was an injunction to free,
then the slave became the freedman of the trustee—an important difference, as will be seen later.   There are many other
minor legal points connected with fideicommissary liberty;
suffice it to say that liberty might be given to others' slaves,
obviously under certain contingencies, and that trusts themselves became restricted by certain legislation to be mentioned
later which applied to wills, but were always less trammelled
than wills proper by formulae and conditions.[4]   The lack of
formality in a trust manumission appears clearly in an inscription found in Sicily.   It is dated A.D. 175, and was copied on the
tomb from a letter.   ' Copy of letter.   Hail to you, father;
farewell to you.   As I dictate this to be sent to you, I guess that

---

[1] 'Testamentum Dasumii.'   Bruns, p. 304; Mommsen, *Ges. Schrr.* i.
442; a fragment is quoted Dess. 8379a, and elsewhere.

[2] An interesting case is given in Pliny, *Ep.* iv. 10.   Pliny and Statius
had been made the heirs of Sabina; she left a legacy to Modestus, her
slave, using the following words: ' Modesto . . . quem liberum esse
iussi.'   She had nowhere commanded the manumission of this slave.
Was he free ?   The lawyers refused to admit it.   Pliny, as a good heir,
freed the slave, on the ground that Sabina's intentions were clear.

[3] Restrictions as to *institutio*, e.g.

[4] e.g. it may be given by word of mouth before witnesses, and will
bind a *heres*.   *Dig.* xl. 5. 47. 4; cf. Buckland, *Slavery*, pp. 460, 513 sqq.;
Textbook, p. 350.

you are as sorrowful as you were when you sent me to this place. I beg you to make a monument worthy of my youth. I beg you to manumit Eutychianus my *alumnus*, and free him by ceremony ; also Aprilis, who alone survives of my servants. I write this at Sirmium on March 18 in the consulship of L. Calpurnius Piso and Publius Salvius Julianus.' [1]

In the early Empire [2] a slave could raise the question of his liberty in the courts, if he could find a representative (*assertor*), for, since his status was doubtful, he could not act himself. But in the case of fideicommissary liberty overdue, but withheld by the trustee, the slave could himself apply to the praetor. In A.D. 103 the SC. Rubrianum provided that, if the trustee failed to appear in the court, the praetor could himself declare the slave free, but free by will, and therefore the freedman of the testator, not of the trustee. If the absence of the trustee was not culpable, the SC. Dasumianum gave the praetor power to free the slave as though completing the trust for the trustee ; the slave then became the freedman of the trustee.[3] Here, at any rate, the slave is no mere chattel ; he can take the initiative in legal proceedings.

Manumission by will was fatally easy.[4] At the beginning of the Empire it called for special legislation. Masters manumitted slaves to avoid the expense of keeping them, or liberated

---

[1] In Pannonia. The inscription is given Dess. 8377. 'A curious case of fideicommissary liberty is given in Dess. 3789 : ' T. Dom. Romulus votum posuit quod fideicommissum Phoebum liberum recepit.' Mommsen's explanation is that Phoebus was the natural son of Romulus. Phoebus' master bequeathed him to Romulus, at the same time ordering that he should be freed *per fideicommissum* ; his father, Romulus, thus recovered him ; (' patroni iure quodammodo,' quoted by Dess. *ad loc.*).

[2] Buckland, *Slavery*, p. 611, says ' under the early Empire a set of rules developed,' but admits that the SC. Rubrianum is the earliest known legislation ; ' Si hi a quibus libertatem praestari oportet, evocati a praetore adesse noluissent, si causa cognita praetor pronuntiasset libertatem his deberi, eodem iure statim servari ac si directo manumissi essent,' *Dig.* xl. 5. 26. 7.

[3] Cf. Buckland, *Slavery*, p. 612 ; Bruns, p. 204. The SC. Iuncianum of A.D. 127 dealt with the case in which the slave belonged to some one other than the testator. Here, too, freedom was given *ex fideicommisso*. Cf. Buckland, *Slavery*, p. 613 ; Bruns, p. 204 ; *Dig.* xl. 5. 28. 4, and xl. 5. 51.

[4] For Persius' protest against the ease of manumission, *vide* iii. 105, v. 75.

favourite slaves with legacies which consumed much of the estate. In days when family unity counted for less than hitherto, the heir often found himself with little of the family property left to him, and the next of kin saw faithful slaves inheriting what he had deemed to be his. Freedmen were threatening to outbid in number and wealth the free population ; and it was not always the best type of slave that was freed. No doubt Dionysius of Halicarnassus, visiting Rome in the reign of Augustus, is expressing the feelings of many Romans when he writes: ' Many are indignant when they see unworthy men manumitted, and condemn a usage which gives such men the citizenship of a sovereign State whose destiny is to govern the world. As for me, I doubt if the practice should be stopped altogether lest greater evil should be the result ; I would rather that it should be checked as far as possible, so that the State may no longer be invaded by men of such villainous character.' [1] The danger was indeed obvious. And so Augustus, in the *Lex Fufia Caninia*, introduced an elaborate scale regulating the number of manumissions permissible under a given will. The owner of two slaves could free both, the owner of two to ten could free half, and so forth.[2] ' Et manumittendi modum terminavit,' says his biographer ; and this rule, as will be seen, was only part of a more comprehensive treatment of the whole question.[3]

It was not necessary, however, to wait till the death of the master brought his will into operation. It was possible to free a slave *inter vivos*, i.e. in the owner's lifetime,[4] by a process known as *manumissio vindicta*. The master yielded his rights. ' It was one of the many fictitious forms of the old capture of property, the primitive Roman method of recovery,' [5] and therefore had much ceremony connected with it. An *assertor*

---

[1] Dion. Hal. iv. 23, translated in Warde Fowler, *Social Life at Rome*, p. 228, whence the above is taken.

[2] 10 to 30, a third ; 30 to 100, a fourth ; 100 to 500, a fifth, and never more than a hundred ; cf. Buckland, *Textbook*, p. 79 ; Gaius, i. 42 sq.

[3] Similar caution was enjoined on Tiberius in the note-books left by Augustus at his death, Dio, lvi. 33.

[4] With certain differences in the consequences, e.g. in the matter of the *peculium, supra*, pp. 103, 104.

[5] Greenidge, *Roman Public Life*, p. 134 ; cf. Buckland, *Slavery*, pp. 451 sqq.

libertatis claimed that the slave was free ; the master made no protest ; the lictor of the magistrate—who might be consul, praetor, proconsul, *praefectus Aegypto* [1]—laid a wand—*festuca*— upon the slave's head, who was then declared free. At some point in the ceremony the master slapped the slave's cheek,[2] and turned him round, the slap being analogous to ' beating the bounds ' and serving to impress the ceremony on the slave's memory, the turning round indicating his changed status. The reference to the turning round appears clearly in the following inscription, and distinguishes this method of manumission from that by will : ' Let those visit my tomb who have been freed by me, both those whom I leave " turned round," or express a wish to be manumitted.' [3]

In both forms of manumission the State so far plays some part at least ; in the first form, manumission by will, its function is not very obvious. It is true that in early Rome the will was made before the public assembly, and ' thus the element of control is traditionally present . . . though, the will of historical times being in an entirely different form, the control has disappeared.' [4] But for the slave, or, indeed, the master, such antiquarian appeal would count for little. It is true also that the State framed rules which had to be observed if the will as a whole was to be valid ; but, even in adding to these rules the limitations of the *Lex Fufia Caninia*, it did not assume any real control of the method or consequences of manumission. Nor was the collection of a tax of 5 per cent. on the value of the slave a method of asserting the authority of the State in any more positive way. Again, the later law, in enforcing a trust

---

[1] Any magistrate who had *legis actio*, which implied *imperium*. In a municipality, manumission could be effected by a Latin before a duovir ; only Latinity could thus be given. A Roman citizen manumitting would have to appear before a Roman magistrate ; cf. Lex Salpens., ch. xxviii. A.D. 81–84 ; Dess. 6088.

[2] Cf. Petr. 38, ' est tamen sub alapa.' This brief account follows the conclusions of R. G. Nisbet, in an article on *festuca* and *alapa*, in *J.R.S.* viii.

[3] Dess. 8268 ; i.e. manumissi per vindictam or testamento, ' hoc sepulchr[um] frequentent a me qui sint liberi c[irc]umversos quos relinquam vel manumitti volam.' Buckland thinks that the ' turning round ' is purely conventional, and plays no part in the legal ceremony. For it, cf. Persius' ' vertigo,' v. 76 sqq.

[4] Buckland, *Textbook*, p. 75.

of liberty overdue, only deals with the destiny of a slave as it might equally well deal with the ownership of any other property disposed of by a similar trust. In the second form, manumission before the praetor, the State plays a more prominent rôle. It is the express declaration of a magistrate of high authority which makes the slave free, though the initiative [1] lies with the owner. And the whole process is made more impressive by an ancient formality which dates back to the earliest days of Roman law.

These were the only two methods under the Empire of turning a slave into a Roman citizen, unless the Emperor, usurping the rights of the Roman people, chose to give citizenship. [2]

Was this the only control exercised by the State ? Was it content thus to allow citizens to be made irrespective of merit or any other qualification ?

To regenerate society by law is an impossible task, and Augustus has often been criticized for attempting the ridiculous ; that is the risk which the reformer must run. To raise fallen standards, to purge and purify false ideals, to bring back piety and religion, to restore self-respect and dignity to a divided State—these are objects which may not readily be realized by legislation. Yet Augustus did not wholly fail; the newly established worship of Rome and Augustus was a powerful link in the unity of Empire, and the very rigour with which the Emperor carried out his legislation cannot but have had a moral influence. But no portion of his social reform had such permanent results as his legislation on the subject of manumission.

To be understood, these measures must be seen in context with the rest, and all in the light of the problems of the times. The political question may be left out of account. The social problems may be shortly put : Senate and knights had suffered in numbers and wealth through the civil wars ; some were ruined, some were excessively rich. Through the whole of the upper strata of society ran a luxury and a licence which were encouraged by the idleness following upon their sullen non-co-operation with the new system. The old family life which

---

[1] Except in the case of a *causa liberalis*.
[2] Manumission *censu* became obsolete under the Empire.

was the basis of Roman religion and law and character was disappearing; licence relaxed the bonds of family affection and duty; the pursuit of pleasure made children an encumbrance, or poverty made their suitable upbringing a burden too terrible to be faced. The best of the senatorial families had been extinguished in the wars, or were slowly fading away through lack of posterity. Luxury meanwhile asked for more servants, and found itself unable to bear the expense of their upkeep. They were sold to those who could at the moment afford them. Or they were manumitted, and the freedmen class was the only section of society which was rapidly increasing. The problem is clear enough; decrease in those quarters where large families were most needed, increase at that level where increase was least desirable. The solution was difficult and has not yet been found. Augustus' attempt was spread over twenty-seven years' legislation.[1] No part of it was so unpopular as his measures to encourage marriage in the upper strata of society. First, penalties for celibacy; later, rewards for children; at every turn in social and political life, in taxation and privilege, the same questions—married or unmarried? —children or no children?—were asked with resulting rights or disabilities. Amid all the restrictions and penalties of the *leges Iulia de maritandis ordinibus* and *Papia Poppaea* appears at least one positive enactment, though its negative form may easily hide its importance, ' qui senator est, quive filius . . . ne quis eorum sponsam uxoremve sciens dolo malo habeto libertinam . . .'[2] No senator or son or daughter of a senator may marry a freedwoman or freedman without the Emperor's leave. But, hitherto, any union at all of free and freed was invalid;[3] now, for the first time, it is recognized as legal marriage —*iustae nuptiae*. The freedman caste henceforth is to be no longer dissociated from the great bulk of the free population. If the upper levels of society will not increase among themselves, they shall be rejuvenated from below. The ex-slave

[1] From the Lex Iulia de maritandis ordinibus of 18 B.C. to the Lex Papia of A.D. 9.

[2] *Dig.* xxiii. 2. 44 pr., where the provision is assigned to the Lex Iulia; in *Dig.* xxiii. 2. 23 to the Lex Papia. Is it possible to determine the date of this concession? For the enactment, cf. Mommsen, *D.P.R.* vii. 13.

[3] Buckland, *Textbook*, p. 115.

class is to be the reservoir from which the depleted free classes shall draw.

At last, but for the first time, there is to be some policy in manumission ; the ex-slave classes are to be given a new function. With a new function a new need arises : the reservoir must have a filter.

The policy of Augustus with regard to manumission has thus a positive side. But, because of the new importance given to the freed classes, restrictions are necessary, if that function is to be justified. As a rule, it is the negative aspect of his legislation that is emphasized ; and this emphasis is probably due to the summary given by Suetonius.[1] ' He attached great importance to preserving the people pure and untainted by any polluting admixture of foreign or servile blood. He seldom gave Roman citizenship, and narrowly determined the limits of manumission. When Tiberius asked for citizenship on behalf of a Greek client, he formally replied that he would not give it unless he persuaded him in person of the justice of his request. When Livia asked a similar favour for a certain tributary Gaul, he refused the citizenship, but offered him exemption from taxes, saying he preferred that the treasury should lose something rather than that the privilege of Roman citizenship should be cheapened. He was not satisfied with putting many obstacles between a slave and freedom, and especially complete freedom ; he made the most elaborate regulations about the number of them to be manumitted, distinguishing and defining their status, and added this provision, that any slave who had been kept in chains or had been tortured should not obtain Roman citizenship, no matter by what method he had been freed.' [2]

Suetonius can never be accused of giving too much information about subjects that really matter. So, too, this passage would be tantalizingly vague were it not possible to fill in the details from the law-books. Suetonius is referring certainly to the *Lex Aelia Sentia*,[3] possibly to the *Lex Iunia* also. Passed in A.D. 4 the *Lex Aelia* was a most comprehensive and important measure—comprehensive, for it deals in detail with a variety of points, and justifies Suetonius' phrase, ' he took the most

---

[1] Suet. *Aug.* 40. [2] *Testamento* or *vindicta*.
[3] For this law, see Buckland, *Slavery*, p. 79 ; *Textbook*, p. 537.

careful precautions '[1]—important, for it is the first to attack the ancient principle that manumission creates a Roman citizen, and introduces some sort of qualification for the slave and some safeguard for the State.

By this law the manumitter must be twenty years of age, the slave must be thirty years, if the manumission is to give Roman citizenship. At the same time, the rule is capable of exceptions which prevent it bearing harshly upon individual cases. Whenever the owner can prove to a legally appointed committee [2] chosen by the magistrate that the slave has rendered exceptional service and is worthy of citizenship, even though under the legal age, then the magistrate declares him a Roman citizen.

If by any chance none of these conditions were fulfilled, the slave, whether freed by will or ceremony, was informally freed, and became a Junian Latin, whose rights will be considered presently.

Lastly,[3] slaves who had been punished by chains or branding or similar penalties, became neither citizens nor Junian Latins, but so-called *dediticii*. They were for ever incapable of citizenship; they had no power of making a will or inheriting under a will, their property reverting to their patrons; they were forbidden, under penalty of re-enslavement, to come within a hundred miles of Rome. They were regarded as incorrigibly bad, and though they might enjoy freedom, they might enjoy few of its rights.

The manumitted fall into three classes : i. citizens ; ii. Junian Latins ; iii. *dediticii*. We may deal with these three classes in the reverse order.

The last class hardly calls for notice. It is impossible to judge their number ; their importance, judging by their status, must have been negligible.

The Junian Latins, however, are numerous. They owe their name to the *Lex Iunia*. It is uncertain whether this law

---

[1] ' Cum et de numero et condicione ac differentia eorum qui manumitterentur curiose cavisset . . .,' Suet. *loc. cit.*

[2] At Rome the *consilium* consisted of five senators and five *equites* ; in the provinces, of twenty *recuperatores*, who were Roman citizens.

[3] The law contains many other enactments less relevant to our purpose. Some are mentioned *infra*, p. 191.

is prior to the *Lex Aelia Sentia*, but it is so closely connected in time and matter that for practical purposes it is possible to regard the two laws as contemporary.[1] Towards the end of the Republic the praetor had intervened to pronounce freedom for deserving slaves whose manumission was formally invalid owing to some flaw in the manumission. They were described as 'in liberty under the protection of the praetor.'[2] Their position is now defined by the *Lex Iunia*; a new status is invented for them. At the same time, a convenient status is discovered into which slaves informally manumitted according to the new regulation of the *Lex Aelia Sentia* may be classed. Junian Latins form a fairly large class and are recruited by a number of methods.[3] In addition to the method already seen arising from the *Lex Aelia Sentia* two others may here be mentioned. It was possible under the Empire to give freedom by two ways other than will or ceremony. A letter of enfranchisement to the slave, or a declaration of his freedom before witnesses gave him informal manumission and Latin status.[4] Such status was seriously limited. Junian Latins possessed the *ius commercii*, and therefore had access to law-courts, but with this exception—that they could neither make a will nor receive under a will. On death they became slaves, and therefore their property reverted to their patron. But their position was not irretrievably determined. The manumission which made them Latins might be repeated without the flaw,[5] and citizenship followed. Again, a Junian Latin freed under thirty, who married a citizen, Latin woman, or freedwoman of his own status and had a child of one year old, could prove

---

[1] Buckland, *Slavery*, p. 534, has a long discussion on the question of date. He sums up with Mommsen's opinion that 'the priority of the Lex Iunia is the solution which creates least difficulty,' though 'certainty is unattainable.'

[2] 'In libertate tuitione praetoris.'

[3] Buckland, *Slavery*, p. 548, gives twenty 'sources of Latinity,' but the list has 'no claim to completeness.'

[4] *Per epistolam* and *inter amicos*. Girard, *Textes*, (3) Appendice, gives an example of *inter amicos*. Possibly Petr. 41, 'Dionyse, liber esto,' would come under this heading, and Mart. ix. 88, 'Modo liberum esse iussi Nastam . . . signa.' Sen. *de vit. beat.* xxiv. 3, 'iustae libertatis an inter amicos datae' certainly is a reference to formal and informal manumission.

[5] For *iteratio*, see Buckland, *Textbook*, p. 95.

these facts before a magistrate. He thereby acquired citizenship for himself, his wife, and his child.[1] No reward is too great for those who will restore family life to a State languishing through dearth of children. Meantime example will relieve the plain statement of law.

Pliny is writing to Fabatus in Picenum: ' Tiro is on the eve of starting for his province of Baetica as proconsul ; his way lies through Picenum. I have good hopes, indeed I am quite confident, that he will yield to me and break his journey to turn aside to you, if you are anxious to free by ceremony those whom you recently freed by declaration in the presence of your friends.' [2]

An inscription [3] records a case of freedom given by will. The man died at the age of thirty-one years and ten days, but care was taken to add that he was freed on March 23, A.D. 86, which day was his thirtieth birthday. It was important for his heirs that his will should have been the valid will of a Roman citizen. A similar inscription [4] tells us that D. Otacilius Felix was freed before a committee of magistrates—*in consilio* ; and therefore, though under thirty years, he was legally a citizen.

At first sight it might be tempting to object that the ages should be reversed, that a man of twenty is somewhat young to be given the right to make a citizen, and that many a slave might become a good citizen before the age of thirty. But the Roman came of age at eighteen, and reached maturity and perhaps discretion at an earlier age than is usual nowadays, when childhood is more and more prolonged. Romans of twenty had commanded armies. Nor is thirty as the age selected for the slave entirely unreasonable. In this regulation is to be found implicit what is seldom, though not never, found explicit in Roman writers—that the Romans had a very definite conception of the functions of slavery in the Empire. The slave is not to become a citizen till he has by very close contact with Roman life picked up enough of Roman tradition and outlook to make it reasonable to believe that he will become a

---

[1] So-called Anniculi Probatio allowed by the Lex Aelia or Lex Iunia ; see Gaius, i. 29. The limitation of age was removed in, perhaps, A.D. 72 by the SC. Pusio-Pegasianum. Buckland, *Textbook*, p. 96.

[2] Plin. *Ep.* vii. 16, *vindicta* as opposed to *inter amicos*.

[3] Dess. 1985 ; cf. 7842.   [4] Dess. 1984.

good citizen. By the age of thirty he will have learnt much ; after that age he has still years enough left to enjoy his new privileges. Nor is the apparently arbitrary scale fixed by the *Lex Fufia Caninia* without significance in this connexion. Of two slaves owned both could be freed; for both would be domestic slaves in close contact with their master. Of a hundred slaves owned only a portion could be freed, for many would be in the lowest of positions, employed as farmhands or in factory.

It would be interesting to know at what age the majority of slaves were freed, whether more were freed as Junian Latins to be turned into citizens later, or whether more remained in slavery till after the age of thirty. The inscriptions of freedmen, which survive in enormous numbers, give in a great many cases the age at death ; this is of no value for age at manumission, though it often suggests that slavery was not so wearing as to prevent a fair chance of a long life. The inscriptions of slaves do not so often record age at death ; but there are enough given in Dessau's selection of inscriptions to make it tempting to take the average. There is one couple, husband and wife, who lived to the ages of one hundred and two, and eighty. But the average age of all, excluding mere infants, is thirty-one years. Such a figure can lead to no real conclusion ; the evidence is very fragmentary ; many slaves' inscriptions give no age ; in other cases the age is recorded obviously because it is noteworthy, ninety-five or eighty-seven or eighty-five. And, unless statistics can take such considerations into account and allow for them accurately, they are of little worth. The best evidence of the frequency of manumission is the number of freedmen's inscriptions ; but from them no precise information can be gleaned as to the age of manumission or the numerical relation of freed to unfreed. On the other hand, with regard to the public slaves at Ostia, there is some evidence that manumission could be counted on with some degree of certainty. An inscription [1] gives a list, headed *publica familia*, of the members of a college ; the names of both freedmen and slaves appear. The freedmen took the name Ostiensis (abbreviated in the inscription to Ost) on manumission. In front of the names of the slaves a blank space is left, in order that the three

---

[1] Dess. 6153.

important letters may be added in the event of manumission, which is at any rate contemplated as not remote. It must be remembered, however, that public slaves were superior in many respects to the ordinary slave.

It has been stated in no uncertain terms that slaves were at liberty to free their *vicarii*.[1] Such a practice seems contrary to the whole spirit of the Augustan reforms, which insist that no manumitter shall bestow a higher status than his own, though he may bestow a lower ; and, if such a practice were to be admitted, the evidence would have to be very convincing. But actually the only evidence cited is one inscription, which the author of this view has strangely misunderstood.[2] It is possible, however, that a *servus publicus populi Romani* may have been allowed to do so, since he could make a will as to half his *peculium*. But little is known as to this, and this type of slave is almost obsolete in the Empire. Possibly Emperors allowed their important slaves to free, but this is no argument for the general law. Further, slaves sometimes had powers of ' alienation,' and it would be easy to alienate the *vicarius* to a free man on the terms that he should free the man ; but in later times at any rate this fraud was punished.[3] But in these possible exceptions there is no reason whatever for believing that manumission of *vicarii* was a general practice.[4]

At this point a parenthesis may be inserted to say something of the manumission of slaves by municipalities and colleges. The fact of such manumission is common enough in the inscriptions : freedmen sometimes directly describe themselves as emancipated by town or college ; in other cases the fact can

[1] ' Rien ne les empêchait de donner ou vendre la liberté à leurs vicarii. . . . C'est ainsi que, par une bizarre contradiction, il leur arrivait de communiquer à d'autres des droits dont ils étaient eux-mêmes privés,' Boissier, *Rel. rom.* ii. 337.

[2] Dess. 1657. Erman writes : ' C'est dans cette inscription que G. Boissier (qui la connaissait par Orelli) croyait trouver des affranchis d'esclaves. Erreur evidente, le *libertis suis* ne pouvant, grammaticalement, se rapporter qu'à Claudia ' (who was free), *Servus vicarius*, p. 464, n. 5. Elsewhere he says, ' Cette erreur, très pardonable à un non-juriste. . .'

[3] *C. Iust.* vii. 11.

[4] Professor Buckland has quoted these possible exceptions in a letter to me, but otherwise agrees in disputing Boissier's statement ; for a discussion, see Erman, *Servus vicarius*, p. 457.

be inferred from the name itself—for a municipal slave took the name of the municipality ; a collegial slave a name derived from the college.[1] Of the details of this emancipation little is known. It is certain that towns freed in Cicero's time.[2] An obscure passage in a law-book refers to an enactment [3] giving them this right, and adds that it was extended to include provincial towns by a *Senatusconsultum* of A.D. 129.[4] Even less is known of the right of colleges to free. Marcus Aurelius is said to have given it 'to all colleges which have the right to meet ';[5] but, as colleges undoubtedly manumitted long before this date, this is probably a general bestowal of a right which hitherto had been given to selected colleges ; now a licence to a college would seem to imply a right to manumit.

Manumission, so far considered, is an emergence from comparative rightlessness to a status of varying rights ; it is at its best a release from a state ' worse than death ' to the privileges of Roman citizenship. Was there a complete break with the past ? Did the master relax all control ? Did the State welcome the new recruit to citizenship on the same terms as those which she gave to her most ancient families ? Or could the slave snap his fingers at his former master, and, turning his back on slavery for ever, rise to the highest positions of office and influence ?

The past was not forgotten. The manumitter still retained

[1] e.g. from towns, Amiternius, Aequiculus, Ostiensis, Sentinas ; occasionally Publicius is used; from colleges, Fabricius Centonius (' collegium fabrorum et centonariorum '), Dess. 7257; Quaestorius Cinyra ('Librariorum quaestoriorum'), 1897; T.Velatius ('accensorum velatorum'), 1956 ; C. Miniarius ('sociorum miniariorum'), 1876, etc. ' Publicius ' ought strictly to denote a freedman of the Roman State ; but *servi publici* is often loosely used to mean municipal slaves ; cf., e.g., Petr. 97. Of the manumission of the old *servi publici* in the strict sense, there is little evidence ; cf. Mommsen, *D.P.R.* i. 369 ; Halkin, *Les esclaves publics*, pp. 22 sqq.

[2] Varro, *de l. l.* 8. 83.

[3] The passage calls it the Lex Vetti Libici, which is variously emended. Mommsen suggests ' Lex veteris reipublicae ' ; *v.* Halkin for other suggestions. *C. Iust.* vii. 9. 3.

[4] The *ordo* of the towns emancipated, just as the *senatus* emancipated the old *servi publici* of Rome. Halkin quotes Senatius as a name. *C.I.L.* v. 2226.

[5] *Dig.* xl. 3. 1. ' omnibus collegiis quibus coeundi ius est.'

some control.   He could expect to receive ' respectful conduct '[1] —a fluid term which tended to crystallize into definite rules. Against his patron the *libertinus* could bring no action at law, unless with the leave of a magistrate.[2]   He was bound to render some ' personal service,'[3] again subject to rules.   If he died without children or intestate, his property reverted to his patron, to whom the *Lex Papia Poppaea* gave varying rights according to an elaborate scale laid down in enactments which again aimed at favouring the possessors of children.[4]   At the same time, the freedman must not be treated like a slave ; the patron's evidence is inadmissible against him ; in time of need the patron must provide for him.[5]

The control from the past was accompanied by a barrier against the future.   The freedman was free, but he was not freeborn, and for many purposes lack of free-birth was a disqualification.   Only the freeborn were capable of holding a Roman magistracy, in Rome or in the townships, of entering the high orders or the army.   But the son of the manumitted slave counted as freeborn, if born after the manumission of his father.[6]   He gained rights, therefore, which his father did not enjoy.[7]   From a legal point of view it took two generations to destroy the disqualifications of a servile origin.

In spite, however, of legal statement of disabilities, there was room for a certain variation dependent on master or Emperor in the rigour with which they were enforced.   It was possible for the patron to waive his rights, or for freedmen

[1] *Obsequium.*   [2] Cf., e.g., Dio, lx. 28 (Claudius).   [3] *Operae.*

[4] Buckland, *Textbook*, p. 89 and p. 376 ; cf. Gaius, iii. 42 ; cf. Nero's murder of Pallas, Tac. *Ann.* xiv. 65.

[5] Buckland, *op. cit.* p. 90.   The *tutela patroni* might be avoided by the *ius trium liberorum* granted to freedwomen in Rome, by the *ius IIII lib.* granted to Roman citizens in Italy.   Cf. Dess. 3952, 5631, 6654, which show the right attributed to a man.

[6] See Greenidge, *Rom. Public Life*, p. 135.   Originally *libertinus* was used to denote the son of a freedman who as such could not be *ingenuus*, the opposite of *libertinus* ; cf. Suet. *Claud.* 24.   But by the Empire *libertinus* denoted the freedman in relation to the community, *libertus* in relation to his patron ; Greenidge, p. 144, n. 3 ; Buckland, *Textbook*, p. 88, n. 9.   Under the Empire, therefore, *ingenuitas* resulted a generation earlier than under the Republic.

[7] And which his brother, born during the slavery of the father, did not enjoy.   See the hard case of Oriens, quoted above, p. 170.

to take advantage of their growing number and diminish in practice the *obsequium* due from them, or for the Emperor to give citizenship freely together with a fictitious free-birth—*ingenuitas*.

Once again the problem confronting Augustus was not simple. As, before, he had to reconcile his wish to increase the birth-rate of citizens with a desire not to incorporate undesirable elements in the citizen body, so now he had to preserve some definite relation between the freedmen whom he allowed to marry all but senators, himself employing them in high offices of State, and the bulk of slave-owners, senators, and others, whom it was his policy to conciliate. So vague a relation as *obsequium*, though it found some concrete expression, rested largely on the prestige and influence, moral and other, of the patron himself. To exalt the freedman and to depress the senator was to overthrow the adjustment of relations between freed and patron, which at its best tended to exercise a guiding influence on the new citizen and at its worst might develop into an intolerable tyranny. Augustus had done much for the best type of freedman : he had regularized his status, he had raised him socially by allowing him marriage above his class, he had created the new and coveted office of *seviri augustales* to encourage him to find an outlet for his powers and ambitions in municipal life, he had granted the *ius anuli* and entry into the knights ; one freedman at least he had raised to be procurator of Gaul—so much he gave and more. But he was nevertheless determined that the freedman should realize that he owed much to his patron, while the patron should realize that he owed it to his freedman to respect his new liberty.

And so, not content with the Republican system which, in leaving the relation of patron and freedman to the authority of the head of the family, also left open the way for rank 'ingratitude' or excessive restraint, Augustus by that same comprehensive measure, the *Lex Aelia Sentia*, allowed a formal accusation to be brought against the freedman. Each case, then, of alleged ingratitude is henceforth to be substantial enough to bear the light of the law-court. In thus leaving the dispute to an outside arbiter the Emperor protected the interests of both sides. It is true that he exempted from personal service the freedman who could prove his marriage and the

existence of two children ;[1] but anything for children.   What
the penalty was for ingratitude is uncertain ; the law-books,
however, never suggest that by this law it was re-enslavement.
It may have been cautioning or fine or flogging,and was certainly
exile in some cases.   Claudius declared that he would always
give judgment against the freedman, and is said to have ordered
re-enslavement in cases where the freedman had suborned
witnesses to dispute his patron's status.[2]   But the whole
question was raised anew in Nero's reign, and formed the
subject of a debate in the Senate, and a wise decision of the
Emperor.[3]

Right to revoke freedom was demanded ; the insolence of
freedmen had become intolerable ; they actually asked their
patrons' advice whether they should entreat them with violence
or as their equals before the law.   The only redress was banishment a hundred miles from Rome.   Such distance did not
exclude the pleasure resorts of Campania ;[4] and the crowning
insolence was the request to patrons for the punishment of
banishment to these places.   Some more powerful weapon
should be given to patrons ; and the worst offenders among the
freedmen should be haled back to slavery.

Such view commanded general consent among senators,
only a few being opposed.   But the consuls had not the courage
to put the question to the vote in the absence of the Emperor,
and merely recorded the general view.   Luckily Tacitus gives
the minority point of view.   The entire class should not suffer
by any subtraction from its rights on account of the guilty
conduct of a few.   The freedman class can be no longer sharply
differentiated ; it has penetrated into high position, civil and
religious, and into every grade of society, not excepting the
senatorial order itself.   The alternative methods of manumission, formal and informal, left room for the refusal or the
gift of the higher type of freedom.   The Junian Latin was still
held, as it were, by the bonds of slavery.   If full freedom had
been given to an undeserving slave, then the master was at
fault.   The whole class of freedmen should not suffer for the

[1] *Dig.* xxxviii. 1. 37, Lex Papia Poppaea : certain conditions are made.
[2] *Dig.* xxxvii. 14. 5, to which cases, perhaps, Suet. *Claud.* 25 is referring.
[3] Tac. *Ann.* xiii. 26 and 27.
[4] Cf. Petr. 53, ' atriensis Baias relegatus.'

bad judgment of the individual master. He should be slow to give what he could not take away.

To the arguments of the minority Augustus would have given full approval, for they were a continuation of the policy laid down by him. Equally would he have praised Nero's decision when the matter was referred to him ; each case was to be dealt with on its own merits : no general rule would be given. The strengthening of the citizen body from the best elements of the slave class was to go on unhindered by reaction. And Nero's practice was consistent with his decision. He, too, judged each case on its merits, even if he judged its merits by his own interests. He was eager to listen while Milichus, a freedman, betrayed his patron Scaevinus,[1] while Graptus brought false charges of treason against Cornelius Sulla.[2] Fortunatus prosecuted his patron L. Vetus, and as a reward for accusing Publius Gallus was given a seat of honour in the theatre.[3] But these were the days of the great fear ; life and throne were threatened.

On the other hand, the freedman often served his patron well during his lifetime, and after death was true to his memory. The Emperors themselves would often have fared ill but for the personal, not merely official, services of their freedmen. A certain freedman, to shield his patron, claimed a peculiarly cowardly murder as his own. ' Magnitudo exempli,' says Tacitus, but it is a pity such devotion had not a worthier object than Octavius Sagitta.[4]

Personal service included often the morning salutation of the patron by the freedman ; it is familiar from the pages of Juvenal and Martial ; but too much emphasis can be laid on it. It occurred doubtless only in the houses of the rich or the ostentatious, and there were hundreds of patrons who had never at any time freed more than one or two slaves. It might be regarded as tactful to dedicate some shrine or statue to the Genius of a patron ; ' Genio Lucii nostri Felix libertus ' may be read on the herm of the coarse-looking auctioneer of Pompeii, L. Caecilius Jucundus ; it was dedicated in his lifetime.[5] But more often the patron was honoured after death with a statue

[1] Tac. *Ann.* xv. 54.
[2] Tac. *Ann.* xiii. 47.
[3] Tac. *Ann.* xvi. 12 ; cf. 10.
[4] Tac. *Ann.* xiii. 44.
[5] See Mau-Kelsey, *Pompeii*, p. 439.

or an adjective—*bene merens, indulgens*, and so on—especially if he had made his freedmen his heirs, as was common. ' Sacred to Aemilia Calliste the freedwoman of Marcus ; her heirs made this in honour of a deserving patroness ; this monument is to pass to heirs of the name of Aemilius only . . . C. Aemilius Euaristus and C. Aemilius Extricatus made it in honour of their patroness.'[1] Often, however, ' personal service ' involved little more than the upkeep of the patron's tomb ; and, as the freedman not unfrequently was provided with a niche in the same tomb as his patron, he had an interest in preserving it from trespass or damage. Such provision is seen clearly in the ' testamentum Dasumii ' ; and, when Trimalchio appointed one of the freedmen to look after that astounding piece of monumental vulgarity which he designed as his tomb, he was true, as so often, to the evidence of scores of inscriptions.[2]

The barrier set up against those who could not prove a free birth could be set aside only by special order of the Emperor. By a legal fiction free-birth was assumed and its privileges given to a freedman. Menas thus received them from Augustus as a reward for betraying Pompey's fleet.[3] Under Tiberius membership of the *equites* was restricted to freeborn of three generations,[4] but under Nero this rule was relaxed. Claudius confiscated the estates of freedmen who had taken on themselves equestrian rank, and beheaded those who falsely claimed Roman citizenship.[5] In the reigns of Tiberius and Claudius, Curtius Rufus rose from obscure origins—perhaps he was the son of a gladiator—through the offices of quaestor and praetor to those of consul and proconsul ; yet, as Tiberius said, ' Rufus seems to me to be his own ancestor.'[6] Such a career was by no means unexampled : Licinus was originally a Gaul, the slave of Julius Caesar, and emancipated by him ; he was later made procurator of his native country, where he amassed for himself a fortune ' with the greed of a barbarian while enjoying the dignity of a Roman.'[7] Felix, procurator of Judaea, needs no mention.

[1] Dess. 8281.

[2] Petr. 71 : ' praeponam enim unum ex libertis sepulchro meo custodiae causa.' An excellent chapter !

[3] Suet. *Aug.* 74 : ' assertus in ingenuitatem.'

[4] Pliny, *N.H.* xxxiii. 2. 8. 32.   [5] Suet. *Claud.* 25.   [6] Tac. *Ann.* xi. 21.

[7] πλεονεξίᾳ μὲν βαρβαρικῇ, ἀξιώσει δὲ 'Ρωμαϊκῇ χρώμενος. Dio, liv. 21, where his retort to Augustus is given.

Galba had little time in which to bestow privileges, but apparently his policy was to give citizenship sparingly;[1] even Vitellius earned the gratitude of people and Senate by restoring exiles and giving them again their rights over their freedmen.[2] Possibly the need of a conservative policy was felt after Nero's extravagance. Several dancers had earned citizenship by their performance;[3] so, too, the judges in musical festivals in Greece had earned similar reward by their just and fair-minded decision when the Emperor had performed.[4] In his reign Narcissus was given quaestorial, Nymphidius was given consular decorations,[5] as, earlier, Posides had received the *pura hasta* for a successful campaign,[6] and as, later, Vitellius raised Asiaticus and Hormus to equestrian rank.[7] From the Senate freedmen were excluded till the time of Commodus.[8] From service in the legions freedmen were excluded because they were not thought worthy of the honour; there were times, however, when circumstances relaxed this rule. Normally they were allowed to serve in the auxiliary corps. The fleet was always the inferior service, and here freedmen served regularly. After Vespasian's time, however, when the fleet was organized on military lines, free-birth was necessary, though it was often fictitious.[9]

When the slave became a freedman, he too became a potential maker of freedmen. Perhaps he acquired slaves after his manumission; often he possessed slaves while he himself was still a slave; these on his manumission would cease to be *vicarii*,[10] and advanced a step towards manumission. But no master freeing his slaves could confer a status higher than his own; if he was a Junian Latin, he could never give citizenship, no matter how formally he freed. It took a citizen to create a citizen. When a freedman manumitted, it was frequently with a view to marriage with his former slave. ' Patronus et coniunx ' is a common combination on tombs : ' Racilia Eutychia made this tomb for Cn. Racilius Telesporus, her

[1] Suet. *Galba*, 14.   [2] Tac. *Hist.* ii. 92.
[3] Suet. *Nero*, 12.   [4] Suet. *Nero*, 24.
[5] Tac. *Ann.* xi. 38, xv. 72.   [6] Suet. *Claud.* 28.
[7] Tac. *Hist.* ii. 57, iv. 39.   [8] Script. hist. aug. *Comm.* vi. 9.
[9] Mommsen, *D.P.R.* vii. 36.
[10] *v. supra*, p. 103. Dess. 7609, e.g., gives a case of an ' unguentarius qui familiam suam manumisit.'

patron and husband, with whom she lived for twenty-one years.'[1] Or a freedwoman freed and married her slave: ' C. Apridius Primus built this for himself and Aristia Arche, his patroness and wife.'[2] The law insisted that a woman freed expressly with a view to marriage could not refuse marriage.[3] An awkward dilemma must often have arisen.

If the purpose of this summary of manumission has not been obscured by detail and illustration, it has become clear that, taken broadly, manumission is selective and that it is a process. Not every slave is freed, and normally the gap from slavery to full and complete freedom and its rights is bridged only after two generations at least have passed. The object in the selection is the creation of good citizens ; the object of the process is to give time for the gradual absorption of Roman culture and the slow training in the use of new privileges and responsibilities.

Theoretic defences of slavery concerned the Roman but little ; even if he could follow their sophistry, he preferred to be honest, perhaps brutally honest. The Platonic defence— and the ideal State constructed by Plato's second thoughts does not suggest that he had advanced very much beyond the normal Greek view of slavery—was that the quality of justice is shown most clearly where injustice is most easily committed, and that just treatment, besides increasing the master's self-respect, elicits goodness from the slave.[4] Of this the Roman was quite incapable ; it might be a description of fact, but hardly a justification ; dearth of labour was to him a sufficient plea, or his own needs. He would willingly convict of inconsistency one line of the Aristotelian defence, that some portion of the race is doomed by natural inferiority to slavery ; for both Aristotle and the Roman were willing to manumit. With the other line of Aristotle's defence, that slavery is on the whole more beneficial to the slave and the master, he would be inclined to agree. ' Thank Heaven for education,' cries a freedman in Petronius[5]—' thank Heaven for education ; it made me what you see me now.' It was the education of his master's office, and the cry was an expression of gratitude that could be echoed

---

[1] Dess. 8219 (cf., e.g., 7488, to his wife and freedwoman, who was also a ' negotiatrix frumentaria et leguminaria ').
[2] Dess. 8259.   [3] *Dig.* xxiii. 2. 29.   [4] Plato, *Laws,* 777.   [5] 58.

by multitudes. The more modern condemnation of slavery, that the capability of a limited social life implies the capability of a larger social life, supposing the necessary training to be allowed, and that such capability implies a right to freedom and to citizenship [1]—this would be acceptable to the Roman provided that he could interpret it in his own way. If there is a right to freedom, there is also a right to slavery. 'Why have you been a slave?' 'Because,' says another of those freed-men in Petronius [2]—'because I went into slavery to please my-self, and preferred being a Roman citizen to paying taxes as a subject-ally; I did my utmost to please my master, a splendid, dignified gentleman, whose little finger was worth more than the whole of you; thanks be to his memory.' If it is just to grant varying degrees of status to free provincials on the grounds of imperial utility, then on those same grounds it is justifiable to enslave the lowest, and after forced contact with Roman ideals to admit them to a status higher than that of the majority of free provincials. From the Roman point of view, to enslave a German and set him free after a training in Roman methods is to benefit him more than his brother, who ran free in the Teutoberg forest, though neither may think so at the time; and he is of far more benefit to Rome, for he becomes the means of spreading still further the culture he has acquired and been rewarded for acquiring. Regarded in this light, slavery is 'a compulsory initiation into a higher culture'; [3] the compulsion is admitted, but the initiation also is indisputable; from slavery only the best elements emerge, but they make their own unique contribution to civilization.

The contribution made by freedmen to the imperial achieve-ment of the first two centuries is too large a subject for an essay on slavery to deal with. To follow the rise and fall of a Narcissus or a Nymphidius—*ipse pars Romanarum cladium*—or an Abascantus, and to trace their influence on the court and politics of the day, would be to pursue a fascinating and varied path which would lead far astray from slavery. But one part of the freedman's destiny is relevant. 'I am extremely glad,' writes Pliny, 'to hear that you profited by the opportunity

[1] T. H. Green, *Principles of Political Obligation*, p. 145; cf. 148, 151.
[2] 57.
[3] The phrase is borrowed from J. L. Myres, *Dawn of History*, p. 98.

given to you by the visit of a proconsul, and manumitted many of your slaves. I am anxious that our native district should be increased in all good things, but especially in the number of its citizens. For that is the surest distinction that a town can win.' Pliny had prevailed upon Tiro to turn aside and give formal freedom to Fabatus' slaves.[1]

When the history of town life under the Empire comes to be written,[2] it will have to take into account two very different types of men. The success of the municipality in the early Empire was in part due to the ex-soldier and the ex-slave. The ex-soldier, turned citizen, brought with him a sense of order, a practical if limited outlook, and an ingrained loyalty. His contribution would be interesting enough. The ex-slave, on the other hand, brought with him a shrewd business instinct, often with its tangible evidence great or small ; he may have been trained as estate agent, or in record-office or customs or bank. His enterprise and quickness must often have balanced most usefully the slower clumsiness, however well intentioned, of many a time-expired Porthos from the legions.

The appeal of the municipality to its citizens was irresistible. Organized by Julius Caesar and Augustus, provided by Augustus with a religion and official responsibilities and honours, adorned by Hadrian, the builder, with monuments and architectural works, it drew forth a devotion and a public spirit which can find few parallels. The local privileges and insignia were eagerly sought for during life, and at death proudly recorded on tombs ; money was poured out in the public use and liberally bequeathed to endow city institutions. One town vied with another in public spirit ; and citizens were happy if they could surpass their neighbours in the splendour of their theatres or their colonnades, and were grateful to the benefactor who gratified their pride.

Modelled internally upon the system of Rome, each town enjoyed the rule of its own magistrates, and waited upon the deliberations of its own senate. From magistracy and senate

---

[1] Pliny, *Ep.* vii. 32 ; cf. for a similar view of the function of manumission, Dio, lvi. 7.

[2] Reid, *The Municipalities of the Roman Empire*, treats it from one point of view ; Dill, *Social Life at Rome*, has a brilliant chapter on municipal life, which is too short.

alike freedmen were excluded,[1] but the ban did not apply to their sons. At Pompeii Numerius Popidius Celsinus rebuilt a temple to Isis ; in recognition of his generosity the decurions admitted him to their rank without cost. He was six years old. The rebuilders were, of course, the parents, but by building it in the name of their son ' they opened the way for him to the city offices for which the father, a freedman, was not eligible,' [2] and to which the son, though eligible, might not otherwise have been elected ; or the child may have been born before the emancipation of his parents, and therefore would not have been freeborn. For freedmen themselves Augustus had provided, in founding the *seviri Augustales*, an outlet for ambition, and a consolation for exclusion from higher offices. The freedman enjoyed the ceremony and external pomp connected with the worship of Rome and Augustus, which this order was designed to foster. He wore its insignia with pride, and valued highly the social distinction thus conferred. No institution of Augustus was so successful ; it cemented the Empire, it occupied the inferior orders, it kept the ambitious freedman in the towns, it called forth his public spirit and unloosed his purse to an end not entirely selfish.[3]

Nothing is more striking in reading the inscriptions than the abundance of money voluntarily spent in the building or restoration of municipal works. After long years in slavery spent in the warehouse or workshop of his master till he reached freedom, and after more years as an independent trader, the freedman found that his accumulated wealth would unlock many doors to the esteem of his poorer but freeborn fellow townsmen. The power wielded by money is obvious in the

---

[1] The Lex col. Gen. Iul. sive Ursonensis cap. cx. (44 B.C. Dess. 6087) allows a freedman as *decurio* probably because the colony was drawn from the city mob ; cf. Hardy, *Six Roman Laws*. On the other hand, the Lex Malacitana, cap. liv., Dess. 6089, makes a freedman disqualified for office. Marquardt, *L'Org.* i. 261, n. 3, mentions Iulia Curubis and Clupea in Africa as also allowing freedmen to stand for office. The Lex Visellia made it illegal for freedmen to stand for office or *decurionate*, A.D. 24. Cf. Plin. *N.H.* xxxiii. 32, and Diocletian and Maximin ad legem Viselliam *ap.* Cod. Iust. ix. 21.

[2] Mau-Kelsey, *Pompeii*, p. 164.

[3] For some account of the *seviri*, see Dill, *Social Life*, p. 216, and Marquardt, *L'Org.* i. 291 sqq.

inscriptions, but equally clear is a certain fraternity and sociability which the apparently timocratic organization of the town could not smother. When individuals do not spend sums to reface a temple or pave a road, colleges of tradesmen, or devotees of this or that cult, combine to undertake some larger work. For club-life, whether for trade or religious or social purposes, played a great part in the life of the freedman. Bequests made to college or township were duly made and duly administered ; small donations to the inhabitants of this or that place are to be made *in perpetuum* to men, women, and slaves alike. Over the whole Roman world these freedmen leave their mark. At Tarvisium several freedmen give a road together with its *crepidines* ; [1] close by at Concordia a freedman and *sevir* contributes to the *crepidines* between a wall and a bridge ; [2] at Pisaurum another dedicates statues of the Augusti ; at Falerii several freedmen join to pave the road with flint setts.[3] And so the list runs on, from Italy into the provinces, to Barcino,[4] to Baetica [5] in Spain, to Sarmizegethusa in Dacia.[6] At Nacolea in Asia, P. Aelius Onesimus left a bequest, 'Though I owe very much to the beloved land of my birth, the state of Nacolea, in proportion to my slender savings I wish . . .' so much to be invested in such-and-such a way.[7] Polycarpus and Europe, slaves of Corbulo's daughter Domitia, obtained the leave of the decurions of Gabii to build a temple and adorn it with statues at their own expense, and when freed they gave to the township a capital sum of which the interest was to be devoted to the upkeep of the temple and to the expenses of a public banquet to be held on the birthday of Domitia.[8] The bequest of the freedman doctor Eros Merula has been quoted already.[9]

In return for such gifts to townships every conceivable honour was voted. Gaius Munatius Faustus, a *sevir* and suburban official, was awarded the right to a seat of double width at the games 'for his services.' The monument put up to him by his wife gives a relief of this throne, evidently the chief pride of his civic life.[10] At Veii a freedman who ' had at

---

[1] Dess. 5370.   [2] 5378.   [3] 5373.   [4] 5486.   [5] 5487.
[6] 5548.   [7] 7196.   [8] 272.   [9] 7812.
[10] He was a *paganus*, and was awarded a *bisellium*. Mau-Kelsey, p. 415, gives a picture of the tomb. For similar *bisellium*, cf., e.g., Dess. 6599 ; cf. Petr. 57, ' sevir gratis factus sum.'

all times aided his township not only by advice and influence but also by money ' was privileged, among other honours, to sit with the magistrates at public banquets, and was exempted from all taxes. The signatures to this official resolution include such aristocratic names as Sempronius Gracchus and Octavius Sabinus.[1] ' Whose deeds cannot be set forth ' is the compliment paid to an ex-slave dignitary at Nola.[2] The monument of another freedman in Baetica boasts that he has been adorned with every honour open to freedmen.[3] Cross over to Africa and the same records are to be found ; Italy, Spain, Greece, Asia—all provide the same testimony.[4] Everywhere slaves are emerging from bondage and pushing their way up into position and privilege.

A great social upheaval has taken place since the Republic. It was no sudden earthquake, no outbreak of revolution on the part of a submerged class becoming conscious of its rights and asserting them by bloodshed and violence, no wringing of privilege from an unwilling upper class by threat or massed action. It was rather steady, almost unconscious, pressure from below, guided and encouraged in certain quarters from above. It was a movement that was inevitable, and the more inevitable according as Rome succeeded in her mission. The imperial achievement was the spread of civilization, and the nearer Rome raised the peoples to her level, the further withdrew into the vanished past the social order of its day. If slavery was one method of initiation into a higher culture, social change was a necessary result and was the measure of initiation. It was but a few years since *novi homines* had thrust themselves to the forefront of success, and Rome still stood. Now was the turn of the ex-slave ; yet miniatures of Rome flourished in hundreds throughout the world.

That the real significance of this upheaval was appreciated by the Romans can be shown by little explicit evidence. Such an idea, if consciously present to his mind, would not easily pass his lips in words. *Pax Romana* is the Latin for the imperial achievement and the imperial mission. *Pacisque imponere*

---

[1] Dess. 6579.   [2] Dess. 6348, ' cuius facta enarrari non possunt.'
[3] Dess. 6914.
[4] The point need not be laboured. Dess. 6663 sqq. will give abundant examples.

morem—peace to the Roman of the Empire is not a mere negative, the absence of war ; it implies arts and crafts, law and order, trade and building, and pleasure. It has been the argument of the chapters on slavery that Rome often gave such ' peace ' to those who earned it in slavery ; that the Romans considered the resulting social change necessary and beneficial has been suggested in this sketch of manumission. Meantime the reflections of the more thoughtful are drowned by the noisy clamour of shallower minds.

Every social change calls forth hysterical protest, which is always likely to take a prominent place in the literature of the day. And in those days, more so than now, those who wrote were also those whose privileges were being attacked and exclusiveness assailed ; if among them there was a minority in sympathy with the new movement, they hid their views, or their mild defence was unheard in the general scream of indignation. And so later generations only hear one side of the question ; and though they may know that the satirist is exaggerating and underlining the features which most excite his wrath, the tendency is to give credence to a case in proportion to the vehemence of its expression. And if by bad luck a Juvenal and a Petronius are born when the social change is at its height, small wonder if the freedman nowadays receives less than his due.

The main charges are vulgarity, ostentation, lack of manners, disrespect for tradition, blatancy ; all true enough, all deplorable, but all inevitable in a period of transition. The real reason for the outcry is jealousy—jealousy of freedmen's success where free men had failed, jealousy of wealth and ability and powers and influence. That the imperial freedmen often deserved the abuse flung at them cannot be denied. When Pliny adds his denunciation of Pallas to the witness of Tacitus, then the gibes of Juvenal and Martial gain in credibility. Originally a freedman of Antonia and brother of Felix, he had early been employed in court intrigues to disclose the plot of Sejanus to Tiberius ; under Claudius he had received praetorian insignia, and fifteen million sesterces as an honorarium for proposing the SC. Claudianum, and public thanks for his condescension in preferring the service of Rome to that of his long line of royal ancestors.[1]

[1] Plin. *Ep.* viii. 6.   For Pliny's praise of Trajan's freedman, Maximus, see *Ep.* x. 85.

What could be more honourable on the part of the Senate, says Pliny, than that they should show that they were properly grateful to Pallas ?   He had promoted the marriage of Agrippina, and secured the adoption of Nero by Claudius in preference to his own son.[1]   'Put in charge by Claudius, he exercised almost the dominion of a king.'[2]   In the next reign he was accused of treason and acquitted.[3]   Of the stories of his arrogance there are many.   At home he did not degrade himself by speaking to his freedmen ;   he expressed his wishes by signs.   Of his mock modesty full details may be found in Pliny, together with the decrees of the Senate which could not satisfy so self-effacing a humility.

' But why should I show indignation ?   It were better to laugh, lest those who have by luck reached such heights as to become ludicrous should imagine that they have secured a position of honour.'[4]

The power given to these freedmen or assumed by them is a commonplace of Tacitus.   ' Claudius placed the freedmen whom he put in charge of his private affairs on a level with himself and with the laws.'[5]   To be known only to Sejanus' freedmen or hall porters was a distinction.[6]   When Claudius could trust no one during the terror of the Silius and Messalina episode, he put a freedman in charge of the praetorians to guard against treachery ;[7]   and Nero made a freedman prefect of the fleet at Misenum.[8]   It needed a freedman to reconcile Suetonius and the new procurator in Britain ;   Polyclitus' orders were to survey the state of Britain, to reconcile Suetonius, to pacify the barbarians ;   he went, his suite was a burden to the provinces through which he passed ;   he was a terror to the soldiers and a laughing-stock to the enemy, who wondered to see an army and a general cringing to slaves.[9]   And so it goes on—Callistus, Narcissus ;   Vespasian insulted by Phoebus for falling

[1] Tac. *Ann.* xii. 25.

[2] ' . . . a Claudio impositus velut arbitrium regni agebat,' xiii. 14.

[3] xiii. 23.

[4] Plin. *Ep.* vii. 29 *ad fin.*   [5] Tac. *Ann.* xii. 60.

[6] iv. 74.   [7] xi. 33.

[8] Tac. *Ann.* xiv. 3.   He was usually an *eques*, but a freedman under Claudius, Plin. *N.H.* ix. 62, and after Nero's death, Tac. *Hist.* i. 87.

[9] Nothing more is known of him except his rapacity, vouched for by Tacitus, Pliny, and Dio Cassius.

asleep at Nero's performance,[1] and later advised by Apollonius the Sage to check the power of freedmen ; [2] Hormus prevailing on the commander of a garrison to release a prisoner [3]—till Geminas and Agaclytus round off our period in the reign of Marcus Aurelius.[4] Of the wealth of these freedmen there is no need to accumulate examples. Their power and the abuse of it, their wealth and the cupidity with which it was amassed, are their crimes.[5] Yet it was those who made their protest who were partly the cause ; their determined refusal to work with the Emperor had originally been a contributory reason for his employment of freedmen. Deliberately standing aloof, they saw positions filled by ex-slaves, capable and industrious, and complained that they were themselves still poor, and still unimportant. We do not make the same complaint ; we deplore rather the servility of spirit which could produce such extravagances in literature as the *ad Polybium* of Seneca, or a poem written upon the lock of an Emperor's favourite by Statius —a boy marked by Venus as worthy of more than mere slavery, fairer than Hylas—a hundred lines of nauseating flattery.[6]

But imperial slaves were not the only target for the wit of the outraged. More details of the extravagance and licence of Zoilus are given than will bear repetition ; but the main argument is the same. Zoilus wears the rings of knighthood— they were better on his feet. If he is a thief now, it is not surprising ; for he was once a runaway slave.[7] Maevius, a poet of real Roman blood, not from Syria or Parthia, must be content to shiver while Incitatus, the muledriver, is resplendent in purple.[8] Rufus may display his fortune on his back, but the brand-marks may still be seen on his forehead.[9] ' 'Tis men like these that fortune, as often as she wills some jest, lifts from lowliness to the pinnacle of success.' [10] Said by Juvenal,

---

[1] Tac. *Ann.* xvi. 5.   [2] Philostr. *Vit. Ap.* v. 36.

[3] Tac. *Hist.* iii. 12.

[1] Script. hist. aug. *Marc. Aur.* xv. 2.

[5] Doryphorus, Dio, lxi. 5. 4 ; Asiaticus, Tac. *Hist.* ii. 95 ; Narcissus, Dio, lx. 34 ; Phaon, Suet. *Nero*, 48 ; Pallas, Tac. *Ann.* xi. 29, etc. ; cf. also Suet. *Otho*, 5 ; Plin. *N.H.* xxxiii. 145.

[6] *Silvae*, iii. 4.

[7] Martial, iii. 29, iii. 82, xi. 37, xi. 54 ; cf. Stat. *Silv.* iv. 5. 47. ' Sunt urbe Romanisque turmis qui Libyam deceant alumni.'

[8] Mart. **x.** 76.   [9] ii. 29.   [10] Juv. iii. 39.

this is echoed by Martial wherever he finds occasion, and it is often, to deal with these parvenu freedmen. But Martial's real meaning is that others are rich, while he is poor; he is distressed not so much by Maevius' fate as by his own. He may make some case for himself when he can cite a Zoilus for his purpose; but he, no less than we, could read the signboards on the shops of freed craftsmen who, by hard work and careful thrift, had built up a modest fortune for themselves, and left their records on the tombstones which he, no less than we, could read. 'Sed liberti scelerati, qui omnia ad se fecerunt.'[1] He may dislike their vulgarity—though neither Juvenal nor Martial would be taken as 'arbiters of taste'—but he should give them their due for industry while he idled, for thrift while he squandered, despising trade in a pride which he could ill afford to maintain.

'It were better to laugh,' said Pliny. Petronius is the only critic whose laughter is not mingled with a fury artificially worked up; his book, therefore, makes pleasanter reading than Martial or Juvenal, and is more valuable because it deals not with the freedmen at court but with the ex-slave who has retired from trade to parade his wealth in the luxurious resorts of the Campanian coast. Petronius is caricaturing their vulgarity and ostentation, and no doubt exaggerates; but in many details he is testifying to literal fact. Several fellow-freedmen of Trimalchio reveal their past history with a frankness which glories in a humble origin rather than attempts to conceal it, and look back upon former hardships as milestones in a prosperous career.

'And now I live such a life that no one can jeer at me. I am a man among men; I walk about bareheaded; I owe nobody a brass farthing; I have never been in the courts; no one has ever said to me in public, "Pay me what you owe me." I have bought a few acres, and collected a little capital; I have to feed twenty bellies and a dog; I ransomed my fellow-slave to preserve her from indignities; I paid a thousand silver pennies for my own freedom; I was made a priest of Augustus and excused the fees; I hope to die so that I need not blush in my grave.'[2] Petronius may laugh, but if this man's claims

---

[1] Petr. 38.
[2] Petr. 57, translated by M. Heseltine (Loeb Series).

are true, he will make no bad citizen.   But, good or bad citizen, he was no doubt happy; ' I am bursting with happiness ' is the triumphant admission of a fellow-freedman.[1]

Meantime Trimalchio's other friends are not to be despised. ' They are very juicy people. That one you see lying at the bottom of the end sofa has his eight hundred thousand. He was quite a nobody. A little time ago he was carrying loads of wood on his back. People do say—I know nothing, I have only heard—that he pulled off a goblin's cap and found a fairy hoard. If God makes presents, I am jealous of nobody. Still he shows the marks of his master's fingers, and has a fine opinion of himself. So he has just put up a notice on his hovel: " This attic, the property of Gaius Pompeius Diogenes, to let from the 1st July, the owner having purchased a house." '   Another guest at the same banquet ' had held a cool million in his grasp; but things had not gone well; the company's pot had gone off the boil. Yet his trade was flourishing once; he was an undertaker. He dined like a king; more wine was spilt under his table than many a man has in his cellars.' [2]   The career of the host, Trimalchio, cannot here be spoilt by fragmentary quotation; it is a superb picture.

Discount some of the figures, cut down part of the extravagance, tone down some at least of the vulgarity, but leave the passion for money and the trades by which it is made, and there is little to distinguish the freedmen of Petronius from the freedmen of the inscriptions. To give a catalogue of their trades and their honours would take pages, and it may be seen in the indices of Dessau; among them will be found the trades of woodcarrier and undertaker.

Slaves emerged from slavery, and made their own contribution to the life of the Empire—a valuable contribution, it has been suggested. Satirists fumed and made their protest, misguided often, exaggerated, mistaking accidentals for essentials. It may be, none the less, that the influence of freedmen was not purely salutary, that the rich crop of ex-slave dignitaries in the townships contained also the seeds of decay; it may be, too, that the protest, spiteful and malignant though

[1] Petr. 75, *felicitate dissilio.*
[2] 38, translated by M. Heseltine.

it was, yet ignorantly contained elements of truth. For beneath the veneer of Roman manners lay the lasting substance of race and descent.[1]

[1] Cf. Dill, *Social Life*, p. 102 : ' We can now see that the rise of the emancipated slave was not only inevitable, but that it was on the whole salutary and rich in promise for the future'; and contrast Boissier, *Rel. rom.* ii. 356: ' l'esclavage ne peut pas être une bonne école pour la vie et pour la liberté,' and, commenting on the passage of Pliny quoted above, p. 197, ' il avait tort de se rejouir ; la patrie n'avait guère a se louer des citoyens nouveaux que lui donnait l'esclavage.'

CHAPTER VIII

THE MINGLING OF NATIONS

οὐδὲ τοὺς οἰκέτας ὑμῖν εὐνοεῖν εἰκός, πρῶτον μὲν ὅτι οἰκέται, εἶθ' ὅτι τῶν
ἐναντίων ταγμάτων οἱ πλεῖστοι· κἀκεῖνοι γὰρ ὁμοίως ὑμῖν ἀπὸ γένους.

Philostratus, Ep. Ap. 41.

πέφυκεν δ' ἡ πόλεων ἐπιμειξία πόλεσιν ἤθη κεραννύναι παντοδαπά, καινοτομίας
ἀλλήλοις ἐμποιούντων ξένων ξένοις.

Plato, Laws, 949E.

ἡ δ' ὁμιλία
πάντων βρότοισι γίγνεται διδάσκαλος.

Eur. Andr. 683.

WE have watched the slaves brought in from most
quarters of the world in endless stream. We have
allotted to them their work, often according to nationality ; we have caught glimpses of their inner and private
life, and reviewed their perpetual struggle to rise from slavery
to the fuller opportunities of freedom. It remains to catch up
and combine these isolated studies, no longer to consider slavery
from the point of view of the agriculturist, or the satirist,
but to view it in a larger context in an attempt to estimate its
effects upon the health of the Empire. For whether its influence
can be traced as it worked upon the fabric of civilization, or
whether its influence was too subtle to leave clear signs, it would
not be a dangerous guess to suspect that such influence was
powerful. But such questions as national characteristics,
heredity, degeneracy of type, racial fusion, disappearance of
Western cult in the face of Eastern mysticism and Roman
' gravitas ' before Asiatic volatility, are not likely to receive
much direct treatment at the hands of ancient authors ; none
the less, there are some materials from which to draw some
tentative conclusions.

The ratio of slaves to free men is one aspect of the
question ; [1] but it is not enough for our purpose ; theoretically

[1] v. supra, p. 20.

the two strata, slave and free, might never have mingled.   Given a vast slave-population, it remains to be seen to what extent the foreign and servile elements fused with the native and free elements, and with each other.

' Of the tombs that line both sides of the military roads from Rome more than half belong to freedmen ' ; [1] here is an object-lesson that may warn the visitor to Rome to what extent the non-slave element was of foreign origin.[2]   But even without a journey to Rome, the reading of the ten thousand inscriptions in Dessau's Select Latin Inscriptions will give a fair impression.   Here, in inscriptions grouped under various headings, can be traced the foreign admixture by a mere study of names.   Under the heading ' tituli virorum ordinis senatorii ' may be seen the good old Roman names to be found in every page of Livy ; under the headings ' tituli sepulchrales ' both the strange and familiar are well mingled ; from ' tituli opificum et artificum ' the old Latin names have to great extent disappeared, till as more are read—' tituli sacri,' ' tituli instrumenti domestici '— the unfamiliar becomes familiar, and Phileros and Philargyrus no longer strike upon the ear with foreign ring, so that, in turning to the later equestrian and senatorial inscriptions, the presence of such names almost passes unnoticed.

The study of names, interesting in itself, may be made to furnish important results.[3]   Certain names become definitely established as slave-names, and in consequence tend to be avoided by other than slaves.   A servile origin may thus often be safely predicated of a man who records his three names with no suffix of ' lib ' to show his manumission.   And even in later generations names may have significance ; because Tacitus

[1] Friedländer, i. 202 (Eng. trans.).

[2] G. Boissier, *Rel. rom.* ii. 355, ' Le Peuple de Rome s'est principale-ment recruté dans l'esclavage.'

[3] On servile names, see Oxé in *Rhein. Mus.*, 1904, p. 108 ; Tenney Frank, *Amer. Hist. Review*, xxi. 689 ; and M. L. Gordon, *J.R.S.* vol. xiv. ; and for names as a clue to Thracian nationality, see Mateescu, *Ephem. Dacoromana*, i. ; Bithus (' molto più in uso di qualunque altro nome tracio '), p. 77, n. 1, 218 ; Cotus ; Davus (Daco-Phrygian), p. 208, n. 6 ; Geta, p. 215, n. 7 ; Teres, p. 86, n. 1 ; Tarula, p. 78, n. 3 ; Medus = Maedus, cf. Juv. vii. 132, Tralis and compounds, p. 221, n. 4 ; Aulupor, Mucapor (' nome tracio comunissimo '), p. 120, nn. 2 and 4.   And many others.

and Statius [1] and Thrasea may have been slave-names, a slave-origin has been assigned to these men. The names given to slaves may be either Greek or Latin in form ; here, too, the choice of name may be a broad indication of race.   It was impossible for the Roman to call a Dacian or an Arabian by his own barbarous name ; and the earlier comedies had provided suitable names for a newly acquired slave, when the wit of his master could not invent one.   ' Carpe, Carpe,' cried Trimalchio to his carver, thereby calling him by his name and conveying a command.   When a native name occurs in the inscriptions it is generally added to the Greek or Latin name assigned by the master or dealer—' nomine Abbas qui et Eutyches,' [2] ' Phoebus qui et Tormogus Hispanus,' [3]—and probably serves as evidence of pride of race and memory of freedom not yet destroyed in the cosmopolitanism of the Empire or the enforced obedience of slavery.   In some few cases the native name appears alone —' Sassa coniunx et colliberta natione Daca.' [4]   Tricunda, according to Dessau, is an Isauric name.[5]

That Greek names are on the whole an indication of Oriental origin has generally been taken for granted.   Some names are in themselves an indication of nationality, though it may be doubted whether careful distinction was always made ; ' Syrus ' would often be accurate enough to describe perhaps an Egyptian or a Carian.   Latin names, on the other hand, seem to be given on the whole to slaves of western or northern origin, Greek names being reserved for the Hellenized East or beyond.[6] But such a rule is by no means absolute. Salvius, Hilarus, Felix, may on the whole denote western origin ; Phileros, Hyacinthus, and the like may suggest Greece or the Levant ; but it is none the less true that a Gaul, not merely a Greek slave in Gaul, is called Syntropus, a Parthian Vividius, a Spaniard Phoebus, a German Nereus, a Persian Mercury.[7]   And at the

[1] Aul. Gell. iv. 20. 12.
[2] Pap. Brit. Mus. 229 (reference taken from Bang). See Dess. iii.(2), 927.
[3] C.I.L. vi. 24162.   [4] C.I.L. iii. 14355 (15).   [5] Dess. 3806.
[6] Bang's collection of passages makes this clear.
[7] C.I.L. vi. 27741, 29112, 24162, 4344.   Mercury's date is A.D. 354. Tenney Frank thinks that Greek and Latin names were given fairly equally to Spaniards. For the meaning of natione Gallus, etc., cf. supra, p. 15. See further J.R.S. xiv. 101, where similar caution as to the value of a name as a criterion is recommended.

same time there may have been a tendency for freed parents of Eastern extraction to give their children Latin names in an attempt to conceal the stigma, if such still remained, of a servile origin ; therefore in many cases a Latin name may conceal an Eastern nationality.[1] It may be, then, that the impression gained by a reading of Dessau hardly represents at its full value the vast number of foreign extraction in Rome. At any rate the impression carried away may be checked perhaps by the precise mathematics of Professor Tenney Frank, who, after counting thousands of inscriptions and making the necessary adjustments and compensations, concludes that nine-tenths of the population of Rome under the early Empire were of foreign descent. Yet this figure may need to be discounted, for, as has been suggested, the foreigner rising from slavery to a position of comparative wealth, if even only that given by a retail shop, had a greater achievement to record, and a greater vanity to impel him to record it, than the humble free man who often saw himself outstripped in the struggle by a despised Oriental.

So, too, with Italy ; Professor Frank's careful counting of inscriptions gives for Latium, excluding Rome, 64 per cent. of Greek names to 36 of Latin; for Calabria to Picenum, 53 Greek names to 47 Latin ; for Cisalpine Gaul, 46 Greek names to 54 Latin. But here again it seems very doubtful whether the inscriptions thus used will really give a good indication. The country slave, as has been seen, does not often leave an inscription when compared with his town-bred artisan brother ;

[1] Tenney Frank, *op. cit.* p. 693, produces the following table from a count of 13,900 inscriptions :

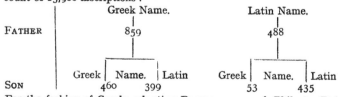

For the fashion of Greeks adopting Roman names, cf. Philostr. *Epistles of Apollonius*, lxxii., and his protest.

Mau-Kelsey, *Pompeii*, p. 337, suggests that Acceptus, together with his wife Euhodia, came from Alexandria, arguing from the number of statues of Isis in his house, and not regarding the Latin name, Acceptus, as an objection.

yet the farm slave is generally of the nationality which would bear a Latin name. The small proprietor leaves little record of himself, and it would be difficult to guess how far he had been corrupted by foreign admixture. Most of the inscriptions come from the towns, and a counting may give some help through the very precision of numerals, but it can never be relied upon to give a close approximation to the truth.

It is a natural tendency to regard the mingling of races in the Empire as centripetal, as moving towards Rome and Italy. On the whole, this is true, and yet there are many influences which draw the foreigner away from Rome and establish him in some remote corner of the earth very far removed from his birthplace. Trade summoned merchants to obscure quarters by the great trade routes, and everywhere are flung up by these currents strange nationalities in strange places : Syrian merchants are to be found in Sicily, Gaul, Dacia, Pannonia ; a Nicomedian at Mainz, a Cappadocian in Gaul ; [1] and many of these traders were freedmen. The movements of legions and their settlement for long years in permanent camps gave ample opportunity for the fusion of races ; nor are the legions entirely irrelevant to the subject, for it has already been seen how often an ex-centurion, after some years as a settled civilian in a land other than that of his birth, married his slave after freeing her. The transplanting of tribes by Trajan and Marcus Aurelius gave less opportunity for complicated interpenetration of races, but was not entirely devoid of consequences. At the low level of slavery the local area over which the fusion of races might take place was as broad as the Empire, though in Rome and Italy and on the main routes of commerce the process may be seen most conspicuously. The manifold causes which might summon a slave or freedman to strange corners have been seen in reviewing the work of slaves on the land, in domestic employment, in business, and in State departments. The train of women servants accompanying the wife of a provincial governor ' converted a Roman army on the march into the likeness of a barbarian progress ' ; [2] officials of the Empire penetrated to obscure regions, and their appearance there is too common to

[1] Cf. M. P. Charlesworth, *Trade Routes and Commerce of the Roman Empire*, e.g. pp. 96, 253, 275.
[2] Tac. *Ann.* iii. 33. Church and Brodribb's translation.

need much illustration ; a Parthian is to be found in Ravenna,[1] a Corinthian among the Allobroges,[2] an Isaurian in Samnium,[3] while a stone found near South Shields records the marriage of a man from Palmyra, on the borders of the Arabian desert, to a woman of the Catuvellaunian tribe in the Midlands of Britain.[4] ' Send my book,' says Martial, ' to Marcellinus '—who now has time to read after a victorious campaign—' by the hand of a Greek slave ' ; he will keep the messenger and send in exchange a captive from the Danube, ' fit to tend sheep on your farm at Tibur.' [5]

Those authors who recommend that family life should be encouraged among slaves also advise that too many slaves of the same nationality or tribe should not be kept within the same household, partly for fear of concerted action, partly to avoid quarrels among the staff.   That such slave-marriages were common and were relied on to maintain the supply of slaves has already been seen.   But, if the staff contained many nationalities, the marriage of *sarcinator* and *sarcinatrix* in the same household may mean the marriage of East and West ; when Flavia Erotis is married to T. Flavius Januarius, or Lais to Fortunatus a gardener, or Optatus to Pyrrhe, or C. Apidius Primus to Aristia Arche, who can tell what mingling of races is taking place ? [6]

Such fusion took place unimpeded, for there was no colour barrier.   If a Syrian or Jewess is despised as a wife by a free man, it is because she comes from a despised race or because she practised barbarous rites, not because her skin was darker. Aristocratic prejudice might abhor a Cleopatra or Berenice as Empress of Rome—chiefly because of the slight to women of Roman stock—but even those senators who raised their protest soon married Syrians and women of mixed descent.   For the Nubian, no doubt, antipathy was felt ; but, on the whole, there was little distinction of nationality as such.   The Greek east led captive the west by more chains than those of literature and art ; and Rome, at first resisting, soon became a willing prisoner.

[1] Dess. 1980.   [2] 4620.   [3] 3806.
[4] 7063.   [5] Mart. vii. 80.
[6] Dess. 1552, 1618, 7400, 8259 ; cf. Tac. *Ann.* xiv. 44, ' nationes in familiis habemus ' ; cf. Sen. *Ep.* xcv. 24.

If there had been a colour bar to draw a rigid line between slave and free, the many avenues by which an ex-slave might proceed from the obscurity of the kitchen or retail shop to high position and influence would have been closed to thousands who actually ascended by them. And wealth and power could open the door to society ; though the grosser type of imperial favourite might be hated by those who hated the imperial régime for producing a Pallas or Narcissus, still many a likeable freedman of moderate fortune must have found that the exclusiveness of self-respecting, even aristocratic, families would open to a golden key, till society was itself so gilded that the only barrier became that of poverty, not of blood. The relaxation of rigid rule has already been observed ; the slave has become knight, praetor, provincial governor. But with such exalted position is given the opportunity of equally exalted marriage ; if marriage to a governor of foreign or servile origin assures wealth and position to the daughter of a once proud family, why look too closely into the origin of that wealth ?— in these days ' money does not smell '—why search too carefully into family history ? *Stemmata quid faciunt?* Felix might ' exercise the dominion of a king with the mind of a slave,' [1] but none the less he was related by marriage to the Emperor Claudius. Slave-blood rose high above its own level, and mingled more and more with the bluest blood surviving, till in the third century senators found it safest to trace their ancestry back to Aeneas,[2] lest in the intervening centuries a Syrus or Geta or Phileros should obtrude his unwanted features.

To such mingling of races each element made a differing contribution. The West was young and lusty. Politically, Italy was the most advanced country, and by the beginning of the Empire had done enough to make other nations realize the genius of the Roman character. Gaul and Spain were beginning to learn the advantages of political life and the opportunities offered by the municipal system. The West, as a whole, was youthful ; seven hundred years was but a childhood, though long enough to show possibilities for good, long enough to have proved that the chosen people were not

[1] ' Ius regium servili ingenio,' Tac. *Hist.* v. 9 ; cf. ' Servis regna dabunt, captivis fata triumphum,' Juv. vii. 201.
[2] Jerome, *Ep.* cviii. 4.

faultless.   In the building of the Empire Rome was trammelled by few traditions of the past ; she inherited no system ; she was free to hammer out for herself by experiment and trial, guided sometimes by imitation,[1] a theory and a practice of government which owed little to any predecessor.   She had quickly broken loose from the despotism of her Etruscan rulers, and, in asserting her freedom, had been the only conquering power which had not been caught in that cycle of dominion and servitude which was the fate of nearly every nation of the East.   Never having been enslaved for any length of time, she had not learnt to play the despot ; never having exercised tyranny, she knew not how to grovel; if she oppressed her provinces, the fall of the Republic was her penalty, and she learnt by experience.   In political and administrative wisdom she was her own tutor ; she could boast neither the reverend years nor the subtle learning nor the blasé worldliness of her more aged subjects.   It was by her youth and freshness that she subdued them, like another new and conquering race from Macedon ; and in her turn she was to fall a victim to the insidious poison of Oriental languor, which rouses itself only to domineer, of Oriental vanity, which swells the more as the object of its pride drops from its failing grasp.

On the East 'let Syria and Asia be in bondage' is the verdict of the Civilis of Tacitus,[2] and it is the verdict of all antiquity, written plainly on every page of Greek and Roman literature.   'Lydia, Phrygia, Pontus,' says Philostratus, 'have always been subject to other nations, and as yet see nothing shameful in slavery.'   The Syrians lived upon the border of Media, where 'they do obeisance to tyrannies, where there is no real conception of liberty.'[3]   Ground down beneath the oppression of successive despotisms, the East was skilled to grovel in adversity, to bully in success ; knowing no form of government but despotism, she had developed no germ of a sound political life ; 'these Oriental monarchies had no room for either Individualism or Freedom.   They wrought great structural works.   They bestowed happiness of a sort upon myriads of men.   They dealt death or bondage to many myriads more.   To political life, to political thought, they contribute

---

[1] A remark of Polybius.   [2] Tac. *Hist.* iv. 17
[3] *Vit. Ap.* viii. 7 (xii) ; vii. 14.

little save lessons of negation.'[1]   And so the Oriental, betaking himself to trade, quickly learnt the advantages of wealth, and, when chance offered dominion and prosperity to each nation, luxury and enjoyment became the sole occupation and the sole right of the predominant power. As the tide of Empire rolled West, it met on the coast the Greek cities of Ionia, where Greek wit had combined with Eastern wealth to build up a civilization of dazzling brilliance, which was later spread by the Macedonian Empire far over the south of Asia Minor and Syria and Egypt. These Hellenized cities of the East reached untouched heights of wealth and outward magnificence ; the Greeks had been caught by the splendour of the barbarians they despised, and by the contributions of their imagination had hastened the pace to degeneracy and corruption. The father of Cicero had observed that the better the Syrians came to know Greek the more abandoned they became ; his fear was lest his own countrymen should meet a like fate from a like cause.[2]

At one great crisis in Roman history these two halves of the Empire threatened to fall asunder. The revolutionary first century B.C., the weakness of the central government and the resulting devotion of vast armies to individual generals had culminated in civil war, which almost split in twain an Empire still loosely bound together. The genius of Augustus by strength of will and sympathetic insight had knit together his Empire ; and for centuries two anomalous elements, East and West, were held together as one unity. Yet the completeness of Augustus' triumph, brilliant as it was, may have meant the certainty of his failure ; it may be that because of the very unity of the whole, the decay of the East penetrated more freely to every part of the West.

It has often been maintained that the mixture of an Asiatic and European race has seldom produced a vigorous and healthy race. The younger race, having no accumulated traditions to

[1] B. W. Henderson, *The Study of Roman History*, p. 12. T. R. Glover, *Virgil*, p. 143, n. 2, contrasts two passages, *Mon. Anc.* 3, ' externas gentes, quibus tuto ignosci potuit, conservare quam excidere malui,' and Aesch. *Persae*, 101 sqq., πολέμους πυργοδαΐκτους/διέπειν ἱππιοχάρμας τε κλόνους, πόλεων τ' ἀναστάσεις.

[2] Cic. *de orat.* ii. 66 (265), ' nostros homines similes esse Syrorum venalium : ut quisque optime Graece sciret, ita esse nequissimum.'

hand on, has little to contribute save its own vigour ; the older race comes laden with the massed tendencies of centuries ; inherited dispositions may lie dormant for generations, remaining in abeyance through sheer absence of vitality to express themselves ; at length, reinforced by a vigour that is not their own, they spring to life, and, fed on a borrowed strength, break out into increased activity, driving with faster impulse the offspring race to destruction. Heredity, climate, institutions have always proved fatal to the Western race rash enough to ally itself too closely with the East.[1]

Every historian of the Fall vends his own variety of apple, and most would agree that somehow or other the penetration of the West by the East was not lacking as a contributory cause. At the same time it is not clearly defined what the influence of the East was. Tenney Frank says 'it would be quite unfair to pass judgment upon the native qualities of the Orientals without a further study.'[2] Rostovtzeff, in his summary review of the causes of the Fall, declares himself incompetent ' to sit in judgment on the problem of degeneration from the biological or physiological point of view.'[3] And he asks what is the criterion for distinguishing between inferior and superior races in the Roman Empire. ' The Celts had a high material civilization of their own.' ' The Germans were destined to develop a high civilized life in the future.' *Grammatici certant ;* and it is rash to intrude. But *is* the Greek race considered superior at this period of history ? From the Roman point of view the Greeks are a part of the decadent East. And when the Roman and Celt combined, they produced as in Gaul, and to some extent in Britain, a civilization as rich in achievement or promise as that of Italy. The judgment of the contemporary Roman is not altogether to be despised ; he condemned Syrians, Egyptians, Cappadocians, Greeks, and the rest ; he felt instinctively that there was a moral and political

---

[1] Cf. a short essay by Nilsson, *The Race Problem of the Roman Empire*, separat ur ' Hereditas,' ii. 1921, since expanded in *Imperial Rome* by the same writer, 1925. Cf. F. C. S. Schiller, ' The Ruin of Rome,' etc., in *Eugenics Review*, April 1925.

[2] Tenney Frank, *Amer. Hist. Rev.*, already cited.

[3] *Social and Economic History*, p. 485 ; cf. Bury, *Later Roman Empire*, i. 311, where the collapse in the West is attributed to ' a series of contingent events,' ' which need not have led to disaster.'

rottenness in these peoples. He may speak slightingly of German barbarism or British ferocity, but it is clear that he saw in the peoples of Gaul and Britain under Roman rule the promise of progress, in the East the decay of stagnation. The instinct of the Roman may have been right, and it is difficult to believe that he did not feel a greater kinship or sympathy with the peoples of the Western provinces than with those of the East. However, the spread of Orientals over the West is a fact ; and whether any value is to be attached to the biological argument or not, any mingling of races is almost certain to have results which may be classed as moral, political, religious. There is not any need to deal explicitly with the moral character of the nations brought into the West by slavery. The Roman opinion of them is clear enough, and slavery was not calculated on the whole to improve that character. But some observations may be made upon the possible effect of Eastern slaves upon the political and religious life of the West ; and their influence upon morals will necessarily be touched upon indirectly.

It has been claimed on an earlier page that the freedman trained in Roman methods and adopting Roman culture made a unique and valuable contribution to the municipal life of the Empire. It is not necessarily inconsistent with this claim to condemn him for bringing the principles of decay which ruined many of the cities of Italy and the nearer provinces. In Asia Minor and Syria the intermingling of Greek and Oriental blood and culture had gone on for centuries ; the result was an urban life marvellous for its outward splendour. Yet those who knew it best knew the decadence within. Condemnation of it may be found in Philostratus' *Life of Apollonius*,[1] but, as the alleged opinions of Apollonius are probably merely those of Philostratus or his worthless sources, we may turn to a more reliable witness, Dio Chrysostom of Prusa in Bithynia. Dio had first-hand knowledge, being a citizen of more than one town and a frequent visitor to many others. His judgment is penetrating and fearless ; he can admire and encourage the good, and outspokenly condemn the bad ; his sincere pleading, expressed in simple if wordy style, is proof of his real anxiety for the true welfare of the towns whose honours he was glad to receive ; his message was neither popular, nor probably effective.

[1] See, e.g., v. 26, iii. 58 ; *Ep.* xxxii. 36, 56.

' Your city,' says Dio to the Alexandrians,[1] 'is remarkable in size and situation ; it stands out as second city in the world. Your city is the head of which Egypt is the body, or rather Egypt is a mere appendage. To such praise you are accustomed ; it is what you expect. Yet it is not you that I have praised ; to dwell upon the excellence of your water is but to praise your wells ; the praise of men is orderliness, gentleness, concord, good government, resistance to the temptations of pleasure. What report do strangers take away from your city ? We have seen a city, they say, wonderful, glorious, but a city driven mad by song and horse-racing, a city engaged in nothing worthy of its greatness.   As soon as her citizens set foot in stadium or theatre, they are bewitched ; after a devastating conflagration of excitement, the turmoil and disorder smoulder on for days, consuming whatever relics have escaped the general blaze. None of you ever handled a horse ; you are like lame men quarrelling over a race. Music is your curse : you are quick enough to condemn a discord in the theatre ; discord among yourselves passes unnoticed.   Your theatre rings with applause and uproar. For righteousness you care nothing ; hence your strife, your unavailing disappointments, your senseless triumphs. Of genuine civic patriotism you know nothing ; empty honours and rewards are expected by your rulers ; those who speak in your assemblies have no thought for the common interest ; they seek merely to parade themselves. To go to Alexandria is like going to see a beautiful house, and finding its master a good-for-nothing slave, not even fit to open the door to the visitor.' [2]

Against other cities similar charges are levelled. At Tarsus [3] birth and wealth give power to men who are incapable of administering even a village ; they gape after the applause of the multitude ; they delight in power and crowns and prominent seats in the theatre ; clothed in purple, they sacrifice in public places and lead processions through the streets. Not content with internal strife, they encourage external jealousies and

<hr/>

[1] Cf. Charlesworth, *Trade Routes*, p. 248, for references to the mixed population in Alexandria.

[2] Very much condensed from Dio Chrys. xxxii. pp. (Dindorf) 400, 401, 406, 412, 413, 414, 416.

[3] xxxiv. pp. 30 to 38.

quarrels with neighbouring cities; whether Tarsus quarrels with Aegae, or Apamea with Antioch, or Smyrna with Ephesus, it is always about a trifle.[1] ' To win some petty triumph over a neighbour reminds me rather of decently bred farmyard cocks than of men.' ' Your petty rivalries and quarrels are those of fellow-slaves wrangling among themselves for first place.' No virtue is more often upon the lips of Dio than unity,[2] no vices more often than luxury and vainglory. The blessings of unity are sung alike to the cities of Nicaea and Prusa and Apamea.[3] The luxury of Tarsus calls forth an impassioned homily, backed by historical example of the decay of empire after empire from this cause.[4]

A picture similar in outline can be reconstructed from the correspondence of Pliny and Trajan. It is possible that senatorial misrule was in part responsible for decay in Bithynia; at the same time, it has been held that conditions there are merely ' a conspicuous example of general disorganization.'[5] Every pretext is used by the populace for wringing from the rich wholesale distributions of money; the rich, in turn, will do anything to secure popularity; a coming of age, a marriage, entry upon office, the dedicating of a public work—all are seized upon as the occasion for lavish bestowal of money and pleasures. Pliny regards the practice as a dangerous kind of bribery, and Trajan agrees.[6] Of the internal strife and jealousy so rife in the Greek cities Trajan is well aware: ' We must remember that the province of Bithynia, and especially city-states like Nicomedia are sorely harassed by faction.'[7] The finances of the cities are in a miserable condition, and it is clear that the main cause is the injudicious expenditure of public money on extravagant works of luxury—theatres, colonnades, and baths—before either the cost had been calculated or compared with revenues. The gymnasium at Nicaea, still unfinished, had begun to sink and crack; the whole of the money spent was wasted. ' All the Greekling peoples,' says Trajan to his persistent Pliny, ' have a weakness for gymnasia; perhaps the people of Nicaea

---

[1] περὶ ὄνου σκιᾶς, φασί, διαφέρονται.   *Ibid.* p. 37.   [2] ὁμόνοια.

[3] xxxix., xl., xli. ; for στάσις at Tyre, Sidon, Cyzicus, cf. Dio Cass. liv. 7.

[4] xxxii.   [5] Dill, *Roman Society*, p. 247.

[6] Plin. *Ep.* x. 116, 117.   [7] x. 36.

have started building on too grand a scale; they must be content with what will answer their needs.'[1] Unfortunately, to cut their coat according to their cloth was an accomplishment unknown to these cities, as many of the letters testify; but their contents are too well known to detain us longer.

Brilliant as was the municipal life of the West in the Flavian and Antonine ages, and profoundly as it affected civilization, there are nevertheless to be found in it the seeds of the decay and the beginnings of the paralysis which settled upon the Roman world for centuries. If it is true that the small provincial towns of the West owed much of their vigorous life to freedmen, it is a remarkable tribute to Rome's power of educating foreign peoples in ideas of self-government that she was able, out of such unpromising material, to make citizens capable of such loyalty to their townships. But it may be a sign that Rome's success was not complete if those causes and symptoms of decay which were discovered in the East are also seen to operate more and more powerfully in the West.

The Oriental nature of the mob at Rome is a commonplace long before the Empire, and not less commonplace is its reputation for idleness and servility, for pleasure-seeking and a growing craving to be fed and amused. It is interesting to notice, too, how the type of entertainment changes, gradually becoming less Italian as music and acting and gorgeous spectacles and pageants become more prominent. But in the provincial towns of the West also those symptoms which Dio notes in the East make their appearance. The voluntary public spirit of the rich is gradually but surely fettered by the exactions of the poorer classes till it becomes a necessary burden to be shouldered by any candidate for office. At the same time, the municipal offices thus obtained depreciate in value and are filled by the wrong type of man; the persistent demand for amphitheatres and musical festivals and public feastings leads to exhaustion of municipal treasuries and to bankruptcy; one township vies with another in the erection of more splendid colonnades; sometimes open enmity, needing the services of an external reconciler, is the outcome, but in any case unwise spending is the certain result. As the burdens of magistrates become greater with the inexhaustible demand of all classes for pleasure,

---

[1] ' Quod possit illis sufficere,' x. 41, 42.

their temptations increase ; resort is made to false balance sheets and irregular practices, till, as local independence is more and more abused, the central Government interferes first by means of *curatores*, later by *correctores*, to check expenditure and regulate finances.[1] Such interference with local liberties may have been in the interests of the towns themselves, but it was a sign that the townships had failed to grasp the first principle of local independence, which is self-control.

There is no need to elaborate the picture. Pleasure as an interruption in a life of hard work gave way to the pursuit of enjoyment as an end in itself ; every small town had its gladiatorial shows and its horse races; the public spirit of leading men is measured not so much by services to the community as by their willingness to spend money in public games, feasts, and distributions of food. Pompeii may be an extreme case, but the imitation of Rome as the pattern produced the same symptoms in provincial towns. At Sitifis in Mauretania, P. Arrius Januarius Mamertinus erected a statue of his dead patron according to the terms of the will, and provided dramatic spectacles and made distributions of presents to the decurions.[2] Feastings and banquets, presents of money, bread, wine, oil, even nuts, sometimes given to the decurions, sometimes to the whole body of the people, sometimes to every person in the town *sine distinctione libertatis*,[3] become monotonous in their repetition ;[4] freedmen are among the givers, but for the most part no doubt they receive.. Such systematic flattery of the rich, such servile dependency on their enforced liberality, is no part of the real Roman character either in Rome or elsewhere, nor as far as can be seen is it a mark of the Western provincial. It is a legacy of the East, a foreign growth made indigenous first in Rome and later in the townships by the imitation of the capital and the ingrafting of foreign stock.

To assign the blame for this decline in the health of municipal life is not easy ; it may have been a temporary phase through

---

[1] Curatores of Italian cities are to be found in the time of Trajan and Hadrian. See Dess. 5502, 5918a, 6725, and cf. 1040, 2768, 2769. The first hint of a corrector under that name in Italy is in the time of Caracalla, Dess. 1159, ' electus ad corrigendum statum Italiae.'

[2] Dess. 6873 ; cf. 6858 for a similar case at Cirta.   [3] Dess. 6271.

[4] e.g. 6654, 6827, 6821, for typical examples.

which an imperial government experimenting with the welding together of peoples and the granting of local liberties was bound to go, and it may be that Rome would have succeeded if she had been given time and opportunity.[1] But, whatever other causes there may have been, the presence of so many slaves and ex-slaves, drawn from peoples devoid of all political sense and brought up through slavery to value money and temporary appearances above all things, contributed to mould the temper and the attitude to life which eventually reproduced in the West some of the worst features of city-life in the East.

The spread of Oriental religions is a subject which has claimed much attention lately. And it is a fascinating study, partly for its own sake, partly as helping to explain the very rapid spread and reception of Christianity among Western peoples. It is not always easy, however, to separate from other agencies the influence of slaves in the spread of these cults, and any distinctions drawn must necessarily be of a general nature. Nor is it easy to date the rise and fall of a given cult in a particular place.

The Egyptian cults may first claim attention. A temple of Serapis was built at Puteoli as early as 150 B.C., and at Pompeii about 105 B.C. From the coast the cult soon spread to Rome, and after meeting with opposition on the part of an official con-servatism secured its triumph by the erection of a temple in the city in 42 B.C.;[2] later, as the cult spreads, Serapis and Isis may be found at places as far distant as Lambaesis, Nemausus, the German frontier, Aquincum. The Egyptian deities leave frequent memorials in Africa, Spain, Narbonensis, Pannonia, Dacia, but are rare in Gaul, Britain, the Rhine, Dalmatia.[3] In Africa they are to be found chiefly in the maritime cities and Lambaesis, in Spain in the most accessible districts.[4] Most of the memorials are due to private devotion ; townships and public bodies play little part in the erection of monuments.

[1] For a pessimistic view of municipal life, see Heitland's *Iterum* (and the very critical review in *J.R.S.*, 1924). Few signs of decay seem to be visible in the first two centuries, in which the municipalities represent Rome's greatest achievement ; my argument is that the seeds of the later decay were sown then, and nurtured by the troubles of the third century.

[2] For a sketch of the history of the cults, *v.* Dill, p. 560.

[3] Toutain, *Les cultes paiens dans l'empire romain*, ii. 18.   [4] P. 19.

Hence it has been concluded, both from the distribution of the memorials and from their character, that though soldiers and officials are to be found as devotees, the great work in the spread of these cults is due to slaves and freedmen.   Thus, at Soissons, a *vicarius* of Hermes Aug. dispensator is found worshipping Isis;[1] at Aequiculi Apronianus, a public slave of the township offers to Serapis statues and a shrine;[2] at Valentia, Isis was worshipped by a *sodalicium vernarum*;[3] and here, too, a slave invoked Serapis for the safety of his master.

The Phrygian cults wielded an enormous influence, particularly the cult of Magna Mater.   Whatever the secret of her power, she made an early appearance in Rome (208 B.C.), and thence spread rapidly through the provinces.   An examination of the inscriptions shows that in the provinces, at any rate, freedmen and slaves are very rare as devotees,[4] and the rareness of officers, soldiers, imperial agents, freedmen, and slaves marks off the Phrygian cults from the Egyptian and Syrian.[5] Hence it has been inferred that the cult came to the provinces not directly from the East, but through higher social circles at Rome than slaves or soldiers.   Whatever the route followed by this cult, its influence is remarkable ; it penetrated far among the natives ; and the secret of its power has been found[6] in the notion of purification and a better life offered by the *taurobolium* and the washing in blood.   And the inscriptions, in one or two of which the formula ' in aeternum renatus ' occurs, seem to breathe a conviction only equalled in the Mithraic cult.[7] In Italy slaves and freedmen are fairly frequent as disciples, and are to be found as priests in the service of goddesses.[8]

The Syrian cults—those of Jupiter Dolichenus and Heliopolitanus, of Elagabal, of Belus and Malagbel, of Dea Syria,

---

[1] Dess. 4376a.   [2] 4381.   [3] *C.I.L.* ii. 3730.

[4] On p. 107 Toutain says he can only find two, *C.I.L.* xiii. 6664 and viii. 5521, but on p. 115 quotes xiii. 509 (=Dess. 4123, 4124), which gives a freedman as priest.

[5] P. 110.

[6] e.g. by Cumont, *Les religions orientales*, p. 102, and Toutain, p. 118, and Dill.

[7] Dill, p. 558, is wrong in saying that this phrase occurs on ' a considerable number of monuments.'

[8] e.g. at Ostia a freedman appears as *apparator*, Dess. 4173 ; at Ostia also a freedman (not an official), 4177.   In Samnium, Tricunda offers to

Astarte, and Baltis—are distributed through much the same provinces as the Egyptian. None are found in Spain ; rare in Gaul and Dalmatia, they occur most frequently in Africa, Britain, Germany, and, above all, in Pannonia, Moesia, Dacia.[1] They are commonest, therefore, where the officials of provincial administration and army garrisons are most numerous. Astarte is found in Britain ; at Lambaesis there was an organized cult of Dolichenus ; Malagbel is found at Sarmizegethusa, Jupiter Heliopolitanus at Carnuntum.[2] The worshippers are drawn partly from the army, but chiefly from the crowds of cashiers and clerks and procuratorial officials, from the staffs of contractors employed by the Government and the assistants of private traders ; most of these were slaves or of slave-origin.

Of the irresistible spread of Mithraic cult it is impossible to give any idea in a short paragraph,[3] nor of the tremendous power of the worship as ' l'incarnation céleste de la conscience.' [4] It was not only a soldiers' religion, though the army claimed thousands of adherents. Brought by slaves to the seaport towns, and flourishing among those who worked in docks and factories and markets, it became so firmly established in these cosmopolitan centres, that at Ostia, for example, there were five *Mithraea* in existence in the second century. In Rome the greater number of Mithraic inscriptions are those of slaves and freedmen,[5] so, too, in such towns as Antium, Rusellae, and Pisa ; in the northern provinces the cult was popular among tax-collectors, cashiers, and slaves engaged in mining and contracting work in obscure outposts of Empire.[6] *Vilici, ferrarii, dispensatores, arcarii*, and *tabulatores* are to be found frequently ; public slaves of townships, *vicarii* of other slaves make their

Bellona (a form of Magna Mater, not the Italian goddess) a lamp and ornaments in A.D. 11, Dess. 3806. At Lactora, in Aquitania, two slaves appear together as priests ; ' Sacrum M(atri) Magnae, Ant. Prima tauropolium fec. host(iis) suis sacerdotib(us) Zminthio Procliani et Pacio Agrippae,' Dess. 4123.

[1] Toutain, p. 55.   [2] Toutain, pp. 51, 53.

[3] Cumont's enormous work is fascinating reading ; Dill gives a brilliantly written summary of it.

[4] Reinach's phrase.

[5] Cumont, p. 274. Cumont inscr. Nos. 53, 69, 75, 175, 415, for *vilici*; *dispensator*, 144, 352 ; *arcarius*, 152, 403 ; *tabularius*, 405 ; *actuarius*, 68.

[6] Cumont, p. 270.

offering—a statue, a pedestal, even a completely furnished *mithraeum*.[1] Carried by these subterranean channels of society, it is difficult to imagine the rapidity with which the cult spread, till it is to be found all over the Roman world in varying density.[2] And to the spread of this intensely spiritual and compelling religion slaves and ex-slaves contributed as much as, if not more than, any other grade of society.

In a world so full of movement as the Roman Empire there is little doubt of the diffusion of Oriental cults over a wide area : troops, merchants, *le diaspora servile*, and the imperial civil service, largely recruited from *le diaspora*, were the chief agents in conveying them. It has been doubted, however, whether the cults made converts in the Latin provinces, though in Italy it is clear enough that thousands of new adherents were made. Thus Toutain is sceptical [3] whether the Egyptian or Syrian or Mithraic cults ever exerted much influence on the native populations ; though he admits it in the case of Magna Mater. His main argument is the lack of native names in the inscriptions. But the test of names is not conclusive ; for a Gaul, for example, who was sufficiently advanced to adopt Roman civilization, together with the Oriental religion which it offered, was also likely to adopt a Greek or Latin name. Again, children were brought up in these faiths,[4] and though of servile birth were absorbed by the native population. When, therefore, Toutain urges that the cults scarcely altered the beliefs or the practice of the vast majority of the inhabitants, he may be right as to ' the practice,' but it would be difficult to say that the introduction of a strange cult can be without influence on the ideas of a people, even though inscriptions may not directly attest such influence. The way in which ideas can act and react on one another is seen in the ' syncretism ' of religion in these and later centuries. Growing familiarity with a growing number of divinities from different countries often with the same attributes and claiming sovereignty not over a portion of

---

[1] Cumont, No. 312a, ' I(nvicto) M(ithrae) spelaeum cum omne impensa Hermes C. Antoni(i) Rufi praefecti vehiculorum et conductoris publici portorii servus vilicus Fortunatianus fecit.'

[2] See Cumont's map.

[3] See, e.g., pp. 34 and 71. He differs from Cumont.

[4] e.g. Dess. 4381.

the world, but the whole, naturally suggested the question whether those divinities might not after all be the same under other names; and alongside with this syncretistic tendency survived an earlier belief in the special protection of local gods for their favourite haunts. It might be safer even in the days when Magna Mater was queen of the earth to placate a local divinity.[1] The inscriptions make clear this desire to propitiate all available gods. One dedication, typical of hundreds, reads: ' Iovi Optimo Maximo, Iunoni Reginae, Minervae Sanctae, Soli Mithrae, Herculi, Marti, Mercurio, Genio loci, diis deabusque omnibus.'[2] And so the first feeling of surprise that so many Oriental slaves worship nominally Italian deities, such as Silvanus, Jupiter, Mercurius, fades away when it is realized that these names have not any longer their former meaning. An *actor*, Sagaris by name, prays for the safety of his master; he prays, as an *actor* appropriately might, to Mercury, the god of gain, but he prays to Mercurius Invictus, and Invictus is the epithet of Mithras.[3] So, too, Callistus prays to Jupiter Optimus Maximus, but his third epithet of the god is Aeternus, and Jupiter Aeternus has been identified[4] as Dolichenus, of Commagene; Silvanus is sometimes ' silvestris,' but also ' castrensis, invictus Pantheus, dendrophorus,' the last an adjective connected with Magna Mater. Most of the gods in the Graeco-Roman pantheon are in some way connected with Oriental divinities. The name of the god counts for little; the gods of Cato's time would hardly recognize their epithets or their ritual. Eastern notions penetrated into the religious consciousness of the day probably much more than inscriptions show.

The moral effect of these religions has been disputed; some writers regret the disappearance of the primitive Italian cults, however emotionless and formal and uninspiring; others point to the licence and quackery practised by some devotees of Eastern cults; others again dwell on the lofty spiritual value of a religion which could call forth the beautiful prayer to Isis given in Apuleius, or lead Plutarch to write so touchingly to his

[1] For one or two striking examples, cf. Friedländer, *Roman Life* etc., iii. 111.
[2] *C.I.L.* viii. 4578. Often cut down to *dis deabusque*, e.g. Dess. 4036.
[3] Another inscription by the same man begins Ἡλίῳ Μίθρᾳ, Dess. 3197.
[4] By Cumont; *v.* note in Dess. 3014.

wife on the death of their little daughter. Or they dwell on the self-sacrifice and sense of brotherhood attested by Mithraic inscriptions. There is little doubt that the old religions of Greece and Rome failed to satisfy the new and genuine aspirations which were everywhere seeking for fulfilment during these two centuries, and that the Oriental religions purged themselves of much that was revolting as they passed West. Though it would be wrong to assume that the highest form of a cult was also its commonest form, yet on the whole, the influence of these religions was a strong force for good in a time when other religion was dead ; what they meant to such men as Plutarch or Aristides or the Lucius of Apuleius they probably meant to hundreds of nameless worshippers, bringing comfort and a new hope to educated and uneducated alike. Indeed, the best proof of their power is to be found in the fierce denunciations of the Christian apologists. And in the spread of these religions slavery played a great part.

The mingling of races was a long process complicated by the action and reaction of a multitude of forces. To discuss the process and its results would be an interesting study, if indeed there is enough material ; the nature of some of the problems raised has been briefly indicated as far as slavery touches them. From a biological point of view, it has been suggested, it is doubtful whether the Roman experiment in the fusion of peoples was likely to be a success ; the moral contribution of the East was not likely to improve upon the old Roman virtues. On the other hand, the religious contribution contained elements of value, and in so far as it influenced morality was undoubtedly a force for good. In the sphere of politics, the East, while providing new and versatile recruits to be trained often most successfully as citizens, sent them out already equipped with an hereditary legacy of tendencies which in the long run helped to destroy the vigorous municipal life of the West.

It is possible that, had more time been given, Rome would have succeeded in her task of fusion, and that out of the cosmopolitanism of the Empire a new and more brilliant civilization might have sprung, embodying the best and the reconcilable portions of the Eastern and Western types. Actually, Roman culture in undertaking the task of levelling the world up to its standard was itself levelled down, or, if it is a case of neither superiority nor inferiority, was itself profoundly modified ; possibly other causes came just at the moment when the venture of civilizing the world was trembling in the balance, and turned what would have been a success into a glorious failure ; or, the dilution of Roman civilization was carried much too far, and taxed too much the savouring capacities of the original Roman element.   Whatever did happen or might have happened, it remains true that slavery was one of the main causes in that mingling of races which was the corollary, possibly the curse, of the Roman Empire.

CHAPTER IX

ANCIENT AND MODERN SLAVERY

IT has been interesting to read the remarkable book of J. E. Cairnes, *The Slave Power*, which was intentionally left to be read after the foregoing chapters were written. Though dealing with slavery in the American States, the book is really of wider interest ; for it tries to determine from observation of the working of slavery there the peculiar circumstances which must be present to make slavery economically practicable, and to discover the laws to which the destiny of slaveowning States is necessarily subject. The investigation includes a few pages comparing ancient and modern slavery, but actually comparison is invited on every page. To summarize his arguments is to rob them of part of their cogency ; and in the main it is with his conclusions that we are here concerned.

Why did the Northern States cease to employ slave-labour while the Southern States continued ? [1] The reasons usually given, it is urged, are invalid ; it is not true that the white man is prevented by climate from working in the South, or that the negro is by nature indolent and will work only under compulsion. The real reason is economic, as will be seen by comparing slave-labour and free. Under the system of slavery the owner has sole power, and enjoys the whole fruit of his slaves' labour ; he can direct that labour to a single end with a definite purpose in view, and he cannot complain that initially it is expensive. But this labour is given reluctantly, and therefore demands superintendence ; [2] dispersal of labourers means greater expense, for overseers must be more numerous. 'The cost of slave-labour thus varies directly with the degree in which the work to be done requires dispersion of the labourers.' Further, slave-labour is unskilful ; when 'fear is substituted

[1] Pp. 35 sqq.   [2] P. 45.

for hope,' there is no inducement to learn a craft; indeed, the slave is intentionally kept ignorant, since thus he gives less trouble. Besides being unskilful, slave-labour lacks versatility; 'the difficulty of teaching the slave anything is so great that the only chance of turning his labour to profit is when he has once learned a lesson to keep him to that lesson for life.' Free labour, on the other hand, has one defect: it lacks co-operation, organization, and singleness of purpose; each peasant proprietor is working for himself. But in every other respect it is superior to slave-labour.

Slavery thus may be made to concentrate on exacting a cotton crop from a rich ground, and will yield better results than the free labour of small proprietors; but it will not produce corn, for here extensive combination of labour is not important. On the other hand, skill and energy and care are essential; the farmer needs extra hands at seedtime and harvest, but it will not pay him to keep slaves all the year round for these purposes.[1]

The climate and soil of the Northern States are adapted for corn-growing; the Southern States produce cotton; hence the disappearance of slavery in the North.

Two further deductions may be drawn before pausing to test the relevancy of these observations to Roman conditions. Slave-labour needs a rich soil,[2] no matter what crop it is engaged in raising. Elaborate cultivation, the exploitation of a poor soil to its utmost, require intelligence, delicate machinery, enthusiasm—in other words, a love of work and a love of the soil. Besides a rich land, slave-labour demands that there should be much of it; the slave can only work at the same job; he cannot adapt himself; rotation of crops is impossible, and new ground is constantly needed.

The broad distinction here drawn between corn and cotton lands has in principle been drawn in dealing with Roman agriculture; there, however, the antithesis is between corn and grazing lands. It was argued that if slave-labour was ever extensively used on corn lands, it decreased rapidly as its failure became apparent. The prospects of the success of slave-labour in general farming were seen to increase only as the slave ceased to be a slave; though in the monotonous unskilled tend-

[1] P. 50.   [2] P. 52.

ing of flocks, which occupied shepherds at all seasons, and in many respects is comparable with labour in the cotton fields, slave-labour persisted and might be economically justified. Both on Italian and American soil slave-labour was given reluctantly, was unskilful and wanting in versatility; whenever the slave in antiquity was trained to supplement his field labour by a craft, his conditions improved, and he was automatically unfitted for labour in the field. If the economic success of slave-labour on cotton estate and Italian grazing ranch depend on that labour being kept ' crude,' it is at once uneconomic to turn crude labour into skilled, and impossible that the same labour should share each characteristic. As for the cost of supervision, that is a complaint frequently made in Roman agricultural treatises.

On the other hand, the principal use to which slave-labour was put in Italian farming did not ask for rich lands; it was the cheapness of grazing lands and their availability in large areas which made it easy for the grazing ranch run by slave-labour to come into existence and to continue.

If the arguments of Cairnes be accepted on general grounds, they would reinforce certain conclusions drawn as to Roman agriculture. The corn land of Italy was limited in extent; there could, therefore, be no exploitation of the soil by slave-labour, which would then migrate to unexhausted areas; it was besides by no means virgin land in the first two centuries; it needed all the science and all the industry available to produce corn or vine, and would not yield crops to unskilled or reluctant labour.

The establishment, then, of slavery in America is explained thus : ' Under certain conditions of soil and climate, cultivation by slaves may for a time yield a larger net revenue than cultivation by certain forms of free labour.' [1] Its maintenance, however, is a different question.

So rigid, the argument continues, are the laws governing the destiny of slave-owning States that for such societies fixed social and economic and political attributes can be deduced by *a priori* argument. If slave-labour must remain unskilled, there can be no industry in that society and no commerce. Apart from other considerations, the training of intelligence and

[1] P. 68.

the bringing together of numbers of slaves in a factory would be dangerous. A certain form of agriculture, therefore, is the sole occupation of the slave-owning State; for in this work the sole merit of slavery—its precise and rigid adjustment to the end in view—finds free scope.

Here are two main points : i. the distinction made between the establishment and the maintenance of agricultural slavery; ii. the exclusion of industry and commerce. That ii. is untrue of ancient slavery is obvious, as Cairnes points out later; but i. need not be so summarily dismissed. In the survey of Italian agriculture in Chapter III. it was insisted that slave-labour in agriculture was introduced and established under circumstances which made it practicable and even profitable, but that as circumstances changed its defects were gradually made apparent; it survived, however, long after it was economically justifiable, simply because the change from one system to another is so difficult in the face of established custom and tradition. There comes a time, however, when the actual presence of slavery on the land ceases to be evidence of its superiority over free labour, and is merely proof of the difficulty of changing one system for another. And the precarious hold of slavery in Italian agriculture was made more uncertain by the presence of slaves in industry—slaves skilled, rich, educated, superior often in every respect to the free man, constantly improving their status and that of slaves in general, and simultaneously reducing the amount of labour available for agriculture and showing the false economy of crude labour. Slaves in industry were a factor with which American slavery had not to deal.

If slavery on the land, the argument continues,[1] requires that whatever operations it is engaged on should be conducted on a large scale, correspondingly large capital is needed; but whereas the employer of free labour need only have in reserve sufficient capital to pay wages between the starting of the enterprise and the first return of profit, the employer of slave-labour must be able to produce at once sufficient capital to buy his slaves—that is, he must buy outright the 'future capabilities of the productive instrument,' and not merely hire the current performance. Plantations must be large and they must be owned by capitalists, who are, however, often driven to borrow

[1] P. 73.

a portion of the initial capital needed.   Capitalists in debt are a feature of slave-owning societies.

On this no comment is needed, for the tremendous initial outlay has been observed in Italian agriculture also.

Such is the anti-social and exclusive influence of slave-labour in modern days that it can admit no free labour ; the two types of labour cannot be blended, since work is the badge of the slave, idleness of the free man.   Hence the growth of the class of ' mean whites,' white men who never had or have lost their capital, and being debarred from wage-earning labour, spend a ' vagrant and precarious life,' living on land exhausted by slave exploitation, thieving, ready for adventure and violence, providing recruits for the expeditions which extend the domain of the slave-power, supporting that slave-system which is really the cause of their own miserable lot, and yet compelled to do so through the artificial conditions which that system sets up.[1]

The simultaneous existence of slave and free labour, and the consequent absence of the race of ' mean whites,' is a feature peculiar to ancient society.[2]   If the conclusions reached in the chapter on slaves in industry are tenable, there was no rivalry between the slave and the free man in this province ; the peculiar conditions of the times made possible the continuance of free labour by the side of slavery.   Thus slaves in industry under the circumstances of the Empire in some measure prevented society from experiencing those disastrous effects of slavery upon the material and moral welfare of both slave and free, which Cairnes traces in the American States.

The pages of *The Slave Power* which are most relevant to this essay are those in which Cairnes formally compares the two systems and finds ' the most deep-reaching distinctions.' [3]

i. In ancient times there was no division of race and colour ; freedom was the only distinction between slave and free : then the difficulty was to alter law, now to alter manners.   Even though slavery were abolished, the modern white man has still three prejudices left—the contempt of the master for the slave,

[1] P. 81.

[2] Perhaps the people for whom Ti. Gracchus tried to legislate most resemble ' mean whites.'

[3] P. 109.

of the European for the non-European, of the white races for the coloured.

This absence of racial distinction has already been seen to have far-reaching results. On the one hand, there was no ineffaceable stamp of slavery to condemn the slave to contempt, or to prevent him rising to position after manumission ; nothing less than a genealogical tree would reveal a servile origin for many high-placed families; there was no danger of ostracism for the half-breed, who in modern days is an outcast from both races. On the other hand, it is possible that the ease of the intermingling of races constituted under the conditions of the Empire a danger none the less real for not being obvious.

ii. In antiquity slaves were trained to commerce and industry, the reason being that the master's progress in enjoyment depended on the slave's progress in knowledge and skill. Nowadays ease of commerce makes modern owners independent of their slaves' craftsmanship, for they can obtain their manufactured goods from elsewhere ; thus the crude labour of the cotton fields is enhanced in value, and it is to the interest of the owner to perpetuate slavery not only of body but of mind and soul.

To bring out more clearly Cairnes' contention, it might be worth drawing the distinction that, while ancient slavery was universal in the sense that there was no limit of place, modern slavery was confined to certain areas, and thus was not exposed to those social and economic influences which steadily improved the lot of the slave in antiquity. That modern slavery was not compelled to develop along the same lines would then be accounted for by the isolation which kept not only free labour separate from slave-labour, but also the industry of Europe and the Northern States from the plantations of the South.

iii. A third difference is found in the circumstances of the slave-trade. Under modern conditions a relatively small area worked by slaves was able to draw upon an enormous reservoir of slave-power in other countries. The merciless driving on the plantations could go on without fear of the supply failing, since waste could easily be made good. Thus the profits of an uneconomic system could be maintained and stability assured. In antiquity, however, the supply of slaves from capture in war steadily decreased, and increase by birth was more relied on ; improvement in the lot of the slave was the result.

Here again the distinction between local and universal seems to hold good ; because slavery was limited to certain geographical areas and consequently limited in the number of slaves employed at a given time, it was uninfluenced by causes which in Roman times created a dearth of slaves by capture and compelled Roman owners to encourage family life.

Indeed, the modern limitation of slavery to certain areas— and here we pass beyond the guidance of Cairnes—seems to be responsible for other differences between the two systems. Perhaps it is not an exaggeration to say that many people in Europe remained in ignorance of the existence of slavery, but it is certain that the majority were unaware of the conditions prevalent. The owners were not likely to advertise their methods, and since the general public had no evidence perpetually before it, it quite naturally was untroubled by any feelings on the subject. It required the utmost effort on the part of missionaries and reformers to rouse public opinion even to interest itself in conditions in the Southern States or the British West Indies ; the press, the platform, the novel, the pulpit took their part in bringing home the facts and in controverting the propaganda of the owners. It was only after slavery was discovered that opinion was brought to bear on it.

But under the Empire slavery was everywhere present and everywhere accepted. Familiarity with an institution may lead to blindness as to its merits or demerits, and an insensibility to its moral justification. But it is quite consistent with this to say that the very proximity of slavery was the cause of much good to the slaves themselves. Religion, law, philosophy, the kindliness of educated owners and the good humour of masters who had themselves been slaves all exercised a steady pressure in favour of more humane treatment of slaves ; there was no need of a sudden campaign to inflame popular opinion ; for reform dictated partly by economic reasons but also by moral considerations was perpetually being put into practice, and from time to time into legislation.

APPENDIX I

A. THE ANCIENT EVIDENCE

THE following lists of references do not claim to record every allusion to slaves or slavery in the authorities, but they contain, I think, the most important passages :

THE HISTORIANS

TACITUS.

(Numbers refer to *Annals* except where otherwise stated.)

Law and practice of torture, ii. 30 ; ii. 71 ; iii. 14 ; iii. 22 ; iii. 67 ; iv. 29. Economy from Tiberius' reign onwards, ii. 33 ; iii. 53 (Tiberius refuses to legislate) ; iii. 55. Tiberius' household, iv. 6. *Lex Papia Poppaea* (allusion to), xiv. 65. Debate in Senate on freedmen, xiii. 26 and 27 ; cf. xiii. 47 ; xv. 54 ; xvi. 12, cf. 10. SC. Claudianum, xii. 53 ; xiii. 32. Nero's refusal of trial on slave's prosecution, xiii. 10. Murder of Pedanius Secundus, xiv. 42. Information against master, xvi. 18 ; *Hist.* iv. 1. Accusation of patron, xvi. 10 ; xvi. 12. Foreign worship, ii. 85. Menace of city slaves, iii. 36 ; iv. 27 ; vi. 11. Slaves and Emperor's statue, iii. 36. In provincial governor's suites, ii. 80 ; iii. 33. Enslavement, iv. 72 ; xii. 17. Tax on sale, xiii. 31. Slave war, iv. 27 ; *Hist.* iii. 47, 48. Cruelty, iv. 54. Disturbances on latifundia, xii. 65. Prevent suicide, *Hist.* iv. 59. Devotion, xiv. 60 ; xv. 57 (Epicharis) ; *Hist.* iv. 50 ; *Hist.* i. 49. Impostor, ii. 39, 40 ; v. 10 ; *Hist.* ii. 9 ; *Hist.* ii. 72. Treachery, xii. 26 ; xv. 54 ; *Hist.* iii. 77 ; *Hist.* iii. 84 ; *Hist.* iv. 1. Manumission, xv. 54 ; xvi. 19. In the army, *Hist.* i. 31. In the camps, *Hist.* i. 49 ; ii. 68 ; iii. 33 ; iv. 23 ; iv. 60. *Servi publici, Hist.* i. 43 ; iii. 71. Private slaves for public work, *Hist.* iii. 58. Vernile Dictum, *Hist.* iii. 32. Galba and rights of *patroni, Hist.* ii. 92. Demand Otho's death *ut si in circo, Hist.* i. 32. The prophet's advice to Vespasian, *Hist.* ii. 78. Slaves among the Germans, *Germ.* 24, 25. *Actor publicus,* ii. 30 ; iii. 67. Nurse, *Dial.* 29. Imperial bodyguard, i. 24 ; xiii. 18 ; xv. 58. Luxury and number, xv. 69 ; *Hist.* ii. 78. Murder of master (law), xiv. 42. Expulsion of freedmen, ii. 85. Tax on freedmen in proportion to their slaves, *Hist.* ii. 94.

Reff. to imperial freedmen are not collected here.

SUETONIUS.

Imperial policy in relation to manumission, *Aug.* 40 ; *Tib.* 47 ; *Cl.* 25, 28. Slaves and freedmen in the army, *Aug.* 25 ; *Nero,* 44. In navy,

Aug. 16.   Enslavement, *Aug.* 21, 24 ; *Tit.* 8.   Slave pretender, *Aug.* 19 ;
Tib. 25.   Assertus in ingenuitatem, *Aug.* 74.   Attitude to slaves, *Aug.* 42 ;
Claud. 25 ; *Tib.* 58 ; *Calig.* 32 ; *Nero,* 11, 36 ; *Galba,* 4.   Kidnapping
for *ergastula, Aug.* 32 ; *Tib.* 8.   Killing of masters, *Dom.* 14.   Mutilation, *Dom.* 7.   Wealth, *Otho,* 5.   Price, *de Gramm.* 3.   Nationality,
Calig. 57, 58.   Vitellius' origin, *Vit.* 2.   Freedmen, *Claud.* 25, 28 ; *Nero,*
48, etc.   Nero and civitas, *Nero,* 12, 24.   Galba and civitas, *Galba,* 14 ;
de Gramm. passim, for freedmen rhetoricians, etc.   Vespasian bought
freedom of poets, etc., *Vesp.* 18.   Claudius' paedagogus, *Claud.* 2.   Sale,
Aug. 69.   *Lex Papia Poppaea, Claud.* 19.   Roman citizenship, *Calig.*
38.   Number in Rome, *Aug.* 42.   To help suicide criminal, *Dom.* 14.
One-third of farm labour to be free, *Iul.* 42.   Expulsion of freedmen, *Claud.* 25.   Banished in famine, *Aug.* 42.   Imperial bodyguard,
Iul. 86 ; *Aug.* 49 ; *Calig.* 43 ; *Galba,* 12.   Libertinus, *Claud.* 24.

See also *Galba,* 10 ; *Tib.* 4.

Dio Cassius.

Enslavement, liii. 25 ; liv. 5, 7, 31, 34 ; lxix. 22.   Fire brigade, liii.
24 ; lv. 8 ; lv. 26.   In army, lv. 31 ; lvi. 23 ; lvii. 5 ; lxvii. 13.   Banished
in famine, lv. 25.   Augustus' regulations about manumission, lv. 13 ;
lvi. 33.   Marriage of free and freed, liv. 16.   Evidence against masters,
lv. 5 ; lvii. 19 ; lx. 15.   Tiberius' attitude, lvii. 11 ; Claudius', lx. 12.
Nero's, lxiii. 3, 4a.   Domitian's, lxvii. 14.   Hadrian and manumission,
lxix. 16.   Slave pretender, lvii. 16.   Licinus, liv. 21.   Vedius Pollio, liv.
23.   Antonius Musa, liii. 30.   Polybius, Asiaticus, etc., lxi. 29.   Doryphorus, lxi. 5.   Hermogenes, lxix. 22.   Shorthand writers, lv. 7.   Freedwomen, as priestesses of Vesta, lv. 22.   Tax on sale, lv. 31.   Saturnalia,
lx. 19 ; lx. 25.   As rowers, xlvii. 17 ; xlviii. 17, 49 ; xlix. 1 ; l. 11.   As
presents, lxi. 18.   Imperial bodyguard, liv. 24.   Cruelty, liv. 3.   Nurse,
lxvii. 18.   Function of manumission, lvi. 7.

Scriptores Historiae Augustae.

Hadrian's attitude, *Hadr.* xvi. 1 ; xxi. 2 ; xxi. 3.   Pius' simplicity,
Pius, vi. 4 ; vii. 5.   In army, *M. Aur.* xxi. 6, 7.   In camps, *Hadr.* xiii. 7.
Hadrian attacked by slave, *Hadr.* xii. 5.   Verus' treatment, *Ver.* vii. 5.
Phlegon, *Ver.* xx. 1.   Pertinax' economy, *Pert.* viii. 8 and 10.   Freedmen, *Pert.* viii. 1 ; xi. 5 ; xiii. 9 ; xiv. 6.   Accusation of masters, *Pert.*
ix. 10.   Geminas and Agaclytus, *M. Aur.* xv. 2.   Law, *Hadr.* xviii. 7,
8, 11.

Velleius Paterculus contributes nothing except one good sentence,
ii. 67. 2.

Josephus gives some numbers of Jewish captives sold into slavery,
e.g. *B.J.* vi. 9. 2–3, and information about imperial freedmen, e.g. *Ant.*
xviii. 6. 6.   Essenes condemn slavery, *Ant.* xviii. 1, 5.

SATIRE

HORACE.

Slaves on journey, *Sat.* i. 1. 47 ; i. 6. 101 ; v. 11 ; vi. 208. *Fugitivi,* i. 1. 77 ; v. 65. Numbers, i. 3. 11 ; vi. 116. Cruel punishment, i. 3. 80. Horace's origin, i. 6. Murder of patron by *liberta,* i. 1. 99. True freedom, i. 6. 110 ; *Ep.* i. 16. 63. Horace's slaves, *Sat.* i. 6. 116 ; ii. 6. 66 ; ii. 7. 118. Burial, i. 8. 8. Treatment, ii. 2. 66. Rich ex-slave, ii. 5. 15. *Mercennarius,* ii. 6. 11. Nomenclator, *Ep.* i. 6. 50. Horace and Davus on slavery and freedom, *Sat.* ii. 7. Cappadocians, *Ep.* i. 6. 39. Horace and his *vilicus, Ep.* i. 14. Price, *Ep.* ii. 2. 5 ; *Sat.* ii. 7. 43. Nationality, *Sat.* i. 7. 20. Colonus, *Od.* i. 35. 6 ; *Sat.* ii. 2. 115 ; *Ep.* i. 14. 2. Food, *Sat.* i. 5. 65. Dedicating chains, i. 5. 65. Enslavement and employment, *Ep.* i. 16. 69.

PERSIUS.

Manumission *per vindictam,* v. 76 sqq. Protest against ease of manumission, iii. 105. Ease of manumission)(true liberty, v. Compitalia, iv. 31. Sale and nationality, vi. 77.

MARTIAL.

Vilicus, etc., at Bilbilis, xii. 18. Faustinus' country house (*vilica, lactei vernae,* etc.), iii. 58. Sale, vi. 29 ; ix. 60. At table, ii. 37 ; iii. 23 ; vii. 48. Cursor, iii. 47. Cappadocian litter-bearers, vi. 77. Litter-bearers, iv. 51. Nationality, i. 42 ; v. 78 ; vi. 39 ; vi. 71 ; vii. 30 ; vii. 80 ; x. 76 ; xi. 11. Nationalities in Rome, vii. 30. Saturnalia, v. 19 ; v. 84 ; vi. 24 ; xi. 6 ; xiv. 1 ; xiv. 72 ; xiv. 79. ' Sit mihi verna satur,' ii. 90 ; cf. ii. 48. In praise of a slave's life, ix. 93. Reflections of slave who has bought his liberty, ii. 68. Branding, ii. 29 ; iii. 21 ; viii. 75 ; x. 56. Zoilus, once a *fugitivus,* iii. 29 ; xi. 37 ; xi. 54. *Fugitivus,* iii. 91. Manumission, i. 102 (on death of slave) ; ix. 88. Price, iii. 62 ; vi. 66 ; viii. 13 ; x. 31 ; xi. 38 ; xi. 70. Luxury and vice, ii. 57 ; iii. 82 ; vi. 66, etc. etc. Favourite redeemed from slavery, ii. 34. Treatment, ii. 66 ; ii. 82 ; iii. 94 ; viii. 23. ' Domine ' to slave, v. 57 ; cf. i. 82. Boys in the amphitheatre, ii. 75. To announce the time, viii. 67. Euclides in the Knights' seats, v. 35. Domitian and mutilation, ix. 7. Colonus ii. 11 ; vii. 31. Number, viii. 75. Dedication of chains, iii. 29. See also vi. 52 ; vi. 68 ; xii. 66.

JUVENAL.

Fugitivi, viii. 172 ; xi. 81. Syrian character, iii. 62, 296 ; viii. 160. Nationality, i. 104 ; v. 52, 131–2 ; vii. 14–16 ; xi. 147. Cruelty, x. 60 ; x. 183 ; xiv. 16–24. Lecticarius, i. 64. Cursor, v. 53. Flos Asiae, v. 56. For appearance' sake, vi. 352 ; vii. 141. Number, iii. 10 ; iii. 141 ; viii. 180 ; ix. 64, 142 ; xiv. 305. Price, v. 55. Have slaves souls ? xiv. 16. Mutilation, x. 307. *Vernae,* v. 74. Slave in consul's car, x. 41. Other reff. may be found in the index to Mayor's *Juvenal.*

PETRONIUS.

The book is full of slaves and freedmen. A few references are given :
Slave *caupo*, 62. Tax on manumission, 58, 65, 71. Price, 65, 68.
Sale, 74. Number, 37, 47, 53. Various functions, 27, 40. *Vernae*, 53.
Education, 46, 58, 75, 76. Nationality, 22, 31, 34, 36, 57, 63, 68, 102.
Saturnalia, 58. *Contubernalis*, 62, 71. Punishments, 28, 30, 52, 53,
54, 107, 115. Law, 53. Common humanity, 71. Careers of *liberti*, 38,
57, 58, 61. *Servi publici*, 78, 97. Banishment of freedmen to Baiae,
53. Manumission, 38, 41, 42, 54, 65, 71.

LETTERS

PLINY THE YOUNGER.

Attitude to master, i. 4. Care for household, viii. 16, 19. Attitude
to freedmen, ii. 6. To Zosimus, v. 19. Medical treatment, viii. 24.
Reader, ix. 34. Pantomimists, vii. 24 ; ix. 17. Pallas, vii. 29 ; viii. 6.
Public slaves, x. 19, 20, 31, 32. Slaves in army, x. 29, 30. Nurses, v. 16 ;
vi. 3. Exposure, x. 65, 66. Manumission, iv. 10 ; vii. 16, 32.
Requests for citizenship, x. 6, 7, 10, 11, 104, 106, 107, 108, 109. Evidence
and torture, vii. 6. Attack on master, iii. 14 ; vi. 25 ; viii. 14. Murder
of patron, viii. 15. Trajan's freedmen, viii. 6 ; x. 27, 28, 63, 85, 87.
Shorthand writers, iii. 5. Slaves as dowry, vi. 32. Pliny's villa (slave-
quarters, etc.), ii. 17 ; iii. 19 ; cf. ix. 20. Hermes, his agent, vii. 11.
Purchase, i. 21. Apology from another's freedman, ix. 21. Appeal to
Emperor's statue, x. 74. Recommendation of a freedman, ix. 24. Not
in chains, iii. 19. Salary, x. 31.

OTHER WRITERS

For reff. to Columella and Varro *de re rustica*, see the footnotes to
Chapter III. ; and for reff. to Frontinus *de aquaeductibus*, see Chapter V.
pp. 137–141.

For the comments of Tacitus, Quintilian, and Plutarch (?) on slaves in
education, see Chapter II. pp. 39–41.

PLINY THE ELDER could hardly fail to include some relevant information in his comprehensive *Natural History*, e.g. wealth of a dispensator, vii. 129 ; xxxiii. 145. Vedius Pollio, ix. 77. Prices, vii. 39.
Ingenuitas, xxxiii. 32. Luxury, xix. 19.

References to the legal writings may be most conveniently found in
W. W. Buckland's *Law of Roman Slavery*.

APULEIUS, *Metamorphoses*.

Names *in familia*, ix. 2. *Paidagogos*, x. 5. Acquired by dowry,
x. 4. At table, ii. 19 ; ii. 31. Shepherds on estate, viii. 1 sqq. Enslavement, vii. 9. Sale, ix. 31. The gardener, ix. 31. *Vilicus*, viii. 22 (slave-
wife). Details of a large estate, viii. 1, 15, 17, 22, 26. Disclose secrets of
house, ii. 15 ; cf. vii. 23. Slaves in a baker's mill, ix. 12. Devotion to
house, ii. 26. Flight rather than change of master, viii. 15. Torture,
vii. 2 ; x. 7. Law, vi. 4 ; viii. 24. Punishment, iii. 16. *Maritus, con-*

serva, viii. 22, 31. *Fotis*, i. 24 *et saep.* *Vernulae*, xi. 18. *Servi publici*, i. 24. *Conservus*, of an animal, vii. 27. Slave-doctor, ix. 2. *Peculium*, x. 14. See also ii. 2 ; iv. 9 ; ix. 20 ; x. 13–16 ; xi. 10.

AULUS GELLIUS, writing in the second half of the second century, preserves interesting information chiefly quoted from older lawyers. *Servus recepticius*, xvii. 6. See Bruns, ii. p. 66. Adoption, v. 19. Redhibition, iv. 2 ; cf. Bruns, ii. p. 63. ' Statius ' *servile nomen*, iv. 20. 12. Pilleatus, *sub corona*, vi. 3. 1–4. Punishment for theft in the XII. Tables, xi. 18. 8. Famous Greek philosopher slaves, ii. 18. Foreign nurses, xii. 1, esp. 17. Saturnalia, xviii. 2 ; xviii. 13. Plutarch and the slave, i. 26. Trained in philosophy, i. 26.

PHILOSTRATUS' *Life of Apollonius* is of little historical value, but see i. 15 ; i. 20 ; iii. 25 ; v. 36 ; vi. 42 ; vii. 23 ; viii. 7 ; viii. 30 ; *Ep.* xli., xliv.

VERGIL'S silence on slavery is well known, and Mr. Heitland has offered reasons to explain it (see *Agricola*).

PROPERTIUS.

His slaves lent to Cynthia. Treatment, etc., iv. 7. 35–46, 73–75. As lovers' messengers, ii. 22a. 49 ; ii. 23. 3 ; iii. 6 ; iv. 8. 37. Evidence of slave against master ? iii. 6. 19. Wool-working at home, iii. 6. 15 ; cf. iv. 7. 41. Sale, iv. 5. 51. Torchbearers, i. 3. 10 ; ii. 29. 2.

STATIUS.

A *verna*, Melior's adopted son, *Silv.* ii. 1. 72–87. Death of Statius' adopted son, v. 5. esp. 10–12, 66 to end. The father of Claudius Etruscus (imperial servant, the duties of *a rationibus*), iii. 3. *passim*, esp. 43 to end. ' Consolatio ad Flavium Ursum de amissione pueri delicati,' ii. 6. Domitian forbids mutilation, iv. 3. 13. Slavery to knighthood, iv. 5. 47. Appeal to magistrate ? i. 4. 43. Compare also i. 6. 65–74 ; iii. 1. 77 ; v. 1. 158.

SENECA.

Right and wrong treatment, *Ep.* xlvii. *passim*; *de ira*, ii. 28. 7 ; iii. 10. 4; xii. 5; xxix. 1 ; (Vedius Pollio), *de ira*, iii. 40. 2 ; *de clem.* i. 18. 1–3. Torture, *Ep.* xiv. 5 and 6. Suicide, *Ep.* lxxvii. 14 ; *Ep.* lxx. 20, 21, 25, 26 ; *Ep.* iv. 4. Revenge, *Ep.* iv. 8, cvii. 5 ; *de clem.* i. 26. 1. Power of master, *de ira*, iii. 24. 2 and 3. Punishment, iii. 32. 1 ; xxxv. 1–3. Devotion : can a slave confer a benefit ? *de ben.* iii. 18–28. Number, *Ep.* xvii. 3, xxxi. 10 ; *Ep.* cx. 17 ; *de tranq.* i. 8, viii. 6 ; *de vit. beat.* xvii. 2. Baba, *Ep.* xv. 9. Fatua, *Ep.* l. 2. Learned slaves, *Ep.* xxvii. 6–8. Cost of feeding, *Ep.* xvii. 3, lxxx. 7 ; cf. *Cato de R.R.* 56. Athletic trainers, *Ep.* xv. 3 ; lxxxiii. 4, 5. Misericordia, *de ira*, iii. 29. 1. Cursores, *Ep.* lxxxvii. 9. Saturnalia, *Ep.* xviii. 1. Debate as to special dress, *de clem.* i. 24. 1. ' Quot servi tot hostes,' *Ep.* xviii. 15. *Fugitivi*, *Ep.* cvii. 5 ; *de ira*, iii. 5. 4. Appeal to Emperor's statue, *de clem.* i. 18. 1–3. Appeal to magistrate, *de ben.* iii. 22. 3. Master killed by slaves, *N.Q.* i. 16. 1 ;

Ep. lxxvii. 7 and 8.   Diogenes and his *fugitivus, de tranq.* viii. 7.   Immortality promised to freedmen, *ad Polyb.* ix. 8.   Plato and the slave, *de ira,* iii. 12. 5.   Better without slaves, *de Brev.* iii. 2, xii. 2 ; *de tranq.* viii. 8, ix. 3.   *Peculium, de ben.* vii. 4. 4 ; *Ep.* xii. 10 ; lxxx. 4.   Slaves refuse to assist master's suicide, *Ep.* lxxvii. 6–8.   Inventions due to slaves, *Ep.* xc. 25, 26.   Sale, *Ep.* lxxx. 9.   King and slave subject to fate, *de clem.* i. 21. 1.   Contempt for death, *Ep.* xxiv. 14, lxxvii. 7 ; *de ben.* ii. 34. 3.   Poverty, *Ep.* xviii. 8.   *Vilicus, Ep.* xii. 1.   Nomenclator, *Ep.* xix. 11.   Price, *Ep.* xxvii. 7.   Manumission, *de vit. beat.* xxiv. 3.   Nationality, *Ep.* lxxxvii. 9.   *Vicarius, de tranq.* viii. 6.   Slave and king, *Ep.* xliv. 4.   Servus a mere name, *Ep.* xxxi. 11.   Mercenarius, *de ben.* iii. 22. 1 ; vii. 5. 3.

DIO CHRYSOSTOM discusses slavery in *Orationes,* x., xiv., xv.   Brief reff. are :

Insincerity (li. 261 R), resourcelessness (xxxiv. 53 R), disorder in the household (xxxviii. 136 R) are necessary accompaniments of slavery. Also lxvi. 352–3 R, xxxii. 672 R, xxxiii. 5 R, xxxii. 695 R, lxxx. 436 R.

PHILO, *quod omnis probus liber.*   *Passim* for discussion of ' true liberty.'

In EPICTETUS the most important passages are *Diss.* i. 9. 1–17, i. 13, iii. 26. 1–36 ; *Fragm.* xliii.

CHRISTIAN WRITERS
ST. PAUL.
' Neither bond nor free,' 1 Cor. xii. 13 ; Gal. iii. 28, iv. 1, iv. 7 ; Col. iii. 11.   Commands to slaves and masters, Eph. vi. 5 ; Col. iii. 22–iv. 1 ; 1 Tim. vi. 1 ; Tit. ii. 9.   ἀλλ' εἰ καὶ δύνασαι κτλ., 1 Cor. vii. 21 ; the Epistle to Philemon.

The ' DIDACHE.'
Advice to masters and slaves, iv.

CLEMENT OF ROME.
Ransoming of slaves from Christian funds, i. 55.   Attitude of Christians to Government, i. 40.

IGNATIUS.
Advice to masters and slaves, *Polycarp,* iv.

POLYCARP.
Attitude to Government, Philipp. xii. ; cf. ' Martyrdom,' x.   Betrayed by a slave-boy under torture, ' Martyrdom ' (of unknown authorship), vi. 1.

The *Apologies* of ARISTIDES and JUSTIN MARTYR contain nothing directly relevant.

Minucius Felix.

Social status of Christians, viii., xvi., xxxi., xxxvi.

Tertullian, *Liber apologeticus.*

Exposure of children, ix. Funds for relieving and burying *egeni*, xxxix. Effect of Christianity on slave and master, iii. Christians of every degree, i., xxxvii. (cf. *ad Scap.* v.). Attitude to Government, xxx., xxxi., xxxvii., xxxix.

Clement of Alexandria.

Effect of Christianity on masters, *Protrept.* x.

INSCRIPTIONS

The inscriptional evidence is most conveniently found in Dessau, *Inscriptiones Latinae Selectae,* and Bruns, *Fontes iuris Romani antiqui.* Dessau's wonderful indices provide easy reference, but even so there is much of interest even in ' slave '-inscriptions which is uncatalogued.

Most ' slave '-inscriptions may be recognized as such without trouble. The slave describes himself as ' servus ' or ' ser ' or ' S.' Sometimes there are other signs ; a single name together with another name in the genitive is often evidence, though not always ; in the case of public slaves the town appears in the genitive. But in many cases there is doubt, no sign being given, particularly in the case of potters' stamps, whether a man is slave, freed, or free ; our knowledge of the type of labour employed in industry is peculiarly uncertain for this reason.[1]

A few examples of the ways in which slaves are described in the inscriptions are given. Unusual methods must be sought for in the footnotes to the text. Numbers refer to Dessau.

M a r p o r, 7822, O l i p o r, 7823

This is the oldest method of naming slaves. Marpor is formed from *Marci puer.*[2]

P r e p o n A l l e i u s M. s., 9236

The Greek is Πρέπων 'Αλλειος Μαάρκου. The slave adds to his own the Gentile name of his master.

A p o l a u s t u s C l a u d i a n u s, A p o l a u s t u s M o d i a n u s, 4984

Both are public slaves engaged on the same work ; they are distinguished by the additional name formed from the name of their previous master.[3]

---

[1] For slave-names, see Bibliography ; for potters' stamps, see *supra,* pp. 121, 127.

[2] So Marquardt, *Vie privée,* i. p. 24. Oxé in *Rhein. Mus.* 1904, pp. 108 sqq. On the other hand, *-por* in *Mucapor* and *Aulupor* has been lately shown to denote Thracian origin. *Mucapor* in particular is a common Thracian name. See G. G. Mateescu in *Ephem. Daco-romana,* i. p. 120, notes 2 and 4.

[3] The form, Pantagatus Rasini Memmi, would be a variant method of expressing the same facts if Chase (*Boston Catalogue of Arretine Pottery,*

O d e is an *ancilla symphoniaci* and is named after her craft, 9345.

Philadelphus Neronis Caesar. ex horreis Petronian. dec. 1625

A slave of the Emperor engaged in work at the Petronian warehouses. A decurion of his college.

Suavis Caesaris supra formas, 1614

A very vague description of the work of an imperial slave. The canting of waterpipes has been suggested.

Felici Caes. n. vern., 1480

To Felix a *verna nostri Caesaris*.

Ost. Hermes tab., 6153

Is a freedman *tabularius*, once a public slave of Ostia (*Ostiensis*).

Other methods of designating public slaves are—
    c.P.s. 6673, *coloniae Placentinae servus.*
    Epitynchano Telesinorum, 6511
    Felici s. p., mensori, 6480.

Invicto Deo Charito Neviod. summ., 4189

A dedication to Mithras by Charito, a slave owned by the city of Neviodunum.   He was dispensator or *vilicus summarum*.

Narcisso publ. Cilniano, 9049

A public slave once owned by the Cilnian family.

C. Miniarius Atimetus sociorum miniariorum, 1876

Once a slave belonging to a company working vermilion-mines (minium).   On manumission he took a name from his trade.

Crescens ꓛ. ser., 7492

The sign stands for Gaiae=Mulieris.   So, too, M i n u c i a e ꓛ. l i b. C a l e t y c h e, 7392.

For a brief epitaph, notice A n t h u s A u g. a c o r i n t h i s s i b i e t s u i s, 1818.   It tells us that he was a slave of the Emperor in charge of Corinthian ware, and that he provided a grave space for himself and his family.

---

p. 20) is correct.   Pantagatus (and other slave-names also) has been found on Arretine pieces in conjunction with Rasini and Memmi, separately and together.   So, too, Mahes is found in combination with Rasinius, while he is also found as a freedman of Memmius.   The theory is that the slaves of Rasinius passed to Memmius.   But Pantagatus Rasini Memmi is a strange way of putting this.   Perhaps it is a method of preserving the original signature of a famous designer, with the addition of his new ownership.

C. G a r g i l i u s H a e m o n, P r o c u l i, P h i l a g r i D i v i A u g.
l. A g r i p p i a n i f. p a e d a g o g u s, i d e m. l. 8436, is an excellent
example of compressed information. C. Gargilius Haemon was a paedagogus and the freedman of Proculus. Proculus was the son of Philagrus,
a freedman of Augustus, who had previously been owned by Agrippa,
had passed into the possession of the Gargilian family, and had been
freed by this family ; the proof of this is that Proculus' freedman takes
the name Gargilius.

H i l a r u s, V a c c i o, S c a r i p u s, N e r v i u s θ, 7228. These
were officials in a college of slaves (quarrymen) ; Nervius had died.
θ = θάνατος.

B. SELECT BIBLIOGRAPHY

A

BLAIR.—*An Enquiry into the State of Slavery amongst the Romans*. Edin-
burgh, 1833.

DE CAQUERAY.—*De l'esclavage chez les Romains*. Paris, 1864.

BOISSIER, G.—*La religion romaine*, vol. ii. pp. 305–360, 7th edition.
Paris, 1874.

WALLON, H.—*L'histoire de l'esclavage dans l'antiquité*, 3 vols., 2nd edition.
Paris, 1879.

BECKER, W. A.—*Gallus*, vol. ii. pp. 115–186, re-edited by H. Goll.
Berlin, 1880.

MARQUARDT, J.—*Das privatleben der Romer*, vol. vii. of the *Handbuch
d. römisch. Altertumer*, by T. Mommsen and J. Marquardt,
2nd ed. Leipsig, 1886. (*La vie privée des Romains*, in the French
translation.) Chapter iv.

INGRAM, J.—*A History of Serfdom and Slavery*, chapter iii. London,
1895.

HALKIN, L.—*Les esclaves publics dans l'empire romain*. Brussels, 1891.

CICCOTTI, E.—*Il tramonto della schiavitu nel mondo antico*. Turin, 1891.

RATHKE.—*De Romanorum bellis servilibus*. Berlin, 1904.

ERMAN, H.—*Servus Vicarius*. Lausanne, 1896.

BUCKLAND, W. W.—*The Roman Law of Slavery*. Cambridge, 1908.

FOWLER, W. W.—*Social Life at Rome in the Age of Cicero*, pp. 204–236.
London, 1910.

KOOPMANS, J. J.—*De servitute antiqua et religione Christiana capita
selecta*. Groningen, 1910.

OXÉ, A.—' Zur alteren Nomenklatur der römischen Sklaven,' in *Rhein-
isches Museum*, 1904, p. 108.

BANG, M.—' Die Herkunft der römischen Sklaven,' in *Romische Mittheilungen*, xxv. (1910) and xxvii. (1912).

GORDON, M. L.—' The Nationality of Slaves under the Early Roman
Empire,' in *Journal of Roman Studies*, xiv. (1924).

B

SALVIOLI, G.—*Le capitalisme dans le monde antique.* Paris, 1908.

KÜHN, O.—*De opificum Romanorum condicione privata.* Halle, 1910.

TENNEY FRANK.—*An Economic History of Rome*, 2nd ed., revised. Baltimore, 1927.

HEITLAND, W. E.—*Agricola : A Study of Agriculture and Rustic Life in the Greco-Roman World from the Point of View of Labour.* Cambridge, 1921.

ROSTOVTZEFF, M.—*The Social and Economic History of the Roman Empire.* Oxford, 1926.

BREWSTER, E. H.—*Roman Craftsmen and Tradesmen of the Early Empire.* Pennsylvania, 1917.

PÂRVAN.—*Die Nationalität der Kaufleute im römischen Kaiserreiche.*

KÖSER, E.—*De captivis Romanorum.* Giessen, 1904.

TENNEY FRANK.—' Race Mixture in the Roman Empire,' in the *American Historical Review*, xxi. (1916), p. 689.

PARK, M. E.—*The Plebs Urbana in Cicero's Day.* Pennsylvania, 1918.

NILSSON, M. P.—*Imperial Rome*, pp. 317–367 (the population problem). London, 1926.

HIRSCHFELD, O.—*Die kaiserlichen verwaltungsbeamten bis auf Diocletian.* 1905.

REYNOLDS, P. K. B.—*The Vigiles of Imperial Rome.* Oxford, 1926.

WALTZING, J. P.—*Etude historique sur les corporations professionelles,* 4 vols. 1895.

SCHIESS, T.—*Die römischen collegia funeraticia.* Munich, 1888.

DILL, S.—*Roman Society from Nero to Marcus Aurelius*, chapters on ' The Society of the Freedmen ' and ' Colleges and Plebeian Life.' London, 1904.

TOUTAIN, J.—*Les cultes paiens dans l'empire romain* (deals with the diffusion of the cults and the status of their converts). Paris, 1907–1911.

BRUNS, C. G.—*Fontes iuris Romani antiqui*, 7th ed. Leipzig.

DESSAU, H.—*Inscriptiones Latinae selectae*, 3 vols. in 5. Berlin, 1892–1914.

CAGNAT, R.—*Cours d'épigraphie Latine*, 4th ed., pp. 80–87 (slave-names in the inscriptions). Paris, 1914.

APPENDIX II

NOTES ON SLAVERY IN THE WEST INDIES

IN this Appendix a few notes are collected from an abridgment (in four volumes) of the *Minutes of the Evidence taken before a Committee of the Whole House to whom it was referred to consider the Slave Trade, 1789.* The evidence given by a variety of witnesses is of the utmost interest, when not too depressing, and would repay a more thorough study. The passages here noted—and they might have been multiplied at great length—have been chosen to illustrate some point of similarity or contrast with Roman practice. It would be necessary to read the evidence more extensively to form some idea of the amazingly conflicting statements offered both by interested and disinterested witnesses.

Enslavement.

> The usual methods—war, punishment for crime, etc.

> Gamesters become slaves by throwing dice. Cf. Tac. *Germ.* 24.

> Native kings said to breed slaves for the trade.

> A born slave cannot be sold except for a crime (Governor of British forts on Gold Coast, i. 33).

> Factory slaves and their forefathers have been handed down from time to time, and are now mostly born slaves (Gold Coast Company official, i. 16).

> Annual average of slaves imported and retained in West Indies was 15,657, at an average of £35 per head ; in Jamaica, 167,000 in 1768. Tax of 30s. on every negro imported—20s. paid by buyer, 10s. by importer (London merchant, ii. 151).

> A negro woman who said her father was a king in Africa neither conversed nor ate with other negroes, since she could not find her equals among them. Maintained it for twenty years. Cf. Pallas' attitude to his freedmen.

> Phillis Wheatley, an African slave, learnt the English language in less than three years, and wrote elegant English verse which has since been published (a dean, iii. 132).

Family Life.

Relations never parted (a planter, ii. 117).

Never bought more than fifty at once ; chose those between ages of ten and twenty-five years old, but if there were any old parents in the lot for sale he bought them ; never separated families (planter, ii. 131).

Relations always sold together (Grenada surgeon, ii. 81).

By law mother and infant child must be sold together (Chief Justice of St. Vincent, iv. 90).

Relations and even friends go together (sailor, iii. 52).

At sales relations were separated as sheep and lambs are separated by the butcher (master of slave ship, later rector of a parish, iii. 58).

Natural Increase or Fresh Importation.

Slaves on a parson's estate doubled by increase in twenty years (dean, iii. 135).

Children could keep up the supply on a humane master's estate without resort to importation (Chief Justice, St. Vincent, iv. 90 sq.).

Lost 6 per cent. by deaths per annum.

The system of breeding is to the planter's profit (Grenada surgeon, ii. 81).

An annual diminution of negroes on an estate whose owners gave rewards for children (surgeon, ii. 88). Cf. Columella.

Estate A. bought many negro women ; estate B., young males. After fifty years B. had purchased the gang twice over and in such state that it had to be almost replaced (i.e. nearly three times), while on A. few negroes not born on the land, and such was the surplus that the owner hired out his spare labour. But estate A. not common, owing to difficulty of obtaining women who will have children (Antigua resident, ii. 34).

Journals of births, deaths, and work have been kept and sent to him periodically (sugar planter not resident on estates, ii. 55). Cf. Petronius.

Hears of a Frenchman who lived in Grenada pretending that it was to his interest to exhaust his slaves by labour in a few years ; but it was always mentioned as a singular absurdity and is sure no planter acts on a maxim so horrid (Attorney-General for Grenada, ii. 50).

Free and Slave Labour.

The slaves in West Indian islands have a decided superiority as to every comfort of life over the common labourers and poor people of Ireland and Scotland, by being regularly supplied with every necessary of life, clothing, food, comfortable houses, protection in health, the best advice in sickness, and on their decease having a father and protector for their children (surgeon, S. Kitts and Nevis, ii. 91).

A white man in England will do with ease the work of three negroes, because the slave, seeing no end to his labour, stands over the work and only throws the hoe to avoid the lash ; he appears to work without actually working (overseer in Jamaica, iv. 32).

An English family is better served by two or three domestic servants than a West Indian by eight or ten (Attorney-General of Grenada, ii. 52).

Planters would prefer to use free negroes than have the expense of maintaining many women, children, old men, and invalids (ditto, ii. 54).

Ratio, five English workers to nine native (sugar planter, ii. 74).

The Ideal Overseer.

The manager ought to have sense, humanity, and good conduct. He must study the slaves' tempers and know the care of flock and land ; so that he should possess the first abilities. It is the owners' interest and care to get such a man. Planters, knowing it the chief point to have the negroes in good heart, look first to his humanity, without which no planter would employ his own brother (Attorney-General, ii. 61). Cf. Columella.

Absentee Landlords.

Very bad effects from the absence of landlords ; estate left under management of overseers ; loss easily one-fifth of the whole ; for overseers always become rich and overwork the staff (naval captain, iii. 83).

Manumission.

Never knew a field slave buy his freedom (lieutenant, iv. 85, and often).

Tailor bought his freedom (ditto, iv. 85).

Many slaves buy freedom (owners, ii. 46 ; ii. 78).

No desire for manumission, otherwise they could easily buy it ; freedom offered and refused lest they should lose friends and protectors ; knew of a slave who bought his son's freedom and slaves for him, and yet himself still remained a slave (resident of Nevis, ii. 97).

Two hundred pounds given for freedom (native of Antigua, ii. 112).

A humane master cannot do worse by his slave than free him (estate owner, Antigua, ii. 133).

One hundred pounds offered, but refused (dean, iii. 133).

Has known many repent of their being freed, finding it difficult to support themselves and get comforts, when sick, equal to what they had before (resident of Grenada, ii. 64).

General Treatment.

(Atrocities not copied here.)

Laws unjust—evidence of slave against white not admissible—murder of slave not punishable—obstacles deliberately placed in the way of freedom—suggests various reforms, including councils of guardians. Treatment in general humane—cruelty rare—fairly happy family life—advises missionary work (from utilitarian motives)—slaves more kindly treated when owner resident (Chief Justice, St. Vincent, iv. 90 sq.).

Floggings more severe than regimental punishments. A clergyman's wife used to drop hot sealing-wax on her slave-women (lieutenant, iv. 83).

More cruel than any army punishment (a captain, iv. 58).

Law limits lashes to thirty-nine, though regularly exceeded. Redress possible on application to a magistrate—had known it made in towns, not in country (book-keeper and overseer, iv. 35).

Many instances where humanity and a regard for interest joined is providing well for slaves (dean, iii. 130).

Never saw any signs of happiness except at their funerals, when they show extravagant joy from a persuasion that the deceased has escaped from slavery to his native country (naval captain, iii. 4).

Humane master sent injured slave home to Africa; slave refused to stay, but came back to slavery (Attorney-General, Grenada, ii. 50).

A hospital kept by law on every estate ; as good as those in England ; wine and every delicacy ; sick visited thrice a week by doctor, and chief nurse every day (resident, Grenada, ii. 60).

Allotments.

Allotments given to slaves enable them to feed themselves and their wives' children (owner, ii. 31).

Proprietors obliged to allot lands by law (Attorney-General, Grenada, ii. 45).

As much as one-eighth of estate allotted to slaves (estate owner, Grenada, ii. 78).

Peculium.

If the negro wishes to sell the product of his allotment, the master buys from him as from any indifferent master (contractor of slave-labour, Antigua, ii. 31).

Properly speaking, slaves cannot be said to have property—opinion, however, secures to them whatever they possess—no master dares to violate their personal property—bankruptcy of master makes no difference—freedom of bequest—knew of a slave worth six or seven hundred pounds—almost all the small currency in the hands of slaves (owner, ii. 36).

Owners compelled to allot lands—Saturday afternoon and Sunday allowed for the working of them (ii. 45).

A slave who makes proper use of his time may produce goods to value of from £7 to £9 yearly, and even up to £30 and £40 (planter, ii. 59).

Slaves give feasts to a hundred or two hundred other slaves, with every rarity and wines, which witness could not have given for £60—often borrow master's plate and linen (resident, Grenada, ii. 60).

Believes it not uncommon for slaves to be the master of slaves ; remembers a case of slave giving £40 for a slave (resident, Antigua, ii. 37).

INDEX